Additional praise for *The Imperfect Diamond*:

"A dramatic, stirring portrayal of traditional confrontation between labor and management. . . . An absorbing account of a hitherto little-publicized American labor movement."—*New Republic*

"Thorough and comprehensive, the clarity of the prose is a welcome respite from traditional 'baseballese.' . . . An important work, not only for baseball history, but also for U.S. history, the labor movement, and the history of capitalism."—*Library Journal*

"Remains to date the very best. . . . An unprecedented opportunity to see beyond the scrim of handlebar moustaches and 'Casey at the Bat' nostalgia."—*Aethlon: Journal of Sport Literature*

"For those fans trying to understand baseball's labor-management underbelly, but who feel the current situation has blown beyond their comprehension, a more readable and relevant book would be hard to find."—*Louisville Times*

The
Imperfect
Diamond

A History of
Baseball's Labor Wars

LEE LOWENFISH

Foreword by Robert W. Creamer
With a new introduction and epilogue by the author

University of Nebraska Press
Lincoln and London

Library of Congress Cataloging-in-Publication Data
Lowenfish, Lee, 1942–
The imperfect diamond: a history of baseball's labor wars / Lee Lowenfish; foreword by
Robert W. Creamer; with a new introduction and epilogue by the author.
p. cm.
Originally published: New York: Stein and Day, 1980.
Includes bibliographical references and index.
ISBN 978-0-8032-3360-7 (pbk.: alk. paper)
1. Baseball players—Salaries, etc.—United States. 2. Baseball—Economic aspects—United
States—History. 3. Industrial relations—United States—History. 4. Collective bargaining—Base-
ball—United States—History. I. Title.
GV880.15.L69 2010
331.2'81796357640973—dc22
2009049566

This Bison Books edition follows the original in beginning the foreword on arabic page 13; no
material has been omitted.

INTRODUCTION

I don't remember where I came up with the title *The Imperfect Diamond*
to describe the long and often bitter history of professional baseball's labor relations. I do know that I have always thought that comedian Mort
Sahl's memorable comment about Richard Nixon's memoir *Six Crises*—
"It should have been published in a loose-leaf edition so you could just
add the crises"—could have easily been said about baseball's history of
owner-player struggles. As respected Boston Red Sox broadcaster Ned
Martin said so well in the introduction to the first edition of this book,
"Baseball must be a pretty remarkable sport to have survived itself. . . .
On the field, it's the prettiest game there is. Off the field, quite often not
so pretty." He concluded, "*War and Peace* it is not, but maybe in theory, it
is." Certainly the continuing story of threatened lockouts and strikes and
actual lockouts and strikes culminating in the mammoth 1994–95 strike
that wiped out a World Series made Martin's remark prophetic.

It has now been three decades since the first edition was published,
and I think that some of the backstory about it and the second edition is

worth telling. In 1980 my collaborator Tony Lupien (the former Boston Red Sox first baseman who had recently retired as Dartmouth College baseball coach) and I both thought that we had timed the market perfectly because it seemed inevitable that baseball's first in-season strike would occur sometime that season. On management's side an outraged core of owners wanted to return to the days when they controlled everything in the shop. On the other side, Players Association leader Marvin Miller was talking retirement—"He hears drums," Ned Martin would later tell me—and he wanted to leave baseball with a legacy of permanent contractual freedom and expanding riches for the players.

However, our timing was off by a year. A strike was averted in May 1980 when a joint player-management committee was established to investigate the issue of compensation for free agents lost by Major League teams. Like most committees in baseball, this one was not successful; the strike ultimately occurred on June 12, 1981, and lasted for fifty-one days.

Baltimore Orioles manager Earl Weaver was a rare member of management who sympathized with the players' position in the strike. During spring training 1980 I gave a copy of the book to Orioles press secretary Phil Itzoe to present to the manager. The next day I asked Weaver if he had received it. "You mean 'Broken Diamond'?" he replied, making reference to the original cover depicting a baseball diamond with a fissure in it. He not only had started to read it, but he began telling his longtime coach Cal Ripken Sr. about Clark Griffith and Connie Mack supporting players' unions in their early days. "Can you believe that?" Weaver chortled. I was and still am an Oriole fan, and Weaver's response to my book as he sat in the home team spring training dugout in the old shed of a ballpark that was Florida's Miami Stadium remains one of my favorite stories about the first edition.

Ten years later when DaCapo Press proposed a second edition of *The Imperfect Diamond* to include a chapter on the 1980s, I agreed with the suggestion that a new subtitle, "A History of Baseball's Labor Wars," would be more comprehensive than the original, "The Story of Baseball's Reserve System and the Men Who Fought to Change It." DaCapo didn't think that "Tony Lupien's Thoughts for the Future," the last chapter in the first edition, belonged in a history book, and I couldn't convince them otherwise. Tony and I had a falling out over the issue because he felt I didn't fight hard enough to include his essay, but I knew that I wanted my historical take on the beautiful if troubled game of baseball to have a second life.

I had an acutely personal interest in a second edition. During the 1981 strike I had written a piece, "And What If Landis Were Around?" for the June 21 edition of the *New York Times* Sunday sports section. I speculated that if Commissioner Landis were still alive, he and Marvin Miller might have found a common ground to end the strike though both came from opposite ends of the labor-management spectrum. A few years later I found out the hard way how fanciful my conception had been.

In August 1987 I was contracted by a major New York publisher to assist in the writing of Marvin Miller's memoirs. As a storyteller who loves the connection between baseball and history and who was obviously sympathetic to Miller's story and accomplishments, I was thrilled by the assignment. I started immediately taping his reminiscences and did so through March 1988. Though Miller was ostensibly retired from the Players Association, I soon came to realize that his grudges against baseball management remained very fresh, in particular toward former commissioner Bowie Kuhn, whose memoir *Hardball: The Education of a Baseball Commissioner* had just been published and contained some very unflattering descriptions of him.

The collaboration was not successful because it became clear to me that Miller's main interest was in settling old scores and berating outrageous management conduct whenever he could. He was obviously not a retiring type able to recollect his achievements in tranquility. We worked together during the period when collusion against free agents was at its peak and the Players Association had filed grievance cases against it. I certainly sympathized with why he was enraged by collusion but sensed he was no longer in the daily loop of the Players Association.

I didn't think that a successful book could be sustained by tirades alone. Neither did my editor, who after reading early drafts of the manuscript commented, "What is missing is Marvin himself." He urged me to create a better voice for the story and maybe find some anecdotes about Miller from friends and associates. But Miller disdained the concept of literary voice. "What do you mean by 'voice'?" he snapped. "I have hundreds of newspaper clippings here in my apartment that you haven't consulted. You can find my voice there." When he found out that I had talked to some of his former Players Association colleagues, he was enraged. "What do you think you are? An investigative reporter?!"

It was a disheartening experience that ended with me having to sue when I was fired after writing nearly 100,000 words. Yet no one person, not even my erstwhile hero, could permanently damage my lifetime love of baseball, of its thrilling and at times heart-breaking sagas. When the second edition of *The Imperfect Diamond* came out during the 1991 season, *Radio-TV Interview Report* headlined on the front page of one of its issues "Are Pro Baseball Players Paid Too Much?" I was gratified to be deluged with dozens of requests for phone interviews. I particularly remember vigorous conversations with on-air hosts in Pittsburgh, where the Pirates would soon lose to free agency three of the key components of their recent pennant-contending teams—sluggers Barry Bonds and Bobby Bonilla and pitcher Doug Drabek. I understood the anger of the fans faced with the loss of local heroes, yet I tried to explain the basic principle that after a finite period of years a ballplayer, like an employee in any industry, should have the right to choose his own employer. I wished the local Pittsburgh fans well as the team sought to replace older stars with younger ones developed by good scouting and a well-functioning farm system (a process that in Pittsburgh and too many other Major League cities remains painfully slow).

Almost twenty years later, I am glad that the stories in this book are going to get another life in this expanded Bison Books edition and that the tales of John Montgomery Ward and David Fultz, union organizers in unfriendly times, can be told again. Ward's story, especially during his time in the Players League, is an amazing tale worthy of cinema treatment, and I want to commend two biographies written on the subject earlier this decade: Bryan DiSalvatore's *A Clever Base-Ballist* (Pantheon) and David Stevens's *A Radical for All Seasons* (Scarecrow). At some point during David Fultz's career as head of the short-lived Baseball Players Fraternity, he made the poignant observation that playing baseball prepares you for nothing in this life. It is a comment that puts into sharp focus why professional ballplayers from the earliest days of their profession possessed such a passionate desire about earning a pension. Thanks to the exhaustively researched 2008 book by Robert M. Gorman and David Weeks, *Death at the Ballpark* (McFarland), the figures Fultz gave for fatalities in the 1915 Minor League and semipro baseball seasons cited in *The Imperfect Diamond* have been slightly downgraded to thirty deaths, twenty-three from head injuries, but Fultz's courage and thoroughness in raising the issue remains exemplary.

Finally, I am glad to have the opportunity to add an epilogue in this Bison Books edition that tells the story of the cataclysmic strike of 1994–95 as well as baseball's recovery and resurgence—even if it is now increasingly likely that many of its home run–happy highlights were fueled by performance-enhancing drugs (PEDs). I am not now nor have I ever been a zealot on the issue of steroids in baseball or, more accurately, PEDs. Though I don't like what their excessive usage may have done to the record books, once baseball expanded to ten teams in each league in the early 1960s—with the resulting unbalanced schedules—I believe that the core of the record book was changed forever.

The public health aspects of PEDs do concern me deeply, yet I doubt whether there is an easy solution to the problem given the unrelenting pressure to win by both owners and players. Yet perhaps, just perhaps, both sides on the inevitable owner-player divide have found a program in baseball to reduce the dangers of PEDs in the seasons ahead.

I want to pay homage to many valuable books that have come out since the second edition of *The Imperfect Diamond*. Among them are Howard Bryant, *Juicing the Game* (Viking, 2006); Robert Burk, *Much More Than a Game* (University of North Carolina, 2001); John Helyar, *Lords of the Realm* (Villard, 1993); Jerome Holtzman, *The Commissioners* (Total Sports, 2000); Paul Staudohar, ed., *Diamond Mines: Baseball and Labor* (Syracuse, 2000); and Andrew Zimbalist, *In the Best Interests of Baseball?* (Free Press, 2006).

Special thanks to Royse Parr, who shared valuable excerpts from his biography of Allie Reynolds.

I offer warm thanks to Judith Anne Dills and Jean Hastings Ardell for their editorial help and thoughtful suggestions for the new introduction.

Finally, special thanks to my sister Carol Norton, who at the last minute generously allowed use of the photo of herself, future Angels owner Gene Autry, and yours truly, her baby brother.

To the memory of my parents, and to the memory of Tony Lupien

I lovingly rededicate this newest edition to Tony Lupien, born Ulysees John Lupien. (During Italian Night in Louisville, Kentucky, where Tony was playing just before his call up to the Red Sox, every player got an Italian nickname; the name "Tony" stuck.)

He was a stubborn idealist, a Harvard-educated, uncompromising northern New Englander whose character resembled one of the gnarled sturdy oak trees in his beloved Vermont that may bend but never break. He deeply cared about the game of baseball and never lost his love for it despite the bad treatment he received during his Veterans Act case after World War II, a story that is told in this book.

His passionate, no-nonsense last words in the first edition are worth repeating: "The owners have proven that their power structure is not 'for the good of the game.' Can the players quench their thirst for leadership temperately? Perhaps this could be a very sobering thought for some young men who have never even read the contracts they have signed."

Ulysees "Tony" Lupien died in July 2004. He went out in style with his favorite Dixieland jazz music filling St. Denis Chapel near the Dartmouth College campus during his funeral service. As Dartmouth coach he led the team to a College World Series appearance in 1970 and tutored three future Major League pitchers—Jim Beattie, Pete Broberg, and Chuck Seelbach. Tony Lupien uttered many wise and inspirational words in his long and accomplished life. The ones that resound the most to me apply not just to the playing of baseball but also to the conduct of one's life: "Show me somebody without emotion and I'll show you a nothing."

Acknowledgments

Several members of the Society for American Baseball Research were extremely generous in sharing materials. Professor Eugene Murdock of Marietta College (Ohio), whose forthcoming biography *Ban Johnson, Czar of Baseball* will make a major contribution to the study of baseball history, wrote several helpful letters. So did Joseph Overfield of Buffalo, New York, who sent on copies of his well-researched and clearly written articles on late nineteenth century baseball. SABR members Harrington "Kit" Crissey, L. Robert Davids, and Jack Kavanagh contributed useful information and offered encouragement. Sheldon Sunness shared some of his research on the Players League.

James Rowe generously provided photos from his impressive archive. Mary I. Fleming and Winifred J. Watson sent on a very appreciated studio portrait of their cousin, John Montgomery Ward. We extend warm thanks to Danny Kaye for permission to reproduce his and Jack Benny's ball park picture of 1947.

George Alexander of Camerama Photo in New York City made swift reproductions of several pictures in the photo section.

Baseball was not invented in Cooperstown, New York, but researchers and writers should be very happy that the National Baseball Hall of Fame Library and photo archive exists there and that such cordial and helpful people as Clifford Kachline, John Redding, and Sally Campbell work there. Retired Hall of Fame historian Ken Smith also supplied quick and friendly answers to queries.

Special thanks to William H. Scherman who read the final draft and offered extremely helpful editorial suggestions.

Eliot Asinof's leads on interviews turned out valuably.

Lawrence Ritter gave cordial permission to quote from his classic *The Glory of Their Times.*

Portions of the manuscript profited from the constructive reading of Dr. Norman H. Bruce of Boston, Professor James Cox of Dartmouth College, and Colonel Red Reeder.

Without the kind use of the West Hartford, Connecticut, apartment of George "Jocko" Stangle, this collaboration between New York and Vermont authors could not have been completed.

The following people were interviewed either in person, by phone, or by mail. Of course the judgments in this book are the responsibility of the author alone, but for background and honest opinion, thanks are offered to: writers Jerome Holtzman, A.L. Rainovic (editor of *The Diamond Report,* published in Milwaukee, Wisconsin), Tracy Ringolsby, and Harold Rosenthal.

During 1979, Bowie Kuhn was interviewed along with Marty Appel and Frank Cashen, assistants in the office of the commissioner. In August 1990, baseball commissioner Fay Vincent provided an informative interview as did Charles T. O'Connor, director of the Player Relations Committee. Carol Coleman of the commissioner of baseball's office swiftly supplied photographs of the last three commissioners.

Also in August 1990, former federal mediator Kenneth Moffett shared memories of the baseball conflicts of 1980 and 1981 and his short tenure as executive director of the Major League Baseball Players Association in 1983.

From the Major League Baseball Players Association: Executive Director Marvin J. Miller, former Association counsel Richard M. Moss, Jim Bunning, Allie Reynolds, and Robin Roberts, three players active in the formative years of the Association; J. Norman Lewis, the first counsel to the Association, and Mrs. Duffy Lewis, his sister-in-law who helped to arrange the interview.

Other baseball management officials who were interviewed were Jack Dunn III and Henry J. Peters of the Baltimore Orioles, William Y. Giles of the Philadelphia Phillies, and Bill Veeck of the Chicago White Sox.

Former players interviewed were Cy Block, Hank Camelli, Don Drysdale, Danny Gardella, Bob Harris, Newell Kimball, Sandy Koufax, Al Lopez, Hugh Luby, Al Niemiec, Rich Nye, and Greg Pryor. The following players who were active during the 1990 season shared their experiences in baseball's labor relations: Jeff Ballard of the Orioles; Phil Bradley of the Orioles and the White Sox; Brett Butler of the Giants, and Paul Molitor of the Brewers.

From the rising world of player representation and agentry, the following people were interviewed: Mac Barrett, Nick Buonoconti, Dr. Skip Connor and Ronald M. Shapiro of Professional Management Associates (Baltimore), and Professor William Weston of the University of Baltimore Law School, founder of ARPA (the Association of Representatives of Professional Athletes).

The following participants in the legal side of this story were interviewed: Former Congressman Emanuel Celler, Frederic A. Johnson, and Peter Seitz. Stephen L. Mann, founder of The Baseball Brain company in Philadelphia and an incisive writer in his own right, shared his insights from working as an analyst on both sides of the labor-management fence in baseball during the 1980s.

Lawyers and students of law and history who provided useful information and ideas were Jim Curtis, Alan M. Kaufmann Jr., James R. Kearney, Stanley I. Kutler, Ted Meckler, Jeffrey B. Morris, Clark Shaffer, John Strawn, Steve Tischler, Mary V. G. Walsh, and Stephen Vicchio.

Bill Cooper of the manuscripts division of the University of Kentucky forwarded excellent material from the Happy Chandler Papers, a kind gesture which spared the expense and time of a research trip. The Cornell University archives sent a detailed obituary of Harry Leonard Taylor.

From Stein and Day—Art Ballant, who supported this project from the outset; Daphne Hougham, Judika Konowe, Laura Lamorte, and Robert McBroom, who saw it to completion; Henry Engel who copyedited the book; and Jerry Weinberg, who proofread it impeccably. From Da Capo Press, Yuval Taylor was a cheerful but incisive editor who supported the new edition of this book enthusiastically.

In closing, Lee Lowenfish would like to acknowledge the interest and friendship of his nephew, Eric B. Norton, part of another generation learning to love baseball. Lee cannot fully express in words his gratitude to his wife, Greta Minsky, whose patient editing and understanding were sorely tested at times throughout this venture but never were found wanting. These words still hold true even if she is now my ex-wife.

CONTENTS

FOREWORD

One of the most important books on the history and development of major league baseball is *The Imperfect Diamond*, written by Lee Lowenfish, a New York City writer, teacher, radio broadcaster, and jazz buff. Lowenfish has a profound affection for baseball and a deep-seated resentment of the way ballplayers are manipulated by club owners, particularly in the dark days when the infamous "reserve clause" bound the players to a contract for life. A student of American history, he also possesses a keen understanding of the turbulent relationship between labor and management in the United States.

The Imperfect Diamond, first published in 1980 and now happily reissued with 20,000 words of new, updated material, gives those who love baseball both as a game and a way of life the opportunity to see beyond the scrim of handlebar moustaches and Casey At The Bat nostalgia that blurs the reality of baseball history. It reveals the depth and intelligence and courage of such ballplayers as Curt Flood and Hall of Famers Jim (Orator) O'Rourke and John Mont-

13

gomery Ward, who off the field fought the unfair strictures imposed by the powerful entrepreneurs who controlled the game.

Today in our era of free agency and high salaries, it is easy to forget what it was like to be a ballplayer in "the good old days" of the reserve clause. *The Imperfect Diamond* will help you remember.

Robert W. Creamer
author of *Stengel* and *Babe*
October, 1990

PROLOGUE

The Messersmith-
McNally Decision

*RICHARD M. MOSS, Attorney for the Major
League Baseball Players Association: "You mean
players might have to be paid what they are
worth?"*
*LELAND M. MACPHAIL, JR., President of the
American League: "No. They might have to be
paid more than they are worth."*
*—from an exchange during the Messersmith-
McNally arbitration hearing, November 1975.*

Thanksgiving 1975 was only days away. The last rustling of autumn
leaves could be heard in New York's Central Park. Across the street in a
hearing room of the Barbizon-Plaza Hotel, there was a conspicuous lack
of holiday spirit. At issue was a grievance of two veteran major league
baseball pitchers, Andy Messersmith and Dave McNally.

Messersmith had won 39 games for the Los Angeles Dodgers during
the 1974 and 1975 seasons. Dave McNally had retired from the Montreal Expos during the 1975 season. From 1962 to 1974 he had been a star
hurler for the Baltimore Orioles, winning 20 games or more four times
and amassing 181 victories. If a three-man arbitration panel ruled in
behalf of Messersmith and McNally, the century-old restrictions of
baseball's reserve system could be ruptured.

Neither Messersmith nor McNally had signed a contract for the 1975
season. The Dodger and Expo managements had renewed their services
under the provisions of Section 10(a) of the Uniform Player's Contract.
The Major League Baseball Players Association argued that both
hurlers should be free agents because Section 10(a) allowed renewal only
"for the period of one year."

Baseball officials and their lawyers hotly contested this interpretation. Veteran National League attorney Louis Hoynes said that to isolate one clause of the contract from the totality of major league rules and regulations "was to describe the human skeleton omitting the backbone," which was the reserve system.

The dictionary defines reserve, "To keep for future use." Variously called in baseball practice a rule, a clause, or a system, the reserve was defended as necessary for "competitive balance" between teams in a league. The reserve also was deemed necessary to protect the investment baseball owners had made in the skills of baseball players.

Historically, the first reserve clause had been introduced in September 1879. Arthur Soden, owner of the Boston National League club, won the support of his colleagues for a plan to reserve five players on each club in the League. The owners agreed to respect each other's reserve clauses and not to try to lure the protected players with better offers.

By the middle of the 1880s, baseball management had extended the reserve clause to every contract. The provision enabled the owners to control the players indefinitely. It also was an effective device for holding salaries down because players were denied an alternative market for their services. Although many trade wars had dotted baseball history, the reserve clause still dominated the business of professional baseball in November 1975.

The prospect of losing the Messersmith-McNally grievance horrified baseball's magnates. Their strategy before the arbitration panel was to emphasize the historic propriety of the reserve system. They entered as evidence the 1891 contract of baseball's winningest pitcher, Cy Young, stressing the perpetual reserve in the document. They submitted the official card on which Cincinnati Reds' star outfielder, Edd Roush, had been reserved throughout his career. Baseball management's position was that Roush had been reserved even during the 1930 season when he did not sign a contract during an extended holdout for better pay.

During the hearing, forecasts of doom were voiced by baseball officials. Walter Alston, Andy Messersmith's manager, was quoted, "If he wins his case, baseball is dead." National League President Charles S. "Chub" Feeney testified that if competitive bidding were allowed for players' services, "We might not have a World Series if it gets to be that disastrous." "The loss of a major league is quite possible," added Baseball Commissioner Bowie Kent Kuhn, an attorney who once worked in the same office as National League lawyer Louis Hoynes.

Players Association advocates scoffed at these arguments. Executive Director Marvin Julian Miller, who had become the permanent representative of the major league players in 1966 after years with the United Steelworkers of America, considered organized baseball a unique monopoly. "Unlike most antitrust conspiracies, this one is written down on paper—even printed," Miller had once observed about the National Agreement, the portentous-sounding document which bound all players and clubs in the major and minor leagues.

Miller and Players Association counsel Richard M. Moss refuted baseball's arguments in favor of the reserve system. They argued that it had not achieved the goal of "competitive balance." In the twentieth century, only four teams had won 60 percent of the pennants, with the New York Yankees far in the lead.

Miller and Moss also resented the suggestion that a free market for ballplayers would make them compete less enthusiastically against teams they hoped to play for in the future. Baseball players were competitors by nature, they argued. They would not give less than their best under any circumstances. Moreover, players' good performances would always enhance their market value, their advocates stressed.

Peter Seitz, chairman of the arbitration panel, listened to the conflicting arguments carefully. He was an experienced lawyer and had been a full-time professional arbitrator for twenty years. Under the law, it was his duty to make a prompt decision on the merits of the case. It was not his job to worry about the skyrocketing salaries owners would have to pay the players if management lost the case. Seitz realized his assignment was as awesome and as final as an umpire's call on the diamond: Safe or Out.

Seitz never lost his sense of humor during the three days of frequently acrimonious hearings. When additional evidence was suggested for submission, he rejected it on "environmental grounds. Whole hillsides are being decimated for the exhibits in this case." But he knew the burden of a weighty decision would soon fall upon him. On the three-man panel, Marvin Miller would surely vote for the players and John J. Gaherin, the owners' delegate, a former president of the New York City Newspaper Publishers Association, surely would side with management.

After the hearing ended on December 1, 1975, Seitz made some initial judgments. He rejected the owners' contention that the arbitration panel had no jurisdiction over a grievance on Section 10(a). He believed there was nothing in prior negotiations between players and management that excluded the renewal clause from arbitration.

But Seitz believed that the renewal question was only a narrow part of the central problem of the reserve system itself. His first reaction to the Messersmith-McNally grievance had been that neither side had sufficiently bargained the question. Seitz hoped that the basic question of modifying the reserve system could be worked out through collective bargaining rather than by the quasi-judicial fiat of arbitration.

He discussed the matter with John Gaherin and asked management's representative to take a letter to the owners' end-of-year meeting in Florida. Gaherin gladly obliged and carried to Tampa a carefully written eight-page missive from the arbitrator.

Peter Seitz hinted strongly in his letter that he was leaning to the Players Association's position in the specific Messersmith grievance. He defined the issue as "whether a player, after the expiration of his 'option year,' on further renewal of his contract, can be 'reserved' by his club to play for it, exclusively."

The purpose of his letter was to suggest a compromise. He asked the owners to take advantage of a "fortuitous circumstance." The Basic Agreement between players and owners was expiring at the end of December. He urged management to open up the entire reserve question for negotiation in the interests of future accord with the players. Seitz noted that Commissioner Kuhn's testimony before his panel had strongly endorsed the method of collective bargaining.

Seitz wrote, "Clearly, it would be vastly more desirable and profitable for the parties to take advantage of this coincidence of events, to endeavor to accommodate their objectives and interests in their bargaining than for this Panel to make a final Award on what has been an unusual state of facts affecting the Reserve System." He concluded, with emphasis, that if his suggestion were ignored, "The Panel will not shrink from the performance of its duty, which is to make a decision *promptly* on the merits."

The owners were unimpressed with Seitz's letter. They had railed at him in December 1974 when he declared Oakland Athletics' masterful pitcher Jim "Catfish" Hunter a free agent because Oakland owner

Charles Oscar Finley had committed a material breach by not delivering a contracted insurance policy. They knew that the Messersmith case was far more ominous because the renewal clause's interpretation would affect every contract.

However, the baseball owners chose to believe that the traditions of the sport would never change. The modern establishment consisted of the descendants of the men called magnates and moguls in the late nineteenth and early twentieth centuries. Like their forebears, the modern owners considered themselves benevolent rulers creating jobs for players who otherwise would be poor, unskilled workers. Many wished that Marvin Miller and the Players Association would simply go away. They had greeted with cries of rage and doom every advance by the players since the late 1960s: the first Basic Agreement in 1968, outside arbitration like the Seitz panel in 1970, and salary arbitration for players in 1973.

Although outfielder Curt Flood of the St. Louis Cardinals had lost his antitrust case against baseball in 1972, the tide of public opinion clearly had changed in behalf of the players. That Dave McNally, a *retired* athlete who had left Montreal in midseason because he could not regain the form which made him a star with the Baltimore Orioles, would attach his name to the Messersmith grievance should have been further evidence to management that a time for change had come.

It is said that those whom the gods would destroy they first make mad. The major league owners proved the dictum by rejecting Seitz's offered compromise, leaving him with no choice but to decide the grievance on the merits.

On December 23, 1975, he issued a sixty-one page decision siding with the Players Association in behalf of Messersmith and McNally. He ruled that they were free to bargain with other teams because organized baseball could not maintain a player's services indefinitely. Seitz compared the owners' assertion of a perpetual reserve to "the claims of some nations that persons once its citizens, wherever they live and regardless of the passage of time, the swearing of other allegiances, and other circumstances are still its own nationals and subject to the obligation that citizenship in the nation imposes." On the contrary, Seitz wrote, "This 'status' theory is incompatible with the doctrine or policy of freedom in the economic and political society in which we live and of which the professional sport of baseball ('the national game') is a part."

Seitz emphasized that his ruling did not obliterate the reserve system or make any judgment on the validity of such restrictions. He urged again that both sides bargain in good faith on this crucial complex question. "The clubs and the players have a mutual interest in the health and integrity of the sport and in its financial return," he concluded. "With a will to do so, they are competent to fashion a reserve system to suit their requirements."

Baseball was not quite ready to admit defeat. The moguls fired Seitz as the arbitrator, and they sought out courts hoping for a decision to overturn Seitz's award. They were rejected every time. In March 1976 the last appeal was lost. Missouri Federal Judge John W. Oliver said it was "ludicrous" for the owners to claim that the players had no right to grieve on the reserve system. He added, "Congress did not entrust this court or any other court with the responsibility of looking out for our national pastime."

The owners, faced with the inevitable, dropped their hard-line stance. They had locked the players out of spring training in a show of force, but the training camps were opened by mid-March in a rare edict of independence by Commissioner Kuhn. Negotiations for a Basic Agreement without the reserve clause continued into the start of the 1976 season.

Free to negotiate with all teams, Andy Messersmith at first was met with a conspiracy of silence by the owners. Once his freedom became irreversible by the court action, he signed a lucrative, long-term pact with the Atlanta Braves. The owners dreaded the end of the season when theoretically, according to their direst predictions, all the good players could walk away from their teams for riches elsewhere.

The fears proved exaggerated. In July 1976 a new Basic Agreement was signed by the Players Association and management, though seven owners voted to reject the pact. The benefits of the Seitz decision accrued to major league veterans with six years experience. A "reentry draft" was established for each November. All eligible major league veterans could be drafted by up to half of the major league clubs. The teams selected players in inverse order to their standing in the pennant race to assure, at least theoretically, that the top clubs did not get all the available stars. During the first reentry draft in November 1976, 24 major leaguers were chosen by other teams, a far cry from the mass exodus and chaos that the old guard had feared.

20

Not surprisingly, the creation of free agency has led to rapidly rising salaries for the players. The average salary had been only $12,000 in 1972, but thanks largely to the coming of salary arbitration in 1973, it had risen to almost $50,000 in 1976. Through the pressure of free agency, the average approached $150,000 in 1980. It continued unabated to the stratosphere of nearly $600,000 by 1990, with some experts forecasting an average salary of $1,000,000 a year by the year 2000.

Yet management has also prospered under the new system. Attendance in the major leagues set a new record for each of the first four years of free agency, reaching almost 44 million in 1979. Throughout the 1980s, attendance went ever upward so that by 1990, over 55 million fans attended major league baseball games. Television revenue, from both network and local sources, reached record levels. Starting in 1990, every major league club owner was assured over $14 million in television money before the gates of the ballpark were even opened and one hot dog put on the griddle. The off-season publicity generated by free agency kept baseball in the news almost all year round, a big plus in the competition for news among professional sports. The baleful predictions of management during the Messersmith-McNally arbitration hearing simply did not come true.

The on-field performance of the first free agents proved the validity of the old baseball axiom: You cannot buy a pennant. Catfish Hunter pitched well for the Yankees during the first two years of the five-year contract that he signed in December 1974. Then his production fell off markedly, and he retired after the 1979 season. Andy Messersmith was constantly plagued by injury and never regained his old form. On the other hand, Reggie Jackson performed spectacularly under pressure after coming to the Yankees in the first free agent reentry draft.

In later free agent drafts, the same mixed results applied. As it should be, managerial talent is at a higher premium than ever before in baseball. Who should get the big bucks in the open market and who should be satisfied before he tries to reap the golden harvest of free agency are crucial questions for baseball evaluators to confront and resolve. Wise managements decide to treat free agency as another tool with which to build a successful ball club, but the traditional methods of team building—minor league development and trades—remain a dominant part of the baseball business.

Despite the seeming equity in the new system, management was not happy with the new arrangement. Lost power can drive men wilder than lost money, especially in a business that for over a century had developed traditions free of governmental restrictions. "Baseball 'law' is illegal, contrary to civil law, in direct violation of the Federal laws regulating combines and the blacklist, and, in principle, directly in defiance of the Constitution and of the Rights of Man," future Hall of Fame second baseman Johnny Evers admitted in *Touching Second: Inside Play in Big League Baseball*, a book he wrote in collaboration with sportswriter Hugh Fullerton (the man who played an instrumental role in cracking open the 1919 World Series scandal). "Yet, because of the nature of the peculiar business, the greater part of baseball law is necessary," they concluded.

It was almost inevitable that management would try to reverse the gains made by the players in the 1970s. In the 1980s, baseball made it through a strike of the last days of the spring training season (1980), a 51-day in-season strike (1981), a 2-day work stoppage (1985), management collusion against free agents (starting in 1985), arbitration decisions that struck down the collusion with damages of more than $100 million levied against the owners (starting in 1987), the return of wild free agent spending (1989), and a spring training lockout (1990). Yet the game continues to prosper. The old saying seems truer than ever: "Baseball has survived world war, depression, and over a hundred years of mismanagement; it can survive anything."

In the perspective of the great gains made (and maintained) by the players in recent years, three questions arise:

Why did it take nearly a hundred years for basic marketplace freedoms to come to baseball players?

Who are some of the forgotten players and spokesmen who fought the battle for equity in less auspicious times?

Why was the monopoly called organized baseball so unyielding and convinced of its sacred status?

22

The Imperfect Diamond intends to address these questions in a perspective sympathetic to the player. The story of the life and work of the professional baseball player has been generally shrouded in illusion. To many fans, the ballplayer leads a life of envious ease. He plays a boys' game for two hours a day and then is adored by an admiring public. To many owners, the ballplayer is an expensive toy to be wound up and sold and traded at whim. Too many sportswriters have spread these distorted viewpoints over the years.

This work hopes to present the baseball player as a real-life individual and a unique phenomenon, a worker in an industry and a part of the product. He is also a businessman with a rare but will-o'-the-wisp skill. But until the emergence of a strong Major League Baseball Players Association in the late 1960s, the player had very little leverage against the ownership of major league baseball.

The Imperfect Diamond is written out of faith in the future of America's greatest game. Baseball has always been a common denominator in our country. It has kept the interest of young and old, of urbanites and country dwellers. It is my hope that this work will contribute to an understanding and the future sustenance of one of the longest running dramas in American history, the baseball enterprise.

Part I

*John Montgomery Ward
and the Bitter Legacy
of the Players League
Revolt of 1890*

1

The Rebellion of the Brotherhood
of Professional Baseball Players in 1889

*"By a combination among themselves, stronger
than the strongest trust, the owners were able to
enforce the most arbitrary measures, and the player
had either to submit or get out of the profession in
which he had spent years attaining proficiency."*
*—Manifesto of the Brotherhood of Professional
Baseball Players, November 6, 1889.*

"I believe that all men who have ever lived and achieved success in this
world had lived in vain if they knew not baseball," exclaimed orator
Chauncey Depew. The occasion was a banquet early in April 1889 at
New York City's fashionable Delmonico's restaurant. The guests of
honor were America's greatest baseball players just returned from a
six-month tour around the world.

Albert Goodwill Spalding, sporting-goods entrepreneur and president of the Chicago National League Club, had planned this trip thinking that American baseball's great surge in popularity in the 1880s could
be duplicated overseas. It did not work out that way. Egyptians yawned
at one game played near the pyramids. Italians indignantly refused to
tear up the Colosseum turf to create a baseball diamond.

Back home, though, the tour members were received as conquering
heroes. After future United States Senator Depew finished his discourse,
Mark Twain told his fellow banqueters, "Baseball is the perfect expression of the conquering age of Americans." New York City Police Chief
Theodore Roosevelt nodded in agreement.

The three hundred diners at Delmonico's had not come for oratory;
they had come to gaze at the players. And none of the players received a
larger ovation than did the captain of the All-America team, John

Montgomery Ward. "When John M. Ward was announced," wrote *The New York World,* "the cheering made the dishes jingle." Ward was the shortstop of the New York Giants, baseball's current world champions. In 1888 Ward had led the New York National League club to a pennant and a victory over St. Louis of the American Association in the postseason World Series. He was a swift base runner who led the National League in stolen bases with 111 in 1887. He was an accomplished fielder, credited with making many refinements in the technique of the double play. He would amass 2,123 hits in a career lasting through 1894.

Ward was a man of exceptional talents. Born in Bellefonte, Pennsylvania in 1860, he entered Penn State College, near his home, when he was only thirteen. In 1875 he left school to become a professional baseball pitcher. In three years, he was pitching for the Providence Grays, a charter member of the National League founded in 1876. Ward hurled a two-hit shutout in his first game in the major leagues. In 1879 he led the league in victories and winning percentage, compiling a 44-18 record. In 1880 he pitched one of the first perfect games on record en route to a 40-23 season.

John Montgomery Ward was a pioneer in pitching technique. He threw one of the first successful curve balls. He has been credited with designing the raised pitching mound, which allows the hurler the advantage of throwing down at the batter.

After the 1882 season, Ward was sold from Providence to New York. During 1883 he developed arm trouble, but the resourceful pitcher, after having compiled a 158-102 record in seven major league seasons, made the rare shift to everyday player. Rosters rarely exceeded fifteen players per club in these days, and Ward played both the infield and the outfield before settling on shortstop as his best position.

His versatility off the field was equally impressive. Ward could speak five languages and between baseball seasons, to compensate for his early departure from Penn State, he earned two bachelor's degrees from Columbia College, in law in 1885 and in political science in 1886. In 1887, Ward, who appreciated good baseball talent, tried unsuccessfully to convince the Giants to sign George Stovey, a brilliant Negro pitcher.

Ward contributed articles regularly to national magazines and also published the first baseball book for young people, *How to Become a Player.* His piece in the October 1888 issue of *Cosmopolitan* magazine, "Our National Game," exemplified his eloquent style and obvious love of the game. In one particularly adept passage, he observed:

Looking back over the brief history of base-ball [*sic*] we are at once struck by its marvelous growth. Like everything else American it came with a rush, and it is today as firmly established in this country as cricket is in England. . . . The game is suited to the national temperament. It requires strength, courage and skill; it is full of dash and excitement and though a most difficult game in which to excel, it is yet extremely simple in its first principles and easily understood by every one.

Robert Smith, in his fine 1947 history, *Baseball,* has given a vivid portrait of the charismatic Ward, "a slender, handsome Irishman with a mossy mustache, high cheekbones, and eyes of an amazingly light and lucid blue. He exuded honesty and purity in every gesture."

Actually, Ward's ancestry was English and Scottish. His parents migrated to central Pennsylvania in the 1850s. It did not hurt to look Irish in New York City. Ward's good looks also made him a favorite of the theatrical crowd, which had started to flock to the ball games. Comic actor DeWolf Hopper, whose rendition of Ernest Thayer's *Casey At The Bat* made him nationally famous in 1888, often came to root for Ward and the Giants.

Another frequent patron was young actress Helen Dauvray. In 1886 she donated a cup to the winner of the National League-American Association World Series. Most people thought Helen simply loved baseball in general. Soon, her specific eye for John Montgomery Ward was evident. *The New York Times* described her at Giants' games: "Her tiny hands beat each other rapturously at every victory and her dark eyes were bedewed at every defeat."

Ward's teammate, pitcher Tim Keefe, was Helen Dauvray's brother-in-law. He arranged an introduction, and a storybook romance ensued between the attractive actress and the handsome star ballplayer.

John and Helen wed after the 1887 season, but the perennial problems of celebrity marriages doomed their relationship. The ballplayer wanted his wife to give up the stage. But Helen had always been an actress and wanted to continue her career. They lived together for barely a year, but were not officially divorced until 1903.

As John Montgomery Ward prepared to start the 1889 season, domestic problems were far from his mind. He and his fellow players faced serious threats to their livelihood. While the stars had been on the overseas tour, the baseball owners had passed stringent new regulations against the players. Since 1885 Ward had been the president of the

Brotherhood of Professional Base Ball Players. When he learned of the turn of events during the tour, he had been so upset he considered leaving for home immediately.

The owners' new rules intended to put a lid of $2,500 a year on player salaries. Although star players like Ward would get $4,000 or more under the table, the owners wanted to keep the majority of their players under $2,500. Indianapolis owner John T. Brush, a wealthy clothing merchant, had also succeeded in passing a "Classification Plan" which assigned players to salary levels below the "A" of $2,500. The lowly "E" player, receiving $1,500 or, likely, less, would be assigned menial tasks like sweeping up the ball park after the game. Arthur Soden of Boston even used his marginal players as turnstile attendants.

In his 1962 volume, *Baseball In America,* Robert Smith has described the owners of the 1880s as "men whose fingers tightened automatically over a dollar, and who checked their receipts secretly and put on a poor mouth to the players." Because of the reserve clause, the player had no alternative other than retirement if he did not like the contract offer from his owner. The National Agreement, the self-important name baseball moguls gave to the accord of 1882 between the National League, American Association, and various minor leagues, enforced harsh penalties on any player or club who operated without the reserve restriction.

While the Brotherhood of Professional Base Ball Players was not a militant group, it sought to provide relief for the players from the worst abuses of management. Its charter, drafted by Ward in late 1885, promised "to protect and benefit its members collectively and individually, to promote a high standard of professional conduct, and to advance the interests of the 'National Game'." Although Ward declined to affiliate the Brotherhood with the Knights of Labor, the national labor organization of the 1880s, the spirit of the players' organization was akin to the Knights, whose motto was, "An injury to one is the concern of all."

John Montgomery Ward certainly cared about the treatment of common ballplayers. One of the Brotherhood victories had been to win restitution for Washington player Cliff Carroll, whose owner, John Gaffney, had stopped payment on a $100-check written as an inducement for Carroll to sign his contract. In general, the players' organization could do very little about the benign neglect of the fair owners to the practices of their less humane partners. Gaffney once fined a player for missing a game on his wedding day. Arthur Soden, who intended to share little of his roofing fortune with his players, continually made them jump into the stands to retrieve foul balls from the customers.

As the 1889 season started, John Ward realized that the Brotherhood had to respond forcefully to the owners' latest abuses. Ward himself had held such stature that he was able to reject his sale to Washington. New owner Nick Young was willing to pay Ward a $6,000-salary, but Ward did not want to leave New York. The thought that he could be sold as if he were a piece of livestock utterly repelled him.

As he considered what action to recommend to the Brotherhood, Ward thought back to his most militant critique of the baseball system, an article he had contributed to the August 1887 issue of *Lippincott's*. The prestigious Philadelphia magazine had been concerned that a new form of slavery was developing less than a generation after the Civil War. The editor asked Ward to write on the topic "Is the Ballplayer a Chattel?"

Using his considerable powers of persuasion to the fullest, Ward had vented his rage at the abuses baseball inflicted upon the player. "Like a fugitive slave law, the reserve rule denies him a harbor or a livelihood, and carries him back, bound and shackled, to the club from which he attempted to escape," Ward wrote. "He goes where he is sent, takes what is given him, and thanks the Lord for life."

Like the lawyer he would become, Ward piled up case evidence of owner malfeasance. Buffalo had suspended a sick player, Charlie Foley, and then reserved him without pay for two years, effectively terminating his career at the age of twenty-seven. Spectacularly stingy Arthur Soden suspended outfielder Charles Wesley Jones when the player refused to compete until he received back pay of $378. Friends and teammates had to stage a benefit game to tide the victimized Jones through the two years of his suspension until he resumed his career in Cincinnati.

Ward especially condemned the sales system. In 1886 Albert Spalding's sale of colorful outfielder Mike "King" Kelly to Boston for $10,000 had caused much public notice. Spalding would later admit that he earned $750,000 from his Chicago club in the late 1880s, quickly adding that he reinvested $600,000 of his profits. The player sale was becoming common, but the player received nothing. Ward told his *Lippincott's* audience, "The whole thing is a conspiracy, pure and simple, on the part of the clubs, by which they are making money rightfully belonging to the players."

Yet even at his angriest moment in 1887, Ward ended on a note of caution. "The system has become so rooted that heroic treatment may be necessary to remove it." Ward was not ready for revolt, partly because he still felt ambivalent about the reserve system. He observed once, anticipating that famous cliché that baseball owners need protection from each other, "The reserve rule takes a manager by the throat and compels him to keep his hands off his neighbor's enterprise." In 1888, following Ward's recommendation, the Brotherhood had the owners put the reserve explicitly into the player's contract. By mid-1889, John Ward was convinced that the owners would never enforce their own rules and abide by their words. The salary classification plan had violated the reserve agreement of 1888 because Ward accepted the reserve in the contract only if the owners promised not to cut salaries for the option year. Obviously, the freeze on wages was contrary to the spirit of 1888.

Always a man of conciliation, John Ward tried to meet with Albert Spalding to work out the differences between players and owners. Spalding had been a star pitcher in the 1860s and 1870s. In 1875 Spalding himself had walked out on his contract with Boston of the National Association of Professional Baseball Players to accept a better offer from businessmen in Chicago, who wanted to establish a new league. The National League was established in February 1876, which minimized the effect of Spalding's expulsion from the National Association for abandoning Boston.

The new league liked to say that it was "born in rebellion" from the old order, but when National League players in 1889 demanded more equitable treatment, the now established circuit rebuffed them. In early June, Spalding gave Ward the brushoff when the player asked for a meeting to discuss the classification and salary limitation grievances. The owner offered an excuse which would become standard in the course of baseball's labor relations: "Wait until the end of the season and then we'll talk." Of course, by the fall, ballplayers scattered to their homes across the country and lost any chance for collective action.

Snubbed by Spalding, Ward faced rising sentiment for radical action within the Brotherhood. Some militants wanted to call a strike for the Fourth of July, to show their sympathy for two maltreated veteran ballplayers, Deacon White and Jack Rowe.

White and Rowe called Buffalo home. They had played for the National League team in the Queen City for the first half of the 1880s.

During the 1885 season, the entire franchise was sold for $7,000 to pharmaceutical magnate Frederick Kimball Stearns, who moved the team to Detroit. White and Rowe had no choice but to move to Michigan with the team. The players had always been told that the reserve rule and other restrictions of the baseball business were needed to "discipline" them and to "preserve their morale." It was not lost on them that the owners hardly showed restraint by moving franchises. As another example, after the 1885 season, the entire Providence franchise was packed up and moved to Boston.

White and Rowe stayed in Detroit through 1888. They helped the Wolverines to win the World Series in 1887. The next year Stearns decided he did not want to pay the salaries of his champions. At the end of the season, he sold Rowe's contract to William J. Nimick of Pittsburgh and White's contract to Arthur Soden of Boston. Upon reflection, Soden decided he did not want the services of a forty-two-year-old player even if he was an outstanding .300 hitter and versatile fielder; he sold White to Nimick also.

Deacon White and Jack Rowe decided they wanted to play in Buffalo. They owned a share of the International League franchise in that town. Stung by the abandonment of the city by the National League in 1885, new investors were determined to put Buffalo baseball back on the map. White and Rowe had always saved their money. White's nickname "Deacon" came from his abstemious habits and regular churchgoing. They were businessmen as well as players, and they wanted to cast their lot with the Buffalo team. White was so highly thought of that he was named the president of the team.

Frederick Stearns, informed of his former players' plans, bellowed, "White may have been elected president of the Buffalo club or president of the United States, but that won't enable him to play ball in Buffalo. He'll play in Pittsburgh or he'll get off the earth." Less dramatically, William Nimick declared, "If they do not want to play in Pittsburgh, they'll play nowhere."

Deacon White was not cowed. He had studied law and considered suing baseball. He was convinced that the reserve clause and other restrictions that had come to be called "baseball law" would not stand up in court. He declared, "The laws of this country will stop people from preventing me from making an honest living."

Yet as late as June 1889, White and Rowe were not playing. The lords

33

of baseball had sent down the word that every player who competed with or against White and Rowe would be faced with expulsion. The baseball blacklist, the ultimate method of enforcing the reserve rule, had turned White and Rowe into excommunicants from baseball's self-sanctified church. They were "outlaws" because they had refused to accept what baseball magnates considered the legitimate sale of their services to another club within organized baseball.

White and Rowe's undesired idleness enraged many players in the Brotherhood, whose membership had soared to nearly two hundred. While the militants called for a strike, John Montgomery Ward counseled caution. He advised White and Rowe to join Pittsburgh for the rest of the 1889 season. It would be better to play, Ward reasoned, than sit out a whole year. The blacklist was not a threat to be taken lightly. But Ward urged them not to sign any contract with Pittsburgh, "Only honor the 1889 reserve from your 1888 contract," he advised.

A delighted William Nimick welcomed Deacon White to Pittsburgh in mid-June and gave him a handsome salary of $5,000 prorated for the rest of the season. He also announced that $1,250 of the purchase price had been given to his new player. The Deacon made an uncharacteristically pungent comment as he arrived in Pittsburgh. "No man can sell my carcass unless I get half," he roared. Neither White nor Rowe would hit over .260 for a mediocre Pittsburgh team of 1889, but Nimick's property had been delivered.

The owner's jubilation was only momentary, for John Ward was hatching a grand scheme. He had decided that the old leagues would never honor their commitments, and would always find a way to skirt their own rules. Ward knew enough law and sensed enough economic opportunity that he conceived the idea of a new league run by players with owners as partners. At a July 14 (Bastille Day) meeting of the Brotherhood, Ward divulged his plans for the first time, and introduced the players to Albert Johnson of Cleveland, Ohio, a businessman who was most interested in entering baseball.

Johnson was a trolley-car owner and the younger brother of Tom Johnson, Cleveland's reform mayor. Albert Johnson shared his brother's idealism and was genuinely shocked by the inequities of the baseball contract. "If the [National] League can hold a man on a contract for any or all time that it may desire when it simply guarantees to him ten days' pay," he declaimed, "why, then the laws of our land are worse than those of any other nation on earth." Al Johnson believed ballplayers should earn whatever they could get. "Never forget that it is but a few years at best that a ballplayer can last," he said.

Johnson was also frankly interested in baseball for the money he could make. He knew that owning the trolley lines which carried fans to the ball parks would bring great profit. There was also money to be made in manufacturing turnstiles, baseballs and other equipment, and selling concessions at the games. The Brotherhood's idea of the new league was that players and backers (they would not be called owners) would share in all these proceeds. Tim Keefe, secretary of the Brotherhood and star Giants' pitcher, made plans to set up a sporting-goods company which would manufacture the official new league ball. Why should Spalding have the monopoly on everything?

Ward stressed that every city would need new backers, and the players should actively seek investors. By the end of the 1889 season, an impressive lineup of sponsors had been secured. Stockbroker Edward B. Talcott and realtor Wendell Goodwin would head the new league's New York and Brooklyn franchises, respectively. Colonel Edwin W. McAlpin, a tobacconist, realtor, and community leader in New York, was chosen as the new president. McAlpin had a streak of adventure in him; when he was fourteen he ran away from home to become a drummer boy in a Civil War unit. John Addison, a wealthy Chicago contractor, became president of the Chicago franchise and a vice-president of the league along with Albert Johnson.

Although no formal announcement of a new league came during the 1889 season, rumors were flying throughout the baseball world. Albert Spalding and other National League owners professed no concern, but they did announce that the classification plan and the maximum salary of $2,500 had been dropped. However, momentum was building, and on November 6, 1889, Ward made it official in New York, by announcing the birth of a new organization, the Players National League.

"There was a time when the league stood for integrity and fair dealing; today it stands for dollars and cents," Ward read from the new league's manifesto. "Players have been bought, sold, and exchanged as though they were sheep instead of American citizens." By the late 1880s, American society was in ferment with opposition growing to the huge corporations which were crushing many small businesses. Ward's manifesto appealed to the antitrust sentiments of the public when it derided the established owners for their unbridled power. "By a combination among themselves, stronger than the strongest trust," Ward declared, "they were able to enforce the most arbitrary measures, and the player had either to submit or get out of the profession in which he had spent years in attaining proficiency."

The Players League vowed to run their business on cooperative principles. A ten-year charter was drafted with players and backers sharing power on a board of directors. The reserve clause in the contract was scrapped. Instead, each player received a three-year contract. Salaries were guaranteed for the first year and there would be no pay cuts in future years. A fifty-fifty cut of gate receipts was established between visiting and home teams so that the smaller cities were not penalized for their lack of drawing power at home. The backers insisted on a provision which allowed them individually to keep the first $10,000 in profits. John Montgomery Ward reluctantly agreed to this compromise when the backers promised to put all the earnings over $10,000 into the cooperatively managed League treasury.

Almost all the stars of the day joined the new venture. Only Spalding's player-manager in Chicago and the leading hitter of his day, first baseman Adrian "Cap" Anson, remained loyal to the National League. The Players League backers were so confident of success that they went head-to-head with the established circuit in seven cities: New York, Brooklyn, Boston, Philadelphia, Chicago, Pittsburgh, and Cleveland. Buffalo was the eighth city given a franchise. Deacon White and Jack Rowe were players and part owners. So was a journeyman catcher named Cornelius McGillicuddy, also known as Connie Mack, who left Washington to join Buffalo and invested $500 in the new team.

One of the last stars to join the Players League was Charles Comiskey, player-manager for St. Louis of the American Association. Comiskey threw in his lot with the new organization when he decided he would not feel right earning $6,000 from the old regime while his brethren were banding together for a cooperative ideal and a dream of ultimate riches. Comiskey was named player-manager of the Chicago Players League franchise.

The players entered 1890 confident of victory. In the short history of the National League, several clubs had already folded because of mismanagement. In 1884 a wealthy St. Louis manufacturer, Henry V. Lucas, had vowed to succeed with a new league, the Union Association.

36

He promised the players a contract without a reserve clause, which he called "the most arbitrary and unjust rule ever suggested." But Lucas's association lasted only a year, and, in 1885, he had entered the National League with the Cleveland franchise in his pocket.

The players and their backers claimed it would be different this time. They thought they had right and riches on their side. They would learn instead how ruthlessly the baseball monopoly, barely a decade old, would deal with its adversaries.

2

The Rise and Fall of
the Players League of 1890

*"The magnate must be a strong man among strong
men, else other club owners in the league will
combine in their own interests against him and his
interests, and by collusion force him out of the
game."*
*—Albert Goodwill Spalding, Chicago National
League owner, 1890.*

Faced with a full-scale rebellion, the National League abandoned its
initial posture of indifference. It sought to win back the more than one
hundred players who had signed Players League contracts. Indianapolis's John T. Brush, the inventor of the classification plan, was the most
successful. He enticed back three-fourths of his former infield, including
shortstop Jack Glasscock. Glasscock then tried to recruit players back
himself. To meet the challenge of the New York Players League franchises, Brush moved his team to New York where he would compete for
fans against John Ward, player-manager in Brooklyn, and slugging
catcher William "Buck" Ewing, player-manager for New York.

Despite Brush's and Albert Spalding's efforts, only 25 players
returned to the older leagues. The sporting press roundly criticized the
owners for encouraging "double contracting," i.e., urging players to
break their new contracts and sign on with their original clubs.

There were two national sports weekly papers at the end of the 1880s,
St. Louis's *The Sporting News* and Philadelphia's *Sporting Life*. Established in 1886 by the Spink family, *The Sporting News* openly endorsed
the Players League. The weekly loved to poke fun at Chicagoan Spalding. The Spinks had not forgotten that Spalding denied St. Louis a
franchise in the National League earlier in the 1880s. Spalding believed

the immigrant populations of St. Louis and Cincinnati did not deserve National League baseball because they drank too much and did not behave properly. The two cities had to be content with American Association baseball, which was dubbed the "beer and whiskey league."

When the Players League arrived, the Spinks reveled in the prospect of Spalding being conquered by new competition. They had dubbed him "the Windy City fake," and they laughed at his criticisms of the new league. When Spalding had called labor and capital "irrepressible enemies," *The Sporting News* replied, "Of all the boobies in the baseball world Spalding is the biggest. Like the pig under the fence he squeals before he is hurt." They wished the Players League the best of luck when the manifesto was announced: "The child is born. It is a big, strong, lively kicking infant."

Sporting Life, established in 1887, was more cautious. Editor Francis Richter sympathized with the players' desire to be treated as more than "mere machines." He praised the new backers' "surprising aptitude" manifested in the first statements of the new league. He liked the new rule changes which the Players League promised. The pitching mound would be moved back from 45 to 51 feet (the modern 60 feet 6 inches would come later in the 1890s). The introduction of a double umpire system promised to cut down on sly base running tricks like running from second to home when the umpire was following the flight of a ball in the outfield.

Both journals opened their pages to John Montgomery Ward and other Players League spokesmen. Ward explained to an audience in Pittsburgh the rationale for the new league. "That we receive larger salaries and that our hours of work are shorter leaves us none the less workingmen," he insisted. "We are hired men, skilled in a particular employment, who work not only for the profit, but the amusement of our employers." After making this trenchant analysis, Ward returned to the idealistic mode he liked so much. "I would rather work for $10 a week and keep my personality, i.e., have some volition in the conduct of my own affairs than be made a monkey of or simply an animated being by such methods of government as used by the League, for $100 a week." Ward also vowed that the new league would never engage in the double-contracting methods of the Spalding crowd. "Somebody's got to assume a honorable stand or else baseball will degenerate into a disorganized body."

Rivaling Ward in eloquence was another veteran player, James "Orator" O'Rourke. In 1879 O'Rourke had left Arthur Soden in Boston because the owner had reneged on a promise to pay for his uniform. O'Rourke's action had so enraged Soden that it precipitated his introduction of the first reserve clause. O'Rourke would become one of those rare players to compete in major league baseball for four decades, from 1876 to 1904; he then played in the minor leagues until he was 58.

Speaking in his home town of Bridgeport, Connecticut, shortly after the Players League had been proclaimed, O'Rourke explained why the new league had been necessary. Ballplayers often had been suspended without cause and without pay, O'Rourke recalled, yet there was little "the poor defenseless ballplayer without courage to enforce his legal rights" could do. O'Rourke mimicked the standard appeal of his former bosses: " 'Our interests are identical,' owners proclaim. 'We have kept faith with our players (excepting where it was to our disadvantage), and we love the player most affectionately,' when the player has been taught by experience to be extremely incredulous and cautious of you."

O'Rourke predicted that the Players League would succeed and grant the players their richly deserved equity. Like Deacon White and John Ward, O'Rourke had studied law. He believed the reserve clause could only bind players to clubs within existing leagues and then only if the contract was specific on terms. It was "ridiculous and absurd," O'Rourke declared, to claim that the reserve could prevent a third party, such as a Players League, from obtaining players.

Orator O'Rourke proved true to his nickname when he wound up his Bridgeport speech with a flourish. "We have endeavored to build on a foundation even more substantial than Earth itself," he vowed. "Our ascension from thraldom is positive, uncoupled from all doubts, notwithstanding the warning of the master magnates and the snapping of their whip, which has no more terror for the players as they stand today shorn of all physical strength to use them."

Legal decisions early in 1890 seemed to justify O'Rourke's posture of lofty defiance. The National League, once double-contracting had failed to break the rebel circuit, had tried to get courts to enjoin their players from performing elsewhere. In late January 1890, New York State Supreme Court Judge Morgan Joseph O'Brien refused to prevent John Ward from leaving the Giants.

The Giants had hoped Judge O'Brien would rule in their behalf under the precedent of 1852, the case of impresario William Lumley vs. opera singer Johanna Wagner. Lumley had obtained an injunction because the singer had tried to break a contract with him and take her "special, unique, and extraordinary services" to another entrepreneur. The Giants argued that Ward was doing precisely the same thing as the singer, and should be enjoined.

Judge O'Brien cited another part of the Lumley verdict favorable to Ward. "The law cannot compel specific performance under a personal service contract," the judge ruled. He allowed, over the objections of Giants' lawyers, the court to discover that Ward's replacement at short-stop, Jack Glasscock, was earning as much as Ward did in 1889 despite the Giants' admission he was not nearly the player that Ward was.

Most importantly, O'Brien decided that he could not uphold the renewal clause in Ward's 1889 contract. "The failure in the existing contract to expressly provide the terms of a contract to be made in 1890 renders the latter indefinite and uncertain," O'Brien concluded.

In March 1890 a New York southern district federal court further buoyed the Players League. The Giants had tried to enjoin slugging catcher William "Buck" Ewing, later dubbed the "Babe Ruth of his day," from playing for the New York Players League entry. Federal Judge William P. Wallace refused to uphold the renewal clause, calling it "in a legal sense . . . merely a contract to make a contract if the parties can agree, and as such is not enforceable against the employee by injunction against entering into other employment." Such a clause would be inade-quate in a personal services contract "for a lawyer, or doctor, or artist, or laborer," and the judge would not enforce it for a ballplayer.

Interestingly, without mentioning John Montgomery Ward by name, Judge Wallace referred to a "prominent professional player's" descrip-tion of the reserve clause as compelling the "manager by his throat to keep his hands off his neighbor's enterprise." He admitted there were peculiarities in the baseball business because of the need for stability and competition, but he could not uphold the contract as written. Both Judge Wallace and Judge O'Brien also took strong issue with the clause which allowed the owners to release players on ten-day notice while otherwise binding the athletes indefinitely.

Orator O'Rourke was jubilant at the court decisions. "He that hath committed inequity shall not have equity," he crowed. He applauded the legal defeat of the "crafty, astute and unscrupulous magnates . . . who would uphold its white slave trade with a tract in one hand and the National Agreement in the other (both instruments of torture)." Ward was gratified but less vocal. He simply wanted the year to start and felt confident that the Players League would outshine the National on the field.

The National League leaders reacted to the legal judgments with an arrogance that would become characteristic of baseball owners. Philadelphia's Colonel John I. Rogers, a lawyer who had drafted the standard player's contract, was rendered speechless, not believing that a court had struck down his handiwork. But the intractable Arthur Soden announced that the courts simply did not understand baseball. He averred that all players who signed 1889 contracts were still liable for 1890 because of the reserve rule. He also offered gratuitous counsel, suggesting that Ward would have done better to advise players not to sign their 1890 National League contracts but play anyway, and after the season become eligible for a new league in 1891. Soden conveniently ignored management's practice of refusing to allow a player to compete without having signed a contract, and the extreme risk for an athlete to sit out a year and watch his skills erode.

Albert Spalding also discounted the court's judgment. He insisted that the ten-day release clause was "a necessity to guard not only against disreputable and incompetent players but as a matter of protection and justice to those players who combine skill with gentlemanly conduct on and off the field." Spalding was rallying the National League for a war to the finish. He declared in March 1890, "I am for war without quarter. I was opposed to it at first, but now I want to fight until one of us drops dead." To show he meant business, Spalding arranged for the National League schedule to conflict wherever possible with the Players League.

The first returns from the opening series of April 1890 looked promising for the new circuit. Enthusiastic home crowds greeted all the Players League franchises. Since the courts had refused to enjoin the stars from joining the rebel league, the fans flocked to see them in their new surroundings. King Kelly's Boston team, the ultimate pennant winner, developed an attractive rivalry with Ward's Brooklyn outfit, which was less talented on paper but performed so gallantly on the field that they were dubbed "Ward's Wonders." Comiskey's Chicago club signed the most stars perhaps, including infielders Fred Pfeffer and Arlie Latham, and outfielder Hugh Duffy who would hit .438 for Boston in 1894. They would limp in fourth, a testimony to a lesson in baseball lore: All-Star teams on paper don't necessarily play like champions on the field.

The players got a laugh when they learned that the National League was trying to increase its attendance by giving out free passes in saloons, barber shops, and other public places. They remembered when Arthur Soden took away free tickets from the players' wives and made them pay to get in. Soden also tore down the press box in order to increase seating capacity. In a moment of effusion, John Montgomery Ward predicted in late April that the old league "might be in the soup" by the Fourth of July.

However, Albert Goodwill Spalding was a fearsome adversary when he made up his mind to fight. By 1890 Spalding had built a vast sporting-goods empire. His firm had offices in twenty-five American cities and many countries of the world. Spalding and Company was involved with manufacturing turnstiles used at ball parks. It contracted out the making of the official baseball to A. J. Reach of Philadelphia who, with Colonel Rogers, owned the Philadelphia Nationals. By 1889 Reach was in Spalding's employ as a mere adjunct to Spalding's expanding dominion. If the Players League wanted a fight, Spalding was prepared to give them one.

In *America's National Game,* his autobiography published in 1911, Spalding recalled the tactics of the 1890 season: "In place of powder and shell, printers' ink and bluff formed the ammunition used by both sides." He also doubted whether either league ever made a truthful statement in reporting attendance, as each inflated its own figures and discounted its rivals' spectators.

Spalding engineered a propaganda campaign against the very idea of a league run by players. He installed sportswriter O. P. Caylor as the head of a new weekly, *The New York Sporting Times.* Caylor bombarded his readers with tales of the wasteful living of the Brotherhood players, living it up with the security of long-term contracts.

Henry Chadwick went even further. An English-born sportswriter who had devised the first box score for baseball, Chadwick could be seen at ball games with a solemn expression on his bearded face and always wearing a top hat. Some players thought he was Father Baseball himself. The voice of the old order decried the Brotherhood as a "secret terrorist organization" which had forced many unwilling players into joining the new league.

Harry C. Palmer was another journalist who picked up the cudgels in the ideological war against the Players League. Why should players complain, asked Palmer, when they are engaged "in a business that is really a pastime and unquestionably a pleasure." Palmer painted a picture of the carefree player's happy life off the field "full of good things," yet the greedy ones want more money, he railed. *The Sporting News,* still hopeful in mid-1890 of the success of Spalding's competition, dismissed Palmer's ranting as the work of a man as close to Spalding "as a leech is to its appurtenant."

Though attendance figures from 1890 are unreliable, there is little doubt that the Players League outdrew the National League throughout the season. One estimate said it was 913,000 to 853,000 in the final count. The key to the survival of the fledgling organization remained the steadfastness of the backers. When Buck Ewing, one of the last to join the Brotherhood, was rumored to be returning to the National League, *Sporting Life* observed accurately, "Twenty Ewings are not worth one McAlpin." The players seemed to be holding strong through the summer, as Ewing stayed. King Kelly had earlier refused Spalding's offer of a blank contract and a $10,000 bonus, and remained with his Players League team in Boston.

By the end of July both leagues had set up emergency war committees but many writers thought a truce might be near. The established leagues had lost plenty of money, probably in the hundreds of thousands of dollars. But William Conant, one of Arthur Soden's partners, spoke for most of the older owners when he stated his willingness to lose for at least five more years if necessary rather than to compromise with the rebels.

On the other side, Colonel McAlpin reflected the wavering among the players' backers. He and most of the Players League businessmen told a *New York World* survey that they wanted a compromise with the National League, but the problem was that the older circuit wanted to restore their monopoly of all players. "Four courts of justice declared the old jug-handled contract void," complained McAlpin. "And two justices practically said it was infamous. The trouble with the National League is that its business was conducted on lines not permitted by the Constitution of the United States. It has aimed, and is still aiming, at a monopoly of the business."

In the fall of 1890 the Congress of the United States would pass the Sherman Antitrust Act to declare its legislative opposition to all combinations in restraint of trade. But this law was not yet in the books, and it would not have mattered, given the will for domination manifested by Spalding, the National League mastermind.

Spalding's behavior was reminiscent of Commodore Cornelius Vanderbilt, the empire-building railroad mogul of this same period, who, when asked about the propriety of some of his maneuvers, snapped, "Who cares about right? Hain't I got the power?" In Spalding's office hung the motto, "Everything is possible to he who dares," and the magnate plotted strategy of divide and conquer, sensing that the Players League backers were already vacillating.

Before leaving for a midsummer business trip to Europe, Spalding addressed the players through the newspapers. "It is folly pure and simple, this Brotherhood sentiment of sticking together. It is always manliness to acknowledge it when you're done," he pontificated. The time has come, he continued, when the players "should go to the men whom they induced to put up their money, and say in a straightforward way that they will not ask for another dollar to be spent on them in a venture that is already lost."

In August *The Sporting News* observed, "The baseball cat is an animal of much interest just now. Everybody is looking to see which way it will jump." Rumors abounded that the Players League might amalgamate with the American Association. St. Louis, perhaps the only stable franchise in the circuit, had considered joining the Players League in 1889, but John Ward distrusted the reliability of the owner, Chris von der Ahe, a colorful brewer who often lavished gifts on his players. The new circuit was not interested in taking on more partners at a critical juncture in 1890.

The players continued to put on a brave public face. They insisted that by 1891 theirs would be the dominant league. Buck Ewing vowed, "If we don't disappoint a few people who hope to attend our funeral I don't know much about baseball." Charles Comiskey added, "To my mind the most prominent feature of the good which has been done by the organization of the Players League is the personal responsibility it has placed on the shoulders of the players."

John Montgomery Ward was reached for comment in Boston during a series against Kelly's Boston club. The *Boston Globe* had saluted the two leaders for the fine quality of their teams' play. In spite of the war of words engaged in with the National League, "There is no doubt that the game has been pure."

At a postgame banquet for both teams at one of Boston's fancier hotels, John Ward voiced a revealing lament. "The N.L. magnates would have stopped their warfare on the Players League long ago," he said, "if they could only get over the idea that they owned us." Ward understood why they would not compromise: "Because we went into business for ourselves after our contracts with them had expired we treated them shabbily—in fact robbed them of all their stock in trade, so to speak." Although he would battle to the end, his Boston remarks were a remarkably candid and prescient analysis of the established owners' feelings.

The only chance for the Players League survival was a strong September finish. The pennant race between Boston and Brooklyn was close, but the weather ruined them. Many key games were rained out and never rescheduled. "Ward's Wonders" faded in the stretch and finished six and a half games behind Boston.

Since a World Series was not scheduled—the National League contemptuously turning down a Players League suggestion for such a contest—the new circuit planned some exhibition all-star games in Cincinnati for early October. Albert Johnson had bought the failing N.L. franchise in September, and was eager to introduce Players League baseball into his new market. But the games drew poorly, hastening the panic of the fearful Players League's Eastern backers.

The National League moved in for the kill. Its regularly scheduled meeting was slated for New York on October 9. Albert Spalding, back from Europe, suggested an informal meeting beforehand with Players League backers. Albert Johnson agreed as did two of the backers of New York teams, Wendell Goodwin and E. B. Talcott. Using his considerable backslapping charm, Spalding suggested to the backers that they compare notes on the losses of the season. Spalding had loaned $60,000 to the Giants in August 1890 to keep the Giants' franchise from falling into enemy hands. However, he surely did not want to bail out other failing teams and hoped to get an inkling of how his opponents had really fared.

To his astonishment, the novice backers put all their cards on the table, telling of losses of thousands of dollars and projected deficits perhaps into the millions. Spalding was prepared to mention some of his losses, but when his opponents revealed everything, he merely talked in generalities. The rest of the informal meeting was devoted to loose talk about the merger or amalgamation of the leagues. Al Johnson was not opposed to compromise, but he rejected Spalding's idea that the result of

47

any combination should be called, simply, the National League. Since this was merely an informal gathering, the parties decided to meet formally on October 22 when all representatives would have official powers from their respective leagues.

At the regular National League meeting, the magnates could not contain their glee at the news Spalding brought them. They no longer feared compromise; they could simply pick apart their adversary. Brooklyn's owner Charles Byrne, called Napoleon for his imperious manner, started to draft a resolution for the return of the reserve clause, but it was tabled as premature. Byrne was told to wait for the formal peace meeting before introducing the new restrictions.

Robert Smith writes that the manipulation which led to the demise of the Players League "reads like something out of the private diary of a jailed utilities magnate." Even before the scheduled October 22 meeting, the backers were bailing out and Spalding stood by picking up the pieces. Talcott sold his franchise to Spalding, who immediately merged it with the troubled New York National franchise. John Addison sold out his interest to Spalding in Chicago, who promptly gave Addison and his associates season's passes to games in the Windy City. Addison became a long-time minority stockholder in Chicago National League baseball, and a street near today's Wrigley Field is named after him. The Wagner brothers of Philadelphia, George and J. E., who had rescued the Players League team there in midseason, became owners of the National League franchise in Washington.

But what of the great experiment in players and capitalists working together? John Ward and Al Johnson were not ready to give up the ideal yet. Ward told Johnson that he, outfielder Ned Hanlon of Pittsburgh, and shortstop Arthur Irwin of Boston wanted to attend the October 22 meeting as representatives of the Players League. Its constitution called for equal representation of players and backers on all committees, and Johnson readily agreed.

Ward admittedly was peeved at how fast the backers seemed to be abandoning ship. He still insisted that most of them had taken their losses like "heroes." Ward felt sure that the "more thoughtful players" would agree to "sink all personal feelings for the benefit of the entire league."

Spalding, in total control of the situation, soon learned of the players' desire to sit in on the truce conclave. The moment Al Johnson made the request for the addition of Ward, Hanlon, and Irwin, Spalding adjourned the meeting, claiming that the composition of the informal group, which had met earlier in the month, could not be changed. This parliamentary maneuver was Spalding's way of rubbing it in to the players that from now on they would have no say in the operations of the game.

Ward confronted Spalding and his allies: "Do these gentlemen wish to go on record as saying that the occupation of a ballplayer bars him from business association with respectable men?" Ward knew that Spalding and one of the American Association representatives, William Barnie, had played big league baseball. Ward asked, "Mr. Spalding, are you willing to place such a stamp of infamy upon the profession of which for years you were a member?" Spalding was adamant. "The question of a compromise should be settled between the moneyed men of both organizations on a purely business basis," he said. He could not resist a parting shot at the Brotherhood, with whom he would never meet because it "had done everything in its power to wreck the National League."

When Talcott and Goodwin upheld Spalding that the players could not be admitted, Al Johnson walked out of the meeting with Ward, Hanlon, and Irwin. The gesture was meaningless; the Players League was effectively dead. Ward belatedly realized that the whole conference had merely been a scheme to solidify the reestablishment of the National League monopoly.

Ward was so disgusted that he did not even bother to attend the annual meeting of the Players League in Pittsburgh in mid-November. He sent a proxy, Judge Edward Bacon of Brooklyn, who attested to the soundness of Players League contracts which the old league had better honor. Edward Prince, a lawyer for the Boston Players League franchise, also argued this point in the weeks ahead, but the hard truth was that the rebellion had ended and the monopoly was entrenched stronger than ever. Adopting a strategy it would employ many times in the years ahead, the baseball owners offered Prince an American Association franchise to placate him.

In hindsight, the Players League might have survived if it knew how serious the National League losses had been. Cincinnati and New York were key markets within their grasp if only they had been equipped with the business skill to exploit this knowledge. If the Players League war committee had insisted on far more than the $2,500 contribution from each club that it exacted in July 1890, it might have had a reserve fund with which to do battle. The backers' inexperience was costly and they were easy prey for the manipulations of Spalding and the more experienced league owners. John Montgomery Ward's initial fear of allowing the backers the first $10,000 of each franchise's profits proved prophetic. When losses came instead of profits, the backers lost faith quickly.

The immediate consequences of the Brotherhood defeat were not as devastating as the players feared. Although their fraternity died with the new league, the owners could not blacklist them all because there were few stars of merit in the National League of 1890. The owners did institute major salary reductions—as much as 50 percent in some cases. They also virtually eliminated salary advances. But most of the players returned to their former homes: Buck Ewing to the New York Nationals, Charles Comiskey to St. Louis in the American Association, and King Kelly to the Boston Nationals. In 1894, only 37 years old, Kelly passed away, meeting the early death to become typical for many of America's celebrity idols.

The long-range effects of the lost Brotherhood war were devastating to the self-esteem of the players. The stigma of the defeated experiment lingered over the players, and the owners lorded their revived total control over them. Professional baseball had its version of the "bloody shirt," which, like Northerners after the Civil War, the moguls waved at the defeated rebels.

Many of the players came to believe that the Brotherhood had indeed been wrongheaded from the start. When Orator O'Rourke retired from playing baseball in 1913, he denied that he had ever been in the Brotherhood. He became an official of the New England League, a minor league within organized baseball's expanding umbrella.

Ned Hanlon also learned to play the ownership game. By the end of the 1890s he was a field manager in Baltimore and a part owner of the Brooklyn franchise. He looked back on the Players League and recalled only a feeling that four weeks into the campaign the whole idea had been a mistake. Lack of discipline among the players proved fatal, he recollected.

The Sporting News accurately prophesized how history would be unkind to the losers. In December 1890, conceding victory to Spalding and the triumphant National League monopoly, it editorialized:

50

Win in the lottery and you are a clever man, for he who triumphs is reveled. . . . Ward and those who fought with him might have been written down in history as great had that one word, Success, crowned their efforts. As it failed to follow them, however, there are no crowns for them and when they are gone they will be thought of as fellows of no great shakes after all.

The obscurity of John Montgomery Ward today bears out the newspaper's prediction. Like the other players, Ward relinquished the collective dream of the Brotherhood. He blamed the defeat on "stupidity, avarice, and treachery," especially by the Players League backers. He recalled ruefully how he had tried to persuade the backers to change the schedule so they would not conflict with the National League, but the early militants like McAlpin and Goodwin had insisted on challenging the Nationals directly. Of course, they would be among the first to succumb to Spalding's October blandishments. As so often in the history of insurgent movements, the most reckless and verbally confident activists had been the quickest to surrender.

Ward played in Brooklyn for two years after the Brotherhood war, and then returned to the Giants. He retired after the 1894 season, and having passed the bar exam, opened a law office in New York's Wall Street financial district, and became a respected and successful attorney. Ward accepted as a client the National Association of Professional Baseball Leagues which, in 1901, had been established as the ruling agency of the minor leagues of organized baseball. In 1909 Ward was seriously considered for the presidency of the National League, but ran afoul of Ban Johnson, American League president and baseball's first czar, who never forgave Ward for representing a Giant infielder, George Davis, whom Johnson believed belonged to his league's White Sox.

In 1912 Ward was selected as president of the Boston Braves, a franchise which had been a chronic tail-ender for a decade and had not perked up with the sale of the club by Arthur Soden in 1905. Ward lasted less than a year with Boston, but he did scout and sign a future Hall of Famer, shortstop Walter "Rabbit" Maranville. In 1913 Ward urged a congressional committee not to investigate baseball as "an autocratic trust." He conceded that organized baseball did violate normal business practice, but it could be run in no other fashion.

Yet John Montgomery Ward's story is not simply that of the young idealist turned older and wiser conservative. He never ceased to oppose the inequities of the baseball contract, and rendered legal services to many ballplayers, including one-time Brotherhood firebrand, infielder Fred Pfeffer, and fireballing pitcher Amos Rusie, who had remained loyal to the National League in 1890. It was Rusie who threw so hard that the pitching mound was moved back to 60 feet, and became 60 feet 6 inches because of a surveyor's error.

In 1896 Ward succeeded in getting his name removed from the Giants' reserve list. Many owners and sportswriters suspected that Ward was about to unretire, and warned that the Giants would not be compensated for his lost services if Ward joined another team. Ward had no intention of returning to the game, but was insisting on the principle of being free from the odious rule. He won his case before baseball's in-house arbitration board, in part because his former Giants' owner, E. B. Talcott, an original backer of the Players League, was too ill to attend a hearing.

In 1914 Ward joined the Federal League, briefly, as business manager of the Brooklyn franchise for that upstart circuit. He observed that baseball's "advancement should be credited 25% to the players, 75% to the newspapers, and 0 to the owners," showing that he was still willing to tangle with the entrenched monopoly. In 1916 he served as an assistant counsel in the Baltimore Federal League suit, which in 1922 led to the sustained exemption of baseball from the antitrust laws. Ned Hanlon was one of the Baltimore plaintiffs; the spirit of rebellion had not left him either.

John Montgomery Ward lived until 1925. He died of pneumonia during a hunting trip in Georgia, where, as one of America's leading amateur golfers, he had traveled to play in a local golf tournament. Eloquent and lyrical to the end, Ward left a note to his second wife to the effect that he wanted to be "buried where a pheasant might run across my grave." In 1964 he was belatedly enshrined in the National Baseball Hall of Fame at Cooperstown, New York, along with his one-time Brotherhood comrade and brother-in-law, Tim Keefe. His experience in the Players League, not surprisingly, was omitted from his Cooperstown plaque.

Yet the inequities of the baseball contract and the triumphant smugness of the owners in the wake of the victory over the Brotherhood created enough discontent to spur a new rival to the National League within ten years. The emerging American League did not stir the players' hearts with calls for cooperation as the Brotherhood had done. It did promise them a fuller pocketbook. In 1900 the master strategist of the new league, Byron Bancroft Johnson, would even endorse a cautious new players group, the Protective Association, to woo athletes to his side. By 1902 the National League monopoly would be seeking a truce. But the economic and legal condition of the players would barely improve.

Part II

*The Age of
Fitful Fraternity,
1900-1920*

3

Ban Johnson and the Rise of the American League and the Failure of the Players Protective Association

*"Whenever I go to a baseball meeting, I never
forget to check my money and valuables at the
hotel office before entering the session chamber."
—Ferdinand Abell, co-owner of the Brooklyn
National League club, c. 1900. Quoted in Lee
Allen,* The American League Story.

Within a year of the demise of the Players League in December 1890, the National League enjoyed a total monopoly of major league baseball. The American Association, always plagued by weak leadership, folded after the 1891 season. The Association had broken away from the National Agreement in the middle of 1891 in protest of the National League teams' refusal to return to them players who had played in the A.A. during 1889. When Pittsburgh did not return to the Philadelphia club infielder Louis Bierbauer, the team acquired its present nickname, the Pirates. The Association could not cope with the power and money of the National League and so ended operation.

The National League absorbed four teams into its circuit: Louisville, Baltimore, Washington, and St. Louis. It operated as a twelve-team circuit for the rest of the 1890s, but business sagged noticeably. Douglass Wallop has observed in his informal history, *Baseball,* "Monopoly could be ruthless, unprofitable, stupid, and often extremely dull." The addition of four teams only assured four more losers. Although the Baltimore Orioles emerged by 1894 as an exciting and successful team, there were many mismanaged franchises in the League as well as startling indifference to gambling and rowdiness at the ball parks.

Major league baseball was ripe for competition and, by the end of the

57

1890s, a definite new star loomed on the horizon. Albert Spalding had dominated the first fifteen years of National League baseball with his imperial designs and careful selection of partners. By 1902 Byron Bancroft Johnson was to be reckoned with as the leading figure in major league baseball. Having succeeded in turning the minor Western League into a superior major American League, Ban Johnson would dominate baseball for almost twenty years.

Born in Marietta, Ohio, in 1864, Ban, as everyone called him, was the son of a college professor. Although Ban never played baseball professionally or amassed the great wealth of Albert Spalding, he would leave a lasting imprint on the operations of the game.

Upon graduating from college, Ban started his career as a sportswriter for the Cincinnati *Commercial Gazette*. He observed the Players League war closely. Although he was sympathetic to its cause, he never expected the circuit to last. No idealist, Johnson felt that equal division of gate receipts in the Players League was foolhardy. He also criticized the unfair division of travel schedules in the league, a point where equality should have been followed. Chicago had to travel 2,000 miles more during the season than did Brooklyn, he observed. Ban Johnson dreamed of one day running his own league with his iron hand and capable brain to assure success.

In 1892 Johnson made the acquaintance of Charles Comiskey, who after the failure of the Players League, had come to manage the Cincinnati National League team. Comiskey and Johnson frequented a restaurant known as The Ten-Minute Club, where someone at every table had to order a round of drinks every ten minutes. Cincinnati, a charter member of the defunct "beer and whiskey" league, the American Association, was such a beer-drinking town that prohibitionist Carrie Nation was said to have given up saving souls there after walking down just one block of the city.

In the liquid atmosphere of The Ten-Minute Club, Comiskey and Johnson forged a friendship and discussed their mutual ambitions. "Within their veins flowed the dauntless blood of the old Spanish conquerors who knew no danger and dared impossible feats," wrote writer Allan Sangree.

Ban Johnson was one of the first examples of a phenomenon of the baseball business, the sportswriter turned executive. He was probably the ablest. After the 1893 season, Comiskey recommended Johnson to

Cincinnati owner John T. Brush as the man for the presidency of the Western League, a minor league in the Midwest.

Brush was the same owner who had introduced the classification plan that provoked the Brotherhood war. He was no friend of Johnson's and would remain a bitter rival until his death in 1912. But he agreed to use his influence to assure Johnson's appointment. It would get him out of Cincinnati, where Johnson's columns lambasting Brush's poor Cincinnati team had proved an embarrassment.

In 1894 Johnson took over a league comprised of Indianapolis, Minneapolis, Milwaukee, Detroit, Kansas City, Toledo, Grand Rapids, and Sioux City. In establishing a career-long pattern of total rule, Johnson assumed the positions of president and secretary-treasurer. He kept 51 percent of each team's stock in the League office safe.

He immediately served notice that the baseball world had found a crisp and authoritative executive at a time of stagnant monopoly. Johnson gave his umpires unquestioned authority on the field. He upheld their decisions and supported their ejections of players. Johnson made it clear he would not tolerate rowdiness from fans or athletes. He wanted to make baseball a gentleman's game.

He survived an effort by John Brush to depose him during his first year. Johnson was enraged when Brush drafted some Western League players ostensibly for Cincinnati and then transferred them to his farm club at Indianapolis. Johnson forced Brush to sell his stock in Indianapolis and thereby earned a signal victory over one of the dominant moguls of the National League.

Charles Comiskey joined his friend's Western League in 1895. Retiring as an active player, he bought the Sioux City franchise and moved it to St. Paul. In 1897 Connie Mack came on board as manager of the Milwaukee team. Though it was still the Western League, a triumvirate that would influence American League baseball for a half century had already formed. They all longed for a piece of the major league action. By the end of the 1890s enough players were grumbling in the National League to make another major league seem feasible.

Salary cutting headed the list of grievances. The $2,500 maximum, introduced ten years earlier, was being rigidly enforced except for the greatest stars who received extra payments under the table. To add to the economic restrictions, the players faced harsh new personal regulations. A temperance pledge was written into the standard contract. Never at a loss for bright ideas, John Brush devised a "purification plan," which would have expelled any player for cursing. Brush's idea never got too far with the other owners, but it was indicative of the authoritarianism spawned by the era of total monopoly.

At the end of 1899 Ban Johnson flexed his muscles and announced that the Western League was henceforth to be known as the American League. He also notified the National League that he was establishing a franchise in Chicago, another sign of his growing ambitions.

When Spalding was ruling the older league, such a move would have been tantamount to war. But Spalding had left Chicago baseball to his associate, James B. Hart, and moved to California, presiding over his sporting-goods empire from there. Chicago baseball was ripe for picking because the National League franchise had fallen into disarray. Cap Anson was fired as manager in 1897, his reward for serving the Spalding interests loyally for nearly twenty years. Anson, a longtime Brotherhood baiter, now said that greedy players paled in comparison to rapacious owners. Chicago's National League team rarely contended for the pennant in the 1890s.

The National League tolerated Johnson's move of the Grand Rapids franchise into Chicago because it feared a revival of the American Association more than Johnson's minor league. In 1898 Cap Anson and John McGraw, the Baltimore Orioles' fiery third baseman, in association with sports editors Charles Spink and Francis Richter, had almost set up a Chicago franchise for a reborn American Association, but they failed to raise sufficient capital. In allowing Johnson to move into Chicago, the National League exacted a pledge from Johnson to abide by the National Agreement and not raid any of its associated clubs for players. Johnson agreed, knowing that the baseball contract would not likely be upheld in court.

As Johnson moved into Chicago in 1900, he struck up a friendship with another of the American League's founding fathers, Clark Griffith. Griffith had been vociferous about the low pay in the National League. He had good reason to complain. He won twenty games or more six times between 1893 and 1899, yet the Chicago Nationals only paid him $2,500 a year. In 1897 Griffith came close to organizing a strike of the Chicagoans for better pay.

1900 would be Griffith's last season in the National League. His record slumped to 14-13, but his mind was preoccupied with the dreams of the new league. He became one of Ban Johnson's most zealous recruiters when full-scale trade war erupted before the 1901 season.

In 1900 Clark Griffith also played a founding role in the Players Protective Association, the first players association since the ruined Brotherhood. Delegates from all the major league clubs convened in New York City in early June amidst caution and near secrecy. They did not want the stigma of the radical Brotherhood upon them. They chose as officers those who had not played in the Players League. Charles "Chief" Zimmer of Cleveland, famous as Cy Young's catcher, was elected president. Griffith and Hugh Jennings, famous for his ball field cry, "ee-yah!," were named vice-presidents. The players seriously considered not giving out the names of their officers for fear of owner reprisal. But they did relent and announced their group's lineup to the press.

Although the players were necessarily careful in their actions, they invited Dan Harris, an emissary of Samuel Gompers, President of the American Federation of Labor, to address their first meeting. Gompers's Federation had been successful in organizing workers in crafts, although labor unionism in American society was still widely viewed with suspicion.

Gompers was a baseball fan. But he deplored the low wages of the players. He sent Dan Harris to the Protective Association to explain how unionism might help them. Harris assured the players that whatever they decided, the new group "would enjoy the moral support of the A. F. of L." They decided against any affiliation with the labor organization, feeling too uncertain of their strength to antagonize the owners. Many players agreed with John Montgomery Ward, now a rising Wall Street lawyer, when he told a reporter that a union of ballplayers might be untenable because of "the peculiar nature of the profession of baseball." However, Ward did think the new group might serve a useful purpose.

Sporting Life expressed its sympathy more strongly. "The wonder is that the union for self-protection against intolerable oppression has been so long delayed," Francis Richter editorialized. When the June meeting adjourned, Hugh Jennings, another student of law among the ballplayers, announced that the new group did not contemplate striking for its demands. "I do say that we'd resort to harsh measures," Jennings added, "if players were abused." He did not specify methods. A month later, the Protective Association convened again in New York with nearly one hundred players in attendance including some from the new American

League and the Eastern League, a minor circuit.

Attorney Harry Leonard Taylor introduced himself to the gathering with a program for the new group. Taylor was a former major league first baseman and utilityman who like the other Association leaders had remained loyal or uninvolved in the Brotherhood war. He played for Louisville of the American Association and then the expanded National League from 1890 to 1893. He pitched in the minor leagues also, and then became an upstate New York lawyer.

Taylor won the delegates over with his strong background as both a major and a minor league player and with his legal astuteness. He convinced them that a new contract was possible and necessary to alleviate the many problems they faced. He vowed to help them in the struggle for higher wages, better working conditions, and freedom from capricious shuttling to the minor leagues.

The problem of farming was particularly nettlesome to the players. Jobs were scarce in the big leagues. Rosters were under twenty per team, and in 1900, the National League had cut back to eight teams. Many good players found themselves sold or hidden in minor league clubs where the big league teams had interests.

As for the reserve clause, Taylor, like John Montgomery Ward, was ambivalent. He called it the "bulwark" of the sport because it protected the investment of the owner in the player. But like Ward he railed at the abuses of the sales system where the player was treated like merchandise. Taylor convinced the Association to go on record in behalf of granting one half of the sale price to the player.

The Sporting News applauded Taylor's position. "The civil law does not permit the sale of a personal contract," it commented, and wished Taylor well in his efforts to bring the baseball contract into the legal mainstream. By the end of the 1900 season, Taylor was chosen as the Protective Association's counsel. He received a promise from all members that they would not sign contracts for 1901 until either the National League granted their demands or Taylor at least approved the individual contracts.

The National League owners greeted the new players organization with contempt. New York's John B. Day said he would raze his ball park before he would meet with "a secret organization of ballplayers." Colonel John Rogers of Philadelphia declared, "When the players band themselves together in an effort to dictate to us the manner in which we shall conduct our business it will be time for the magnates to retire." The ever-direct Arthur Soden averred, "I do not believe in labor organizations or unions. . . . When a player ceases to be useful to me I will release him." Soden's more tolerant partner, dubbed James "Benign" Billings by the sporting press, did not rule out recognition of a deserving players organization.

Of course, the owners would decide which players group would be acceptable. By fall of 1900 they decided that Harry Leonard Taylor was outrageously radical. Taylor's offense was that he had submitted written requests for contract changes more severe than his oral proposals of the summer. He now wanted the ten-day release clause in the contract to benefit the player as well as the owner. He also called for the club to pay physician's fees for players injured in service. And most radically, he wanted the establishment of an impartial arbitration board composed of representatives of owners, players, and third parties chosen by the first two. He also asked that no player be sold, farmed, or traded without written consent. Emphasizing this point, Taylor asked that the word "assign" be stricken from all League-player dealings.

The National League owners had no intention of granting the players' requests, but they agreed to meet with them at the League's annual meeting in New York in December 1900. The magnates created a committee to negotiate with the Protective Association; Soden, Brush, and Rogers formed this body, an indication of the owners' hard-line position. When Arthur Soden casually told Taylor and the Association board that his committee really had no power to grant any concessions, Taylor was incensed. He warned the magnates of his authority to keep all members of the Association unsigned until their demands were met. Clark Griffith said of the owners' condescending attitude, "They treated us as if we had been unruly kids who had to be lollipopped and put to bed."

The players were angry at this rejection; they prepared to recommend a refusal to sign contracts for the 1901 season. For some reason, probably the pressure of other business, Harry Taylor left New York for his office in Buffalo before the Association took any final action. Taylor was only the group's attorney, but his strong position on contract reform had impressed the players. He should have realized that tackling the baseball monopoly would require tenacity and patience.

But Taylor had other clients in Buffalo, and serving the baseball players was not a full-time job. It would be more than sixty-five years before anybody would treat the ballplayers' cause seriously enough to take on the job as a full-time obligation.

The officers of the Protective Association stayed on in New York while the National League held its regular meeting. Ban Johnson had also come to town to seek recognition of his American League, which had enjoyed a successful first season in 1900 as the second major league. The National League owners had no intention of granting Ban Johnson his desires. They slipped out the side door of the hotel to avoid meeting with him. The snub infuriated Johnson, who decided to open all-out war with the National League by invading its Eastern territory.

Clark Griffith became one of Johnson's closest allies and most successful recruiters. Griffith joined Comiskey's American League Chicago club for the 1901 season and regained his old form with a 24-7 record. He performed brilliantly as Ban Johnson's emissary also, winning to the American circuit every National player he sought except Pittsburgh's star shortstop, Honus Wagner, who remained loyal to his owner, Barney Dreyfuss.

Ban Johnson had hoped to win perhaps two dozen National Leaguers to his side. Delightedly, he watched more than one hundred players flock to his new circuit. His alternative market had a lot to offer the players. Johnson vowed he would not enforce an arbitrary salary maximum and he granted one of the Protective Association's most sought-after reforms: the prohibition on farming players without their consent.

The Protective Association withheld immediate endorsement of the new league. If one of the recurrent problems of baseball's early labor relations was a reluctance of outsiders to represent players on a permanent basis, another theme was the understandable wariness of the players themselves to commit themselves to collective action. They knew from hard experience of the perils of fighting the monopoly. Protective Association President Charlie Zimmer cautioned early in 1901, "We don't want a baseball war, and to show that we have no secret agreement with the American League, we have ordered all the National Agreement players to keep from negotiations with Ban Johnson for the present at least." Of course, this decree did not stop a Clark Griffith from pursuing his main chance. It did reflect the concern of National Leaguers for their teams, and their hope that some compromise with their owners could be reached.

64

By February 1901 the National League was already suffering from the trade war instigated by Ban Johnson and his American League. The owners decided another meeting with the Protective Association might be worthwhile. They reasoned, "Perhaps if we recognize the players' group, the tide of defection to the Americans will be stopped."

A National League committee consisting of owners Brush, Soden, and Hart informed Zimmer they would like to meet with him in Cleveland in the middle of February. They added with baronial arrogance, "Don't bring your lawyer"—Harry Taylor. Zimmer accepted this humiliating condition, a graphic indication of how cowed and cautious the players had become in asserting their rights since the destruction of the Brotherhood. Taylor told Zimmer to attend the meeting but to wire him in Buffalo before he signed any National League offer.

The meeting brought mixed results. The owners promised not to farm the players without written consent. They also agreed not to transfer a minor league team to another town unless the level of play and the salaries remained at least the same. The owners even agreed to modify the reserve clause so that the contract allowed only a one-year "option to renew." This was only a surface reform. All players had to sign their contracts before the season began, and the option could thus be renewed indefinitely. The moguls steadfastly refused to consider an outside arbitration of grievances, not surprising if the Protective Association could not even have its lawyer present.

Zimmer granted his biggest concession to the owners when he agreed the Association would expel any member who violated his National League contract by jumping to the American League. Taylor received the proposed agreement by telegram and approved it.

When the accord between the N. L. and the P. P. A. became public in late February, many of the players were critical of Zimmer's willingness to police his own members in the interests of the National League. But Zimmer was strongly defended by Francis Richter who praised the players' leader in *Sporting Life* for dishing out some "humiliating medicine" to the owners. He saw wise method in Zimmer's lobbying for a clause which provided for expulsion of any member who jumped to the American League "pending action on his case by the Association as a body." There was no way the players group would condemn any of their own for getting a larger salary from another team; the Association would never convene "as a body" and players could join whatever teams they wished. Richter called Zimmer's technique "conservative shrewdness" in contrast to the Brotherhood's frontal assault of a decade earlier.

Despite its recognition by the N. L., the Protective Association had a very short and ineffective life. Its inability to prevent players from flocking to the American League caused the older magnates to lose whatever interest they initially had in courting the group.

Ban Johnson, like most of the business leaders of the early twentieth century, had little use for unions or any independent labor organization. But recognizing the Protective Association had been a useful function for Johnson when he plotted his invasion of the East for the 1901 season. Connie Mack came into Philadelphia, new franchises were created in Washington and Boston, and wealthy coal heir Charles W. Somers, Johnson's financial angel, started a team in Cleveland. Once he was successful, Johnson dealt only with the Protective Association to divide and conquer it. He publicly upbraided Zimmer as "one of the worst characters in baseball." Johnson believed the best player was a gratefully submissive player; the czar would later oppose the introduction of Most Valuable Player awards because it might enhance the player's salary-bargaining power.

The beginning of the end for the players group came in early 1901 when veteran second baseman Tom Daly became president of the Association, replacing Zimmer. Daly had not merely ignored his reserve clause, but had walked out on his 1902 contract with the Brooklyn Nationals to join Griffith and Comiskey in Chicago. Zimmer was appalled that the Protective Association would choose a contract jumper to succeed him. But it was part of the sly strategy of Griffith and American League interests to isolate the National Leaguers within the players' group.

A poor turnout at a New York Protective Association meeting in late July 1902 foretold its pending demise. The officers were there, but no players from New York bothered to attend although the meeting was held in a hotel where some of the players lived.

The Protective Association faded out of existence at the end of 1902. On December 1, in a perhaps symbolic reflection of the unhappy history of players' movements in baseball so far, Fred Dunlap, one of the most militant of the old Brotherhood players, died in Philadelphia. Only forty-three years old, the retired second baseman had lost what the sporting pages called his "respectable fortune" from baseball by betting on the horses. His last two years had been spent in "mental gloom and abject poverty," added an obituary writer.

Professional baseball players would enter the forthcoming period of baseball prosperity unorganized and relying totally on their individual wiles to face management. As weak and cautious as the Protective Association had been, the players would soon feel the loss of an organization that could voice their grievances.

A time for truce was nearing as Ban Johnson had made such a great success of the American League that it already outdrew the Nationals. In 1902 Americans counted more than 2,200,000 fans while the Nationals declined to fewer than 1,700,000. In Philadelphia Connie Mack's A's routed Colonel Rogers's Phillies by nearly 300,000 at the gate. The sporting press hailed Ban Johnson as a master leader while poking fun at a National League "dying of dry rot."

The older circuit was indeed having its troubles. Before the 1900 season, it had lopped off four of its franchises—Louisville, Cleveland, Washington, and Baltimore. In 1901 Ban Johnson had gobbled up the last three territories during his Eastern invasion.

The National League was virtually leaderless in the face of aggressive new opposition. Washington's Nick Young, the same owner who had tried to purchase John Montgomery Ward before the 1889 season, had been a figurehead president for years. He was a pleasant man who had no stomach for traditional National League machinations, and would leave meetings whenever something unsavory came up on the agenda; in these circumstances brazen Arthur Soden would serve as acting president. It was Young, in December 1900, who told Clark Griffith, as he left the meeting in which the National League was to spurn both Ban Johnson and the Protective Association, "Griff, your players are not going to get a thing. You will have to fight them."

As the American League battled successfully, the National League was wracked by a bitter internal division. One faction was headed by John Brush, Arthur Soden, and New York transit magnate Andrew Freedman, who had purchased the Giants in 1894. The trio wanted to establish syndicate baseball in the National League. Under this plan, players would be the property of the league instead of the individual clubs. Masterminds in the central office could shift players from team to team as they saw fit.

Other owners like Colonel Rogers and James B. Hart recoiled at this plan. They summoned Albert Spalding from California to lead the battle. Spalding fought this crusade as grandly and self-importantly as always. He put himself forward as a candidate for league president to restore the circuit to its earlier eminence. Spalding had made too many enemies to win the election. He withdrew his candidacy in April 1902, and the backers of syndicate baseball retreated. That fall Andrew Freedman sold the Giants to John Brush for $125,000 (he had paid $49,000 in 1894), and thus one of the more divisive owners in baseball history was removed from the game. Freedman had been involved in several suits throughout his stormy career, some by players suing for back pay and some by other owners suing for libel.

Meanwhile, the National League tried the courts as a way to stop the exodus of players but found little consolation. It fought a major but inconclusive battle for the services of the star second baseman, Napoleon Lajoie (pronounced Lah´-ja-way).

Lajoie played for Colonel Rogers in Philadelphia. Before the 1901 season, he learned that his teammate, slugging outfielder Ed Delahanty, had been receiving $3,000 a year. Lajoie demanded the same amount, considering himself a star of equal magnitude and importance.

Lajoie went into a meeting with Rogers knowing that Connie Mack was ready to offer him $24,000 over three years to play for the A's. Rogers offered his second baseman $25,000 for two years, obviously a better offer. But he refused to give Lajoie the extra couple of hundred to equal Delahanty's 1900 salary. In a gesture of principle, Lajoie spurned Rogers's better offer and went over to the new league.

Lajoie enjoyed a marvelous year in 1901. He won the triple crown with 14 home runs, 125 runs batted in, and a .422 batting average. An embittered Colonel Rogers took Lajoie to court in the fall to prevent his playing further for his crosstown rival.

In April 1902 Pennsylvania Supreme Court Justice William P. Potter granted Rogers an injunction. Judge Potter had undoubtedly seen Lajoie play because in his opinion he wrote, "Lajoie may not be the sun in the baseball firmament, but he is certainly a bright, particular star." Potter stressed that his judgment was based on Lajoie's having signed a three-year contract with the Phillies in 1900. The document was unique because it provided that Lajoie's salary in the reserve years would be at no lower a figure than the initial year.

Instead of appealing the verdict, the astute Ban Johnson shifted Lajoie to the Cleveland Indians. Throughout his career, Ban Johnson influenced player sales and trades in the interests of his view of competitive balance. In this case, he moved Lajoie to keep the law off his tail.

The Phillies tried to find a Cleveland court that would sustain Potter's injunction, but no member of the Ohio judiciary claimed jurisdiction. Covering all bases, Johnson ordered Lajoie not to accompany the Indians to Philadelphia during the season. The second baseman enjoyed a paid vacation in Atlantic City when Cleveland played in Philadelphia. The Lajoie litigation provided little solace to National League owners: They won the case but lost the player.

In early May 1902 the Harper case in the St. Louis City Circuit Court provided a jolting setback to the N. L. Jack Harper was a pitcher who fled the St. Louis Nationals to join the new American League St. Louis franchise. The court denied the older franchise an injunction on the grounds that the ten-day release clause was not mutual for the player. The National League tried to get the court to consider the Lajoie decision. It refused, and leveled a blistering condemnation of the entire baseball industry for its restrictive labor practices. Writing for the court, Judge John A. Talty cited the Fourteenth Amendment to the Constitution, which was passed after the Civil War to prohibit involuntary servitude. He refused to uphold any contract which tied the players down as servilely as organized baseball did.

By the fall of 1902 the National League was ready for truce. It suggested an amalgamation plan to Ban Johnson whereby the National League would absorb his four best teams and another twelve-team National League would be created. Johnson haughtily spurned this offer, and waited for parity.

The compromise announced in January 1903 allowed Ban Johnson to move the American League into New York in exchange for his promise not to move into Pittsburgh. John Brush opposed his old enemy setting up camp in New York, but learning he could hire John McGraw as manager for his Giants, Brush was placated.

In one of the intricate maneuvers common in the history of baseball management, McGraw was available for the National League because Ban Johnson had suspended him as manager of the Baltimore Orioles for most of the 1902 season. Johnson had always felt McGraw's rowdiness reflected poorly on the gentlemanly image of the game. McGraw for his part cared little for the man who wanted to reform him. Shorn of

McGraw, and earlier losing Willie Keeler, Hugh Jennings, and Ned Hanlon to Brooklyn, the Baltimore franchise had slipped to last place in 1902. The American League moved the franchise into New York for 1903, and Clark Griffith became the manager, but McGraw had the satisfaction of piloting the team which was dominant until the early 1920s.

New York would be the only weak link in Johnson's American League. He had succeeded in achieving parity, at least, with the National League. Sportswriter Allan Sangree gushed, "The arrogant message, which Alexander the Great sent to the prime potentate of the tottering Persian Empire that there could not be two suns in heaven, has been refuted."

At that January 1903 peace meeting in Cincinnati, a new National Agreement was signed by both major leagues. The National Association of Professional Minor Leagues, which had been established in 1901, also agreed to abide by the provisions of the new National Agreement. The Agreement's mandate pledged "to perpetuate baseball as the national game of America, and to surround it with such safeguards as to warrant absolute public confidence in its integrity and methods; and to promote and afford protection to such professional baseball leagues and associations as may desire to operate under its provisions." All participating leagues pledged to enforce a reserve clause on its players, and to treat as "outlaws" any clubs that did not utilize such a reserve practice. The concession given to the defunct Players Protective Association, the one-year option in the contract, was consigned to the scrap heap.

The new Agreement established a National Commission to govern baseball, and once again, Ban Johnson showed his ruling hand. The two league presidents and a third party drawn by them would form the ruling triumvirate. National League President Harry Pulliam was no match for Johnson. Another sportswriter turned league official, Pulliam was chosen in 1902 after the end of the Spalding-Freedman internal battle. Plagued by mental problems, he suffered a nervous breakdown in 1905 and committed suicide in 1909. Thus it was Ban Johnson who was able to exert the greatest power on the Commission. Although the chairman chosen was the president of the National League Cincinnati Reds, August "Garry" Herrmann, he was a close friend of Johnson, who shared his love of good food and drink and deferred to him on most baseball questions.

70

Ban Johnson and the Rise of the American League

Ban Johnson presided over the rise of baseball into true modern prosperity. Attendance doubled between 1900 and 1910, reaching over seven and a quarter million fans. Gate receipts for the World Series, established as an annual national event in 1905, increased tenfold between 1905 and 1912. Six cities built stadiums between 1909 and 1913 at an average cost of over $2 million. Francis Richter described these edifices as "excelling in point of spaciousness, comfort, convenience and splendor anything the new or old world has ever seen, not even excepting the historic Roman structures."

In 1905 Albert Spalding, reflecting this period of self-congratulation and unchallenged power, established a commission to prove that baseball's origins were purely American. Former president of the National League Abram G. Mills, who had written the 1888 contract which contributed to the Brotherhood war, chaired the investigation. In 1907, on the basis of scant evidence, Abner Doubleday was pronounced as the inventor of baseball one day in 1839 in Cooperstown, New York.

Thirty years later, Robert W. Henderson made a strong case that baseball had evolved from the English game of rounders, and that New York clerk Alexander Cartwright should be credited with the greatest innovation, requiring ninety feet between bases. Though General Doubleday would have his place in history as the soldier who returned the fire at Fort Sumter to start the Civil War, he probably never came to Cooperstown. If he had, in 1839, he would have been AWOL from West Point. Spalding was privately embarrassed at Mills's inadequate research, as noted by Frank Menke in his *Baseball Encyclopedia,* but like all owners, he wouldn't repudiate a club member publicly.

Why shouldn't baseball moguls of the early twentieth century create a mythical past? They had written ingenious rules to restrict players services in the present. Branch Rickey, who after World War I would add many wrinkles to the techniques of monopoly, spoke volumes when he said that Ban Johnson reminded him of Rickey's pioneer grandfather who had made decisions by slamming the table and bellowing, "That's the way I think it is, and that's the way it is."

To be on the safe side, the baseball establishment also absorbed the leaders of the Protective Association just in case they ever got rebellious notions again. The most outspoken leader, lawyer Harry Taylor, although his failure to serve the players full-time had gravely hampered him, was by 1905 the president of the Eastern League, the forerunner of the important International League. Taylor later became a judge in Erie County, where he lived until 1955. Hugh Jennings who stayed with the Protective Association until the bitter end, left baseball from 1904 to 1906, but returned as the field manager of the Detroit Tigers from 1907 to 1909 and led them to three straight pennants. As a manager, he was like a foreman for the owner. Thus he too was removed from a potential role as an organizer of players.

It was not a friendly climate labor faced throughout the United States. The Supreme Court's 1908 *Lawlor v. Loewe* decision applied the Sherman Antitrust act against a labor union of hatmakers in Danbury, Connecticut, who had sought to organize for better wages and working conditions. The Danbury Hatters case became a battleground for labor activists who succeeded by 1914 in putting enough pressure on Congress for the establishment of the Clayton Antitrust Act, which exempted most labor unions from antitrust injunctions. Traditionally, ballplayers had steered clear of labor unions for many reasons. Many took pride in their status as *professional* ballplayers who were not ordinary working-men. Some resented the comparison to entertainers such as vaudevil-lians, as it was rumored that Samuel Gompers would have placed the two groups together if the players had affiliated with the A. F. of L. in 1900. A larger reason for the players' traditional nonaffiliation was the sea-sonal nature of the work, which kept their permanent home usually far from their workplace. Last but probably most important was the legacy of fear which the destruction of past players groups had engendered.

By 1911 there were unmistakable signs that the players were again becoming restive. Despite the great rise in attendance and the immense popularity of baseball, a player's average salary was still under $2,500. The marginal player sometimes received under $1,000. The press public-ized the $10,000 salaries of Ty Cobb and the Giants' perennial twenty-game winner Christy Mathewson, and the winning World Series share per player regularly exceeded $3,000 by 1910. But the average player and the minor leaguer constantly suffered from the restrictions of the reserve system and the owners' regular practice of not abiding by their own rules. The players were ready to act together again despite the legacy of defeat and disorder.

4

David Fultz and the Creation
of the Professional Baseball
Players Fraternity of 1912

*"Baseball players weren't too much accepted in
those days. . . . We were considered pretty crude.
Couldn't get into the best hotels and all that. And
when we did get into a good hotel, they wouldn't
boast about having us. If we went into the hotel
dining room—in a good hotel, that is—they'd
quick shove us way back in the corner at the very
end of the dining room so we wouldn't be too
conspicuous. 'Here come the players!' you know,
and back in the corner we'd go."*
—*Sam Crawford, star outfielder of the Detroit
Tigers, reminiscing on the early twentieth century
in Lawrence Ritter's* The Glory of Their Times.

1911 spring training was nearing its conclusion when Addie Joss, star
pitcher of the Cleveland Naps, became ill. (Cleveland took its nickname
from second baseman Napoleon Lajoie, whom Ban Johnson had
ordered to Cleveland to avoid litigation in Philadelphia during the trade
war with the National League, and the team did not adopt the nickname
Indians permanently until 1914.) Joss had won 160 games in his nine-
year career compiling a stunning earned-run average of 1.88. Doctors
told him that nothing was seriously wrong but he should return to his
Toledo, Ohio, home to recuperate. The Indians opened the American
League season in St. Louis without him. As they were heading for the
next road stop in Detroit, they received the news that Joss had suffered
spinal meningitis and died. With heavy hearts they arrived in Detroit and
played the first game of the series. Then they voted unanimously to skip
the next day's game to attend Joss's funeral in Toledo.

73

THE IMPERFECT DIAMOND

Ban Johnson learned of the players' intentions and his first instinct was to order them to play as scheduled. Johnson was an intimate of Cleveland owner Charles Somers, the financial angel who had helped to finance Johnson's bold Eastern invasion in 1901. Johnson and Somers decided not to challenge the unanimous sentiment of the Cleveland players, who were backed by field manager Jim McGuire. Johnson announced the regularly scheduled game in Detroit would merely be postponed and replayed at a later date. Several Detroit players joined the full Indians squad at the funeral, and a month later owner Somers held an Addie Joss Memorial Day at the Cleveland ball park. An exhibition game between National and American League all-stars was played with proceeds going to Joss's widow. Although Ban Johnson and Charles Somers had acted prudently, when faced with the united opinion of the ballplayers, there was clearly an atmosphere of ferment building amongst the athletes.

George "Firebrand" Stovall, a veteran first baseman, had conceived the plan for the Indians to attend Joss's funeral. He was named the Indians' manager later in 1911, perhaps to bring him into management and cool down his ardor. He moved on to the St. Louis Americans as a player-manager in 1912. The next year he was one of the first known major leaguers to join the Federal League, which began to seek recognition as a third major league.

Low salaries in an age of baseball affluence was an obvious grievance. Even some of the most mild-mannered players, among them Walter Johnson, began to express this discontent publicly. Ever since he arrived in the big leagues in 1907, Walter Johnson's fans knew he would be an immortal. Nicknamed "The Big Train," the lanky Kansas farm boy won 25 games in 1910 and was on his way to ten straight twenty-victory seasons and a career total of 414 wins, pitching for a mediocre Washington Senators club.

In its July 1911 issue, *Baseball* magazine offered Walter Johnson its pages for his opinions on what he might be worth as a player. *Baseball* had been founded in Boston in 1908 under the editorship of veteran sportswriter Jacob Morse. At the beginning of 1912, it would relocate in New York City, edited by F. C. Lane.

Baseball took pride in its status as "an independent and impartial" journal. One of its editorials pledged:

We will knock the bald-headed magnate who sits on his piles of long green, grasped from the poor downtrodden player, and smokes

25-cent cigars while he hands out pieces of vitrified rope to the newspaper men who interview him. We will also knock with no less energy the humblest peanut seller in the bleachers who bobs up his freckled face and bawls in your eye just in time to spoil your view of a rattling two-bagger and spill the ashes of a mecca cigarette on your shirt front.

Famed actress Lillian Russell praised the national game in *Baseball* because, "It gives one the chance to 'smile out loud' under God's clear sky and to take in life-giving breaths of fresh air every time one empties the lungs with a lusty cheer."

Walter Johnson's contribution to the periodical was revealingly entitled, "Baseball Slavery: The Great American Principle of Dog Eat Dog." He wondered why he was making only $6,500 a year from Washington owner John Noyes (Clark Griffith would not arrive until 1912). The pitcher considered buying his option from the owner for $1,000 because he was convinced that any other baseball owner would pay him at least $7,500. Of course, Noyes had never even considered accepting such a proposition, but Johnson could raise the question, if only theoretically, because the public sympathized with the plight of a great player confined to a poor team.

Johnson did not argue that he deserved as much money as Christy Mathewson, making $10,000 after nine outstanding seasons. If Ty Cobb was worth $9,500, Johnson raised some interesting questions about his own value. They say Cobb plays every day, and a starting pitcher only every fourth day, Johnson said. But a pitcher may handle the ball 150 times a game whereas an outfielder only touches the ball a few times a game at most. If pitching is 80 percent of the game, should not the salary of a pitcher be accordingly high?

Johnson stressed that he was not bellyaching. "I am not making any complaint," he wrote. "This is simply the direct application of the great intelligent American business principle of dog eat dog. . . . The employer tries to starve out the laborer, and the laborer tries to ruin the employer's business. They quarrel over a bone and rend each other like coyotes." He concluded on a plaintive note which revealed the resignation many players felt. "And we are free-born Americans with a Constitution and public schools. Our business philosophy is that of the wolf pack."

The individual dissatisfaction of star and journeyman was building throughout 1911. After the World Series, the triumphant Philadelphia Athletics decided that they should have a share of the motion picture proceeds of the Series. The movies were shown to audiences all across the country. But when the players raised this question before the National Commission, the moguls laughed at their audacity. As long as the players had no organization to represent their interests, they would be forever brushed aside.

In May 1912 a collective action of the players finally erupted and in the cause of a most unlikely martyr, Ty Cobb. At this time, Cobb was the most famous player in America. Before his retirement in 1928, he would amass a record career total of 4,191 hits and a lifetime average of .367. He was a feared base runner whose flashing spikes regularly tore up opposing infielders. He was the leader of the great Tigers' teams which won successive pennants from 1907 to 1909. Yet the Detroit management had not raised his salary for any of these years. Cobb often held out in spring training for higher pay.

On Wednesday afternoon May 15, 1912, the Tigers were finishing a four-game series against the New York Highlanders in New York. Cobb had been taking a severe heckling from New York fans throughout the series. During the middle of the fourth inning, instead of returning to the outfield, Cobb suddenly leaped into the stands behind third base and attacked the loudest fan. His Tiger teammates came out from their dugout ready with baseball bats in case the New York fans rioted, which fortunately they did not. *The New York Times* reported the next day, "Cobb led with a left jab and countered with a right kick. The spectator went to a lawyer's office to make out his will."

Ban Johnson happened to be attending the game and did not find the incident amusing. On Thursday, when the Tigers arrived in Philadelphia for the next series, they learned that Johnson had suspended Cobb for ten days without pay. The fan, Claude Lueker, a former printer who had lost three fingers in an industrial accident, prepared to file suit. When Cobb was advised of the fan's infirmity, he sneered, "I don't care if he has no feet."

The Tigers rallied to Cobb's side and prepared to strike if he were not reinstated and given a hearing by the league office. Cobb was not personally popular with the players, but they knew his value to the team. They also felt Cobb had been sufficiently provoked by the abusive fan. The Tiger players were eager to challenge Ban Johnson on the issue of fan rowdiness because he never tired of taking credit for cleaning up baseball from its unseemly and ungentlemanly past.

Thursday's game was rained out in Philadelphia, and Friday's game was played. The Tigers told manager Jennings that they would not play on Saturday unless Cobb was reinstated. Detroit co-owner Frank Navin, a wealthy stockbroker who shared the team at this time with millionaire lumber operator William Yawkey (foster father of Tom Yawkey, who purchased the Red Sox in the 1930s), hurried to Philadelphia to try to cool heads. Detroit management knew that the team faced a $5,000 fine for every game not played, and they did not doubt that Ban Johnson would try to take over the franchise if the strike were a lengthy one.

On Saturday morning the Tigers reported for business as usual. When strike leader Jim Delahanty, a veteran second baseman and one of five Delahanty brothers who made the major leagues, learned that Cobb was still suspended, the Tigers walked out. Some went home, and some stayed to watch one of the most unusual games in major league history.

Arthur "Bugs" Baer, later a well-known humorist, was a semi-pro baseball player in Philadelphia preparing to play a game when Hugh Jennings reached him and offered him a chance to be a Detroit Tiger. Jennings frantically rounded up as many able-bodied players as possible, including early arrivals among the fans. Baer recalled to Ty Cobb's biographer, John McCallum, "Any ballplayer who could stop a grapefruit from rolling uphill or hit a bull in the pants with a bass fiddle was given a chance of going direct from the semi-pros to the Detroits and no questions asked." Aloysius Travers, a theology student at St. Joseph's College in Philadelphia, became the starting pitcher for the Tigers. He began the game by mumbling to himself not "Let's play ball!" but "Let's pray ball!" Billy Maharg, recommended to Jennings by striking pitcher Bill Burns, played third base for the makeshift Tigers. Seven years later, Burns and Maharg, no longer active as players, would be central conspirators in the Black Sox scandal.

Twenty thousand fans had come to Shibe Park to see an interesting match between the current and former world champions, but by the middle of the third inning, when the score was already 6-0 A's, hundreds stormed the box office trying unsuccessfully to get their money back. The final score was 24-2; manager Jennings came up as a pinch hitter in the ninth inning, only his ninth at-bat in the last eight years.

The first strike in baseball history was headline news all across the country. Ministers discussed the controversy from their pulpits. One clergyman criticized both Cobb and his nasty heckler, using the homily, "He that ruleth his own spirit is mightier than he that taketh a city." *The New York Times* was editorially less charitable. "The sole underlying cause of [the strike] is the growing resentment of all authority and discipline throughout the world," it warned. "If the president of the American League expels the entire Detroit team for breach of contract he will do right."

Ban Johnson held his ground. There was no Sunday baseball in Philadelphia because of long-standing religious objections. And he cancelled Monday's game, but ordered the Tigers to report to Washington for Tuesday's scheduled game with the Senators. He fined the strikers $100 each, and warned that he would expel them from baseball if they continued their strike.

The players' defiance faded quickly. Ty Cobb urged them to go back to work, stressing that their point had been made. When the full squad reported to Washington for the scheduled game with the Senators, Ban Johnson reduced the fine to $50 per player, and he warned Frank Navin not to pay it, as owners often did with league fines. The Tigers won the game, 2-0, and it was business as usual in the sport pages as writers joked about the Tigers' "forty-eight-hour vacation." Ty Cobb was reinstated on May 26, but Johnson warned him that in future instances of fan rowdiness, Cobb should let the umpires restore order. Johnson also announced that special policemen would be hired to maintain proper decorum at the ball parks.

As word spread among the ballplayers of the Tigers' dramatic action, a sense of solidarity grew stronger. During the strike insurgent Jim Delahanty bluntly told the press, "It is about time we got together and formed a union," adding that many discussions had been held during the past year but the players had not decided upon a leader.

Christy Mathewson, one of the active players under consideration for the presidency of a new organization, had declined the office because he lacked the time and the independence to do a thorough job. Mathewson and Cobb pledged themselves to serve any new group as vice-presidents. In September 1912, while the season was still in progress, the second players group of the twentieth century was chartered in a New York courthouse.

Former major league center fielder David Lewis Fultz, a New York

City attorney, was elected president of the group, which chose to be called the Fraternity of Professional Baseball Players of America.

Dave Fultz had come directly to the Philadelphia Nationals upon graduation from Boston University in 1898. Fultz's early experiences in professional baseball made him quickly aware of the contract's inequity. Philadelphia's owner Colonel John I. Rogers had signed Fultz to what the player thought was a $2,400 contract. When Fultz received his 1899 offer, the salary only called for $1,200. Rogers, a lawyer and a notoriously hard bargainer with players, told Fultz that his original contract was for $1,200 salary and $1,200 signing bonus. Fultz objected that there was nothing in writing indicating such a division of money. His case was strikingly similar to the one Atlanta Braves' third baseman Bob Horner brought before baseball's arbitrator Raymond J. Goetz and won in 1979. In 1899 outside arbitration of grievances had barely been envisioned for players, let alone won. Fultz had to sign a contract for $1,200 in 1899. In the middle of the season, Rogers, disgruntled by Fultz's presumption to challenge him, traded the outfielder to Baltimore.

Fultz enjoyed a seven-year major league career. His greatest season came in 1902 under Connie Mack for the Philadelphia A's. He played center field for a pennant-winning club and led the league in runs scored with 109. His career lasted through 1905. Suffering from chronically sore legs—the result of football injuries when he captained Brown's football team—Fultz retired after he sustained a broken jaw in a collision with A's shortstop Kid Elberfeld in September 1905. He passed the bar examination later that fall and set up a shingle in New York's Wall Street district not far from the office of John Montgomery Ward.

At the time of his election as Fraternity president, Fultz was not well known by the active players. He was vaguely remembered as "the man who would not play Sunday baseball," which showed his religious conviction. (Playing baseball on the Sabbath was not widely accepted in the early twentieth century.) Fultz had also served as Brown football coach and as a referee in major Eastern college games. His greatest assets were that he knew the law and that he understood the travails of the ordinary ballplayer.

That the Fraternity answered a need which the players felt can be seen by the large number who joined immediately—288—a majority on all the major league teams except the two Boston clubs and Cleveland. The charter of the new group reflected the cautiousness of its leader and the lingering fears of the players, who knew what the owners thought of player organization. It merely asked that both sides see that "every reasonable obligation of the player's contract is lived up to by both contracting parties."

Remembering that fan rowdiness in the Tigers' strike had been a rallying issue, Fultz urged the owners to insist on crowd control in the ball parks. He vowed that the Fraternity would aim "to instill into the player a pride in his profession and to use the strongest possible influence to induce him to keep himself in condition, and to give his employer the best service of which he is capable." As if these disclaimers were not moderate enough, Fultz publicly disassociated himself from the stigma of the defeated Brotherhood. "Because an organization formed of players twenty-odd years ago temporarily wrecked the national game by persistence in a sweeping policy of selfishness and self-aggrandizement," he said, it did not mean "that any organization of players in any age and clime must be bent upon the same highroad to destruction."

The baseball establishment greeted the new group warily. Albert Spalding wrote in his influential annual publication, *Spalding's Guide* for 1913, "There is no necessity to fear any grave disturbances, but there is a dread . . . that a selfish coterie of players might obtain control of the organization and retard for a moment the higher development of the game." National Commission Chairman Garry Herrmann told the players he had no objection to their forming an association. But he suggested, condescendingly, that the major leaguers really had nothing in common because they consisted of three disparate groups: those on the make, those already at the top, and those on the downslide.

Connie Mack, already a part owner of the A's franchise as well as manager, was not going to take any chances. He assigned coach Ira Thomas, a former A's catcher who would remain in Mack's employ for fifty years, to join the Fraternity and to keep him abreast of its activities. Though one of many vice-presidents of the Fraternity, Thomas stated in late 1913 that there was no great need for an organization as far as A's players were concerned. "Connie does not hold his players by reason of signed contracts; he holds them because he is eminently fair and gives us practically all we ask for."

While he was a careful, too-polite man for the job at hand, Fultz of course disagreed with Thomas that there was no need for a Fraternity. He jibed at Thomas that there was good reason to call Thomas's boss "Connie." In regular columns that editor F. C. Lane gave Fultz in *Baseball* magazine the attorney pleaded the case for the players' needs with eloquence and pertinence. They hold up well almost seventy years later.

Fultz denied that big leaguers were overpaid. He stressed that the publicity over the highly paid stars obscured the reality of the low wages of most of the journeymen. Fultz told his readers that some players still made less than $1,000 a year despite the great profitability of the sport.

He argued that major leaguers deserved good pay because "the big leaguer is a development of years of continual practice. . . . He is the expert, the masterpiece selected from thousands and thousands of players in this country." Fultz took issue with those critics who said the players should be glad to be involved in a game for a living while the average wage earner in the United States earned less than $1,500 a year. The only valid comparison, Fultz maintained, is to what "the three hundred best men in any industry" receive as compensation. To the familiar management complaint that the players had not invested in the game as the owners had, Fultz responded that the athletes had contributed "their skill, their agility, their strength, their mental and physical alertness, qualities which have taken them years to develop."

He twitted the owners and their press allies for constantly complaining about their lack of money to pay decent salaries. "A glance around the league circuits at the stupendous equipment recently completed or now under construction," Fultz suggested, "would convince the casual observer that after paying salaries, the magnate still has enough left to keep the wolf out of the garage."

Fultz was especially forceful in articulating the problems of the minor leaguers. "The minor leaguer is as important to us as the biggest star," he liked to say. The non-major leaguers received paltry pay because all the lower leagues were bound to strict salary limits enforced by the National Association. Fultz condemned the practice by which a player demoted to a lower minor league had to pay his own way to his new club; sometimes this involved a trip across the country. He lobbied in favor of side agreements in the contracts of minor leaguers which would augment their low wages.

Fultz also raised the issue of player safety, imploring owners to construct green backgrounds on outfield fences so that the batter would be aided in picking up the flight of the pitched ball. Minor league conditions were particularly poor. An item in the *Chicago Tribune,* which Fultz noted in his *Baseball* magazine column, estimated that 59 players died during the 1915 season, mainly in the lower classifications and semi-professional circuits; 38 of these fatalities were due to head injuries suffered in the batter's box. In 1916, John Dodge of Mobile, Alabama in the Southern Association died of a similar head injury, another tragedy which Fultz felt could have been prevented.

His sincerity and clear presentation of the issues attracted hundreds of minor leaguers to the Fraternity. By the end of the 1914 season the total membership had swelled to over 1,100, and he reported a treasury of more than $10,000.

Like all the players' leaders so far, Fultz was a moderate on the reserve system. He accepted the argument that without the reserve, players would flock to the biggest cities and the richest owners. But like John Montgomery Ward and Harry Leonard Taylor, Fultz denounced the abuses of the system. He especially condemned the practice of cutting players as much as 50 percent or more for the option year. The magnates, without any players organization to face them for a decade, had long forgotten the Ward-Spalding compromise of 1888, which allowed for an explicit reserve clause only if the option year provided for at least the same salary.

Fultz speculated on a finite term for the reserve, perhaps five years. He knew that without the reserve in a contract, the owners would likely cut players or blacklist them. He thought that the five-year limitation with the right of both parties to extend the reserve mutually could be an alternative. He dismissed baseball's consistent claim that it must remain outside the law as "an absurdity." "Law has been in existence for a thousand years," Fultz averred, "and no complication is too intricate, no ramification too diverse to find precedents by which they can be untangled."

In January 1914 the Fraternity achieved recognition by the National Commission. The reluctant acceptance of the group came after the regularly scheduled business meeting of the governing body of the sport. Eleven of seventeen points in the Fraternity's platform were agreed to by the Commission. Major league owners would now pay for their players' home and road uniforms. They would make green outfield fences mandatory to provide a good backdrop for hitters. They promised to supply written reasons to a player if he were suspended. They said they would not discriminate against any player because of membership in the Fraternity.

Ten-year major league veterans also won the right to unconditional release. The case of great pitcher Mordecai "Three Finger" Brown had caused widespread sympathy in 1913. Brown had been sold to the minor leagues by Chicago Cubs owner Charles Murphy in utter disregard for his thirteen years of great pitching in the majors.

One of the major Fraternity planks rejected by the National Commission was the publication of waivers. Players always wanted to know what teams were interested in them, and it would help them if they learned what teams claimed them on waivers. The owners liked keeping players in the dark, however, so they rejected this proposal.

The Commission also refused to agree to a provision which promised the player his contract would follow him wherever he went. In 1913 Fultz had taken one of his first cases for the Fraternity in behalf of Boston Red Sox pitcher Kurt "Casey" Hageman, who had been sold to Denver of the Western Association but had refused to report at a reduced salary. Hageman finally won a settlement after eight years of litigation, but his career effectively ended years earlier. Fultz believed strongly that the contract must be upheld throughout all levels of baseball. The Commission turned deaf ears, not willing to yield their historic prerogative to control the destiny of the player.

That the Commission even recognized the Fraternity was a reflection of the threat that a new league, the Federal League, began to pose to organized baseball. Ban Johnson had not endorsed the Protective Association in 1900 out of any concern for players' collective rights. At that time he simply hoped to win the players over to his new league. In 1914 Johnson and the National Commission adopted a converse strategy, recognizing the Fraternity in order to keep the players loyal to the established leagues.

Harold Seymour, who had access to National Commission papers for his *Baseball: The Golden Age,* reports that after the Cincinnati meeting granting recognition to the Fraternity, Garry Herrmann called David Fultz and asked, "What are you going to do for us?" Fultz could not and did not want to do much. Although he was erroneously reported to be a future Federal League president, Fultz had no direct dealings with the new league. He condemned players who broke contracts to join the Federals and recommended their expulsion from the Fraternity. As for those ignoring their options, Fultz was not critical. He doubted whether the courts would uphold the reserve clause. All he would do was to advise the players, with characteristic caution, "These are turbulent days in the baseball world, and the players owe it to themselves and their profession to hew close to the line and to exert every ounce of will power and the soundest judgment which they possess." Unfortunately, the sterling qualities of good judgment and sobriety would not be sufficient in the years ahead for the players to cope with the wounded but ever virulent baseball monopoly.

5

The Rise and Fall of the Federal
League and the Players Fraternity

*"The only way to teach a magnate anything is with
a club."*
—*Anonymous player, quoted in* Baseball
magazine, March 1915.

*"Organized baseball is a mighty steamroller. It may
roll slowly, but it crushes everything that opposes
it, sooner or later."*
—*Cincinnati sportswriter William C. Phelon,*
Baseball *magazine, March 1916.*

Initially, the formation of the Federal League in 1913 was treated
benignly by the major league owners. As it called itself only a minor
league, the moguls thought it would disappear like the other recently
formed circuits. Indiana businessman Daniel Fletcher had tried to start a
rival league in 1911 after being enraged that the owners refused to allow
him to arrange a postseason barnstorming tour of major league stars.
Fletcher's effort failed. So had a 1912 Pennsylvania-based circuit, the
United States Baseball League, which barely lasted a dozen games.

Organized baseball thought it best at this time not to utilize its
harshest methods of blacklisting players and stigmatizing owners as
outlaws. In 1912 and 1913 Illinois Congressman Thomas Gallagher was
getting nowhere trying to investigate baseball as the "most predacious
trust in the country." But why ruffle feathers? Ty Cobb's holdout at the
beginning of the 1913 season had not brought baseball good publicity.
Many of Georgia's congressmen and both senators had interceded in
Cobb's behalf, and the dispute was finally settled. There was no need,
owners thought, to put a squeeze on the Federals.

Then, in August 1913 the Federals served notice that they intended to seek major league status. Taking a page from Ban Johnson's book of ambition, the Federals announced plans to expand into the East for 1914.

The new league had some vital demographic arguments as well as the obvious and commendable desire to make a profit out of the baseball business. America's population had grown 15 percent since the 1903 National Agreement. The increase in cities had been much greater. In 1914 the Federals established franchises in Baltimore and Buffalo, which were larger in population than National League cities Cincinnati and Washington. Baltimore itself was larger than Detroit or Pittsburgh. The rest of the circuit consisted of Chicago, Brooklyn, St. Louis, Kansas City, Indianapolis, and Pittsburgh.

There was big money willing to invest in the third major league. Wealthy and dynamic stationer James Gilmore of Chicago headed the league as president. One league vice-president was Brooklyn owner Robert B. Ward, who had made a fortune in the bakery business with Tip-Top Bread. For the 1914 season, Ward recruited John Montgomery Ward, no relation, as his business manager.

The strongest franchise of the league was Chicago, where self-made millionaire Charles Weeghman, owner of a chain of cafeterias, was both able and popular. For the 1914 season, the league hired three famous managers: George Stovall for Kansas City; Ned Hanlon for Baltimore; and Joe Tinker, of the famous Tinker-to-Evers-to-Chance double play combination, for Chicago.

The Federal League was to run like a syndicate, the idea which the National League had rejected in 1902. Players would be hired by the league though the property of the clubs. The new circuit promised players a contract without a reserve, substituting instead long-term contracts with guaranteed salary increases to athletes who made the team. They guaranteed the full salary from the beginning of spring training, which the established owners had always refused.

Despite the attraction of the revised contract, few experienced major leaguers joined the Federals. In the two years of the trade war, only eighteen major leaguers jumped their contracts and only sixty-three ignored their reserves out of a total of two hundred sixty-four players who competed for the Federals. The bulk of the new circuit's competitors came from the minor leagues, whose operations were severely disrupted. Ban Johnson offered the magisterial opinion, since they were not his leagues, that the minors should close down for a year in 1915.

The presence of the inexperienced players affected the quality of play in the Federal League and made major leaguers less likely to join. The new league also had an image problem. Clubs took nicknames from combining the city with the league: Chifeds, StLoufeds, and even, Buffalofeds. The Brooklyn team was dubbed the "Tip-Tops," which almost made the other nicknames look good.

Despite its problems, the Federal League had an enormous impact on organized baseball. In the short run, it nearly doubled every established player's salary. Harold Seymour estimates that the salaries of twenty (unfortunately, unnamed) regulars jumped from approximately $3,800 in 1913 to $7,300 in 1915. In another study, Steven Reiss estimates the average salary rose from $1,200 in 1904 to $2,800 in 1915.

The great stars benefited handsomely. Ty Cobb, squabbling for $10,000 in 1910 and engaging in his celebrated holdout for $15,000 in 1913, reached $20,000 in 1915. Walter Johnson approached that figure too, after signing a contract with the Chifeds. Johnson then allowed Clark Griffith to coax him back into the Washington fold. Swallowing hard, Connie Mack tore up many of his players' contracts during the 1914 season and extended them into long-term pacts with sizable increases in pay. That did not stop his star pitchers Charles "Chief" Bender and Eddie Plank from leaving his 1914 American League champions to join the Federal League in 1915.

The Federal League had a high-powered attorney, Edward E. Gates, who had warned the establishment moguls early in 1914, "Is it possible that organized baseball, through its years of tyrannical rule and usurpation, has secured certain privileges and immunities which do not belong to other organizations in the country?" Gates recommended that Chifed owner Weeghman sue the Philadelphia Phillies for enticing catcher Bill Killifer to ignore his Chifed contract, signed in December 1913, to return to the Phillies for the 1914 season.

In June 1914 federal district and circuit courts upheld the Phillies' right to Killifer. They accepted the argument of organized baseball's equally high-powered chief lawyer, George Wharton Pepper, that Killifer had been "seduced" by the Chifeds to leave Philadelphia. The courts ruled that since Philadelphia had reserved Killifer by the end of October 1913 for the 1914 season, they had developed an "equity" in the player.

The legality of the reserve clause per se was not approved, but only the propriety of the mechanisms under baseball rules by which the Philadelphia club had laid claim to Killifer. Also in June, a Cincinnati federal court enjoined Reds' outfielder Armando Marsans from jumping to the StLoufeds because he had signed a contract with the National League club for 1914.

In July the tables were turned when the Federals won a major victory in the upstate New York Erie County courtroom of State Supreme Court Justice Herbert Bissell. Veteran first baseman Hal Chase had turned the controversial ten-day release clause on the owners, by giving notice on June 15 to the Chicago White Sox that after ten days he planned to join the Buffalofeds.

It has been said that the history of human freedom is the history of fighting for the rights of unsavory characters. Hal Chase was a gifted player but a notoriously incorrigible gambler, often suspected of fixing games though never caught. Commenting on Chase's contract, which was his sole judicial function, Judge Bissell declared, "This case does not present the simple question of a laborer who has entered into a fair contract for his personal services." He complained that a ballplayer under the National Agreement yields an American's basic Constitutional rights to liberty of contract and of conduct. He condemned the notion that "the right and title of a major league club to its players shall be absolute." He called it "peonage," a term which would appear recurrently in the years ahead. He called the attachment of the option rule to the contract "an ingenious device" whereby the player perpetually consigns himself to "the dominion of a benevolent despotism through the operation of the monopoly established by the National Agreement." Interestingly, he did not take issue with the common view that baseball was a peculiar business outside the regulations of interstate commerce. Anticipating the placid exemption the Supreme Court of the United States would give baseball from antitrust laws in 1922, Bissell commented that baseball was basically a local operation and interstate commerce laws should not apply.

In January 1915, buoyed by the Bissell verdict, Chicagoans Weeghman and Gilmore pressed the most dramatic litigation. They asked a massive nine-count, federal antitrust injunction against the major leagues for denying the Federals access to the player market, thereby restraining free trade.

To many people, the suit was an admission of failure, a confession that in the competition for fans the Federals had failed. Some members of the League doubted the wisdom of the strategy. One report attributed John Montgomery Ward's resignation as Brooklyn business manager at the end of 1914 to opposition to the legal action. Ward denied it, and in 1916 he served as an assistant counsel for the Baltimore plaintiffs of the Federal League.

There were some officials in each league who hoped the suit would clear the air. They wished to discover once and for all whether baseball's controversial provisions, the reserve and assignability clauses, waivers and options of players, were legally defensible.

Clark Griffith, on his way to full control of the Washington franchise by 1920, was aghast at the suit. He criticized Dave Fultz, who continued to keep the Fraternity neutral in the Federal League war, for not going to court to praise the wisdom of baseball's traditional management. Griffith suggested Fultz should testify:

> The Players Fraternity is satisfied with the contracts even if the court isn't; they were made in good faith and we will stand by them.

Fultz replied that Griffith must be a "humorist."

Albert Spalding, in retirement in California and to die later in 1915, took an Olympian view of the suits. He had disagreed with the courts' criticism of the baseball contract in 1890. He had not changed his view. Using the nineteenth-century spelling of baseball, he wrote in his 1915 *Spalding Guide*:

> Our policy is . . . to ignore all leagues, clubs and players who are fighting organized professional Base Ball. . . . The real backbone of Base Ball is the American youth and his love for the National Game may be depended upon to protect it against the greed and short-sightedness of its enemies.

In 1910 Spalding had lost a battle—one of the rare times in his life—when he was denied the Republican senatorial nomination in California. In 1915 he faded away, taking a parting shot at the Brotherhood, whose players in 1890 "had conspired to destroy organized ball."

The undaunted Federal League owners chose the Illinois federal courtroom of Judge Kenesaw Mountain Landis. In 1907 Landis had made a national reputation by fining the Standard Oil Company over $29 million for antitrust violations. Although an appeals court overturned his verdict, Landis had earned a national image as "the trust-busting judge." The Federal League thought he would be sympathetic to their prayers.

They evidently forgot to consider that Landis was an avid baseball fan, closely following both Cubs and White Sox. At one point during the testimony in January 1915, Landis declared, "Both sides must understand that any blows at the thing called baseball would be regarded by this court as a blow to a national institution." Another time he cut off an attorney who had discussed the working conditions of the players. "As a result of thirty years of observation," Landis snapped, "I am shocked because you call playing baseball 'labor.' "

Landis took the Federal League case under advisement in late January. Many observers thought he would issue a ruling before spring training began to ease the situation for all sides. However, he deliberately withheld judgment, hoping that the parties would settle out of court. By November 1915 the competing leagues were ready to negotiate and Landis had won the admiration of the moguls, who kept his name in mind for possible future service.

There were many reasons for the out-of-court settlement. The trade war had been costly to all the owners. Only the players were benefiting from the competing markets. Charles Somers, one of the founding owners of the American League and Ban Johnson's financial angel, suffered business reverses which, combined with his rising payroll, forced him to sell the team. None of his original comrades in arms, including Johnson, did anything to save his investment. Connie Mack broke up his 1914 champions, losing Bender and Plank to the Federals and selling star second baseman Eddie Collins to Charles Comiskey of the White Sox for over $50,000.

The biggest fear of the established leagues was a continuation of the war for another season. Millionaire Harry Sinclair had joined the Federal circuit. He moved the Kansas City franchise to Newark in 1915 and was making noises at invading New York for 1916, where the Highlanders remained a shaky operation. Sinclair, later a central figure in the Teapot Dome oil land scandal of the 1920s, posed a serious threat to the established owners. His seemingly endless supply of money and the suit still pending before Landis precipitated peace meetings in the fall of 1915.

Conditions were propitious, as in October of 1915 a key Federal owner, Brooklyn's Robert Ward, had died. Ban Johnson was not very charitable in commenting, "I think it was the Federal League that put him under the sod as he could not stand the strain of worries and losses." Despite his outward show of arrogance, Johnson was willing to compromise as were all the National League owners.

The settlement announced at the end of 1916 proved surprisingly favorable to the third league. The Federal League received $600,000 in return for dropping the action before Judge Landis. Charles Weeghman became a major stockholder of the Cubs, and the stadium he constructed for the Chifeds is now known as Wrigley Field. Phil Ball, the ice-magnate owner of the StLoufeds, received the American League St. Louis franchise.

Although the settlement denied Harry Sinclair entry into the New York baseball market, he was permitted to sell back his best players to the big leagues for hefty sums. He received $35,000 for Benny Kauff, the Federal League's leading hitter.

International League executives bellowed foul at this provision. They complained that the majors were allowing a burglar to raffle off his stolen goods. But the magnates wanted an end to the trade war, and they had decided that placating the wealthy Sinclair was the best method.

The only loser in the settlement was the Baltimore Federal club, the Terrapins. Its owners included Ned Hanlon, the former Brotherhood activist and the Orioles' 1890s manager; and a former magistrate, insurance man Harry Goldman. Goldman and Hanlon and their board of directors decided to sue.

They claimed that the two major leagues and Weeghman and Gilmore of the Federals had conspired to shut them out of the baseball business in direct violation of antitrust laws. Their suit dragged through various federal courts for six years. It reached the Supreme Court where, in 1922, Justice Oliver Wendell Holmes rendered his momentous verdict. Speaking for a unanimous court, Holmes decreed that organized baseball deserved status outside the antitrust laws because it was not interstate commerce.

Organized baseball looked forward to a period of peace beginning with the 1916 season. Although most of the world was at war, the United States was not yet involved. Baseball operators hoped for business as usual, which meant lowered salaries and reduced freedoms for the players.

The high minor leagues, particularly the International League, had suffered gravely during the trade war. When the Federals moved into Baltimore in 1914 and into Newark in 1915, two prime I. L. franchises were shattered. Owner Jack Dunn in Baltimore had to sell his star "Babe," George Herman Ruth, to the Boston Red Sox for a mere $2,500, far less than Dunn would have received ordinarily for such a fine prospect. In 1915 Dunn had to move his franchise to Richmond, Virginia. The Newark franchise also relocated, in Harrisburg, Pennsylvania. The press dubbed the International League "the Belgium of baseball," overrun by the expansionist power, the Federal League.

International League President Edward Grant Barrow was no stranger to trade wars. In 1901 general manager Barrow of the Toronto Eastern League franchise watched Ban Johnson take most of his prime talent to the new American League. Barrow had survived that war, and he managed to survive the Federal war.

War is not just a metaphor in describing the Federal League period. Ban Johnson had allowed his old comrade Charles Somers to go under in Cleveland. With the International League restored in 1916, Edward Barrow forced a $7,500 reentry upon his old friend Jack Dunn, who had brought Barrow into the League in 1910. Dunn paid up, but engineered Barrow's ouster after 1918. Barrow moved on to become the field manager of the Boston Red Sox, and then arrived in New York in 1920, where he presided for a quarter century as the architect of the Yankees' dynasty of champions.

Although owners and baseball operators warred in the wake of the Federal League complications, they shared one common belief: It was about time the players were put in their place. They were ready to take away the recognition of the Players Fraternity, which had been only an expedient action in January 1914. Ed Barrow soon referred to it as a "huge joke," and counseled that if the owners stood together, the Fraternity would "scatter like chickens before a hawk."

In July 1914 Fultz's group had been strong enough to threaten a strike in behalf of a minor league first baseman, Clarence Kraft, who balked at leaving Newark of the International League when sold to Nashville of the lower-rated Southern Association. Charles Ebbets, owner of the Brooklyn Nationals, controlled Kraft's contract, but backed down when the Fraternity threatened its walkout. Ebbets substituted a $2,500 cash payment to the Nashville owner in lieu of delivering Kraft.

By 1916, the Fraternity, though its membership had remained stable,

92

was in no position to take daring action. Fultz still talked bravely of assuring major leaguers who had signed more equitable contracts during the Federal League war that he would see that the pacts were honored. Of course, he lacked any power to enforce the contract. Even big names like Boston Red Sox pitcher Joe Wood and outfielder Tris Speaker were having trouble with management in 1916. Wood held out the entire year and Speaker was sold to Cleveland, refusing to play for what Boston was offering.

Fultz remained concerned about the plight of the lower-classification players. As noted earlier, his basic principle was, "A minor leaguer is just as important to us as the biggest star." Ignoring the hostile climate he was entering in November 1916, Fultz journeyed to the National Association annual meeting in New Orleans to present a four-point Fraternity program to the minor league conclave.

He wanted the minor league officials to eliminate the practice of suspending players for injury; to provide travel expenses to spring training; to make public the clubs' defenses against grievances brought by players; and to enforce the five-day notice provision to players prior to release. The National Association did not deign to discuss the measures. It dismissed Fultz as a "professional agitator," desperately seeking a cause.

Fultz announced that he would appeal to the National Commission to make the minor leagues grant the Fraternity's demands. He threatened a strike of the players, warning that each Fraternity member was pledged not to sign a 1917 contract unless the minor leaguers won these rights. Early in January 1917 Fultz met with Samuel Gompers in Washington. On January 8, 1917, *The New York Times* headlined that affiliation with the A. F. of L. was a distinct possibility. Independent of Fultz, minor league umpires were meeting with the A. F. of L. to discuss a possible union of arbiters.

In mid-January, Fultz tried to meet with the National Commission, but he was rebuffed. National League President John Kinley Tener, former governor of Pennsylvania and in the distant past a pitcher for the Pittsburgh Players League team, said that the Commission had no authority to enforce rulings on the minor leagues. Tener added that to threaten a strike of major leaguers was "inadvisable" and "inexcusable." He struck a familiar chord when he invited individual players to meet with him at any time.

Ban Johnson, who had only recognized the Fraternity in 1914 because of the trade war, was ready for the kill: "I question whether many of the players want to make trouble for themselves, for they are a smart, thinking class of men and have no grievances as far as I can see." Tener struck the same chord, observing, "Professional men don't strike." Eager for a return to the old days, Johnson warned, "None of the players will be permitted to go South until they have first signed their contracts." The National Commission not only refused to meet with Fultz, but announced that the Cincinnati agreement of 1914 had been abrogated.

By the end of January 1917, Samuel Gompers was hedging in his support of Fultz. He announced that the A. F. of L. had taken "under advisement" a suggestion that the Fraternity be recognized. Gompers admitted that owners had written him, suggesting it would be embarrassing for the labor leader to support a strike if the players did show up for spring training.

By February it was clear that Fultz had made a grievous error. Most of the players were signing contracts because the lack of alternative markets for their wares made the choice bluntly easy. Fultz did retain the admiration of many established major leaguers—like Detroit's outfielder Sam Crawford and Brooklyn's first baseman Jake Daubert—but the odds against his crusade were too great. He briefly considered hiring a theater in New York to make his case to the public; he dropped the idea when he realized he was a poor public speaker. On February 20, 1917, after his hurried effort to organize low minor leagues behind the four-point program failed, Fultz formally released the Fraternity loyalists from the no-strike pledge.

Fultz tried to save some face by asking the Commission not to penalize the Fraternity members for their affiliation. President Tener haughtily replied, "We shall not discriminate against anyone, not because Fultz asks for it, but because it involves a principle of justice." The many dozens of unemployed former Federal Leaguers might have been surprised by this statement. The entrenched and totally triumphant monopoly did not particularly care.

David Fultz admitted to *Baseball* magazine that his defeat "was the biggest disappointment of my life." He genuinely thought the National Association could enforce his demands, and the National Commission would compel them if they refused. As a former football referee, Fultz evidently thought rules were rules, and must be enforced no matter whom they hurt. He totally underestimated the vengefulness of the authorities.

There is no doubt that Fultz lacked the temperament to be a successful players' leader. He had a dour personality and was a poor social mixer. He often would lecture to the players about profligate habits. In his *Baseball* magazine columns, he regularly warned the players not to buy automobiles because they could not afford them. He wanted to expel players from the Fraternity for not hustling. He even allowed some players to organize a Prohibition campaign within the Fraternity. How a no-drinking pledge might have advanced the interests of all the players in professional baseball is hard to imagine.

The aborted strike of early 1917 cost Fultz members and his column in *Baseball* magazine. Editor F. C. Lane had a farewell interview with Fultz in March 1917. Lane felt sorry for the organizer, but he attributed the Virginian's defeat to "a malignant form of conscience." Although the Fraternity existed on paper until 1918, its back had been broken before the 1917 season started.

David Fultz went into war service as an aviator. When he returned in 1918, the triumphant baseball monopoly handed him some patronage, the presidency of the International League. Fultz lasted as Ed Barrow's successor only two years. He tired of the job, which he realized left him at the mercy of the major leagues. He moved to Florida where he worked as a lawyer until his death in 1959. Another players' leader had been beaten and chastened.

The few critics of the baseball establishment in the sporting press were also absorbed. *Baseball* magazine, without Fultz's columns, devoted itself entirely to human interest stories about players and owners. Francis Richter's *Sporting Life* had given Fultz a column in the last years of the Fraternity. Once its defeat was evident, Richter counseled the players in April 1917, "Forget what transpired during the war with the Federal League and injurious wranglings about salaries and other issues with the Fraternity. Now play the best ball possible." (American League President Lee MacPhail took a page directly from Richter's book of wishful thinking when he announced at the settlement of the bitter umpires' strike of 1979, "It's all over and has been forgotten.")

Richter shortly left *Sporting Life* for a position on *Spalding's Guide*. His former journal stayed away from controversy under the editorship of Edgar L. Wolff, who wrote under the pseudonym of Jim Nasium. In the fall of 1922 Wolff converted *Sporting Life* into a monthly devoted mainly to news of bowling and billiards.

The Sporting News was now the lone national baseball weekly of any consequence. Under the leadership of J. G. Taylor Spink it became the voice of the baseball establishment. Spink's father Charles had been sympathetic to the Federal League effort, but J. G. Taylor Spink, who took over as editor and publisher upon the death of Charles in April 1914, backed the established monopoly fully.

Regular TSN contributor Joe Vila, sportswriter for *The New York Sun,* was particularly vituperative. He gloated, "When Ban Johnson and John Tener turned the hose on the Fraternity . . . it vanished like old newspapers on the way to a sewer." Vila leveled the traditional charges against the Fraternity: It had taken the spirit out of the game. Vila claimed that for John McGraw and earlier players, "Baseball and not money was the real concern."

The players stood by helplessly as the owners brazenly violated their contracts. It became a common practice to release players or farm them out at sizable pay cuts. Joe Vila chortled that many of the Federal League unemployed assuredly would prefer to be working peons. Just as the owners had scrapped the one-year option to renew at the end of the American League war in 1902, they now summarily discarded the "iron-clad" contracts without the ten-day release clause which some owners had given during the Federal League war and returned the controversial ten-day provision to the contract. Branch Rickey, in his first executive job as president of the St. Louis Browns, introduced his own form of ten-day clause. He sent contracts to players and informed them that the documents were only good if they returned them, signed, within ten days. Twenty frightened players complied within the deadline.

Management again held an unfettered whip hand, with the players lacking once again any organization to express their grievances. Yet before the fifth game of the 1918 World Series, the participating Red Sox and Chicago Cubs almost staged a walkout.

Baseball attendance had plunged two million during 1918 because of the World War. With the outcome of hostilities still in doubt, War Secretary Newton D. Baker advised a halt of the regular baseball season after Labor Day. He gave permission to hold a World Series, but the owners took many peremptory actions which thoroughly riled the players. They had announced that second-, third-, and fourth-place finishers

96

in each league would get a share of World Series proceeds, a common practice today but introduced by fiat in 1918. The moguls had decided to charge regular prices instead of the normal Series' markup, which further diluted the players' pool. When the players learned that the winner's share would be barely $1,000 per man compared to the $4,000 or more of recent years, they refused to come on the field for Game Five.

The National Commission hurried down to the clubhouses. Garry Herrmann informed the players that there was no way that the proceeds could be increased at this late date. A drunk Ban Johnson asked them to consider the wounded servicemen waiting in the Boston stands. After an hour's delay of the start of the game, the players continued the Series. After Boston won the Series, four games to two, a spiteful National Commission refused to send the teams championship emblems.

The 1919 World Series has been well chronicled as baseball's darkest hour. The 1918 Series is a good illustration of the decay into which the baseball business was already tumbling.

Garry Herrmann had lost the confidence of both leagues as an impartial chairman of the National Commission. As far back as 1915 Barney Dreyfuss had been enraged at Herrmann for allowing Branch Rickey to retain first baseman George Sisler for the St. Louis Browns. Dreyfuss had signed Sisler while the future star was still in high school, but the National Commission denied the Pittsburgh owner his prize for signing someone so young. Herrmann had further weakened his credibility when he was believed to have arranged the favorable settlement of Harry Sinclair's Federal League interests.

In 1918 the Commission took another body blow when National League president John Tener resigned. Tener was enraged when Connie Mack defied a Commission ruling that ordered pitcher Scott Perry back to the Boston Braves, for whom he had played before he left to join an independent team and then the A's. Mack obtained an injunction from a Philadelphia court permitting Perry to remain with the A's. Tener was so mad that he wanted to boycott the stormy 1918 World Series; instead, he just resigned, realizing that his only powers had been to supervise the umpires and to sign the league baseballs.

Other owners were beginning to challenge the authority of "baseball law" as interpreted by the National Commission. In 1919 Colonels Jacob Ruppert and Tillinghast Huston, new owners of the New York Yankees, successfully thwarted the once impregnable Ban Johnson. New York

State Supreme Court Justice Robert F. Wagner, Sr. (later the United States Senator) upheld the Yankees' purchase of pitcher Carl Mays from the Red Sox. Johnson had voided the sale because he had suspended Mays for walking out on the Boston club. Johnson insisted that until he removed Mays from the ineligible list, the pitcher could not be traded.

But Johnson could no longer control the American League owners. New magnates like Ruppert and Harry Frazee would ignore his dictates. Johnson had also plunged into a bitter feud with his oldest ally, Charlie Comiskey, who believed the president discriminated against him in his decisions.

In 1919 organized baseball's leadership was in dire straits, with Ban Johnson no longer the strongman, Garry Herrmann under fire, and John Heydler, the former baseball statistician who became National League president, lacking authority. The National Association had also announced it no longer considered itself bound to the National Agreement of 1903.

In the middle of 1919 advertising executive Albert Lasker, a major stockholder of the Chicago Cubs, circulated a report among the moguls. It called for a new ruling body in organized baseball. He suggested encouraging prominent citizens to aid baseball. Lasker was a power in the Republican Party. He knew many people, including Chief Justice William Howard Taft, who might be willing to serve.

Only in September 1920, when the exposure of the fixed World Series of 1919 brought public outrage, did the owners take action. The tale of the "Black Sox" scandal has been memorably told by Eliot Asinof in *Eight Men Out*. Asinof observed how the closing of the racetracks during World War I had led the professional gamblers to flock to the ball parks. The owners did little to watch out for irregularities. Key contacts between gamblers and players were made easily.

What has not been stressed is the abject state of disorganization all the players had fallen into by 1919. Although Dave Fultz was not a great leader, his Fraternity had provided a meeting place and some means for expressing grievances. Without a protective group, the players were at the mercy of tight-fisted owners like Charles Comiskey, also known as "The Old Roman."

With the exception of Eddie Collins, the White Sox weren't paid the salaries befitting their excellence. Collins earned $14,500 annually, a fair salary considering that Comiskey had paid Connie Mack more than $50,000 for Collins' contract after the 1914 season.

Other White Sox were not so fortunate. "Shoeless" Joe Jackson, the outfielder whose hitting was compared to Ty Cobb's, earned less than $6,000, though his contract had been purchased from Cleveland for $65,000. No other White Sox player earned even half of Collins's salary. A clique formed against the second baseman, from which grew the nucleus of the fix. Eddie Cicotte, who won 28 games in 1917 and 29 in 1919, had been promised a $10,000 bonus for 30 victories or more in 1917. When he neared the magic number, Comiskey ordered manager Clarence Rowland not to pitch him.

Cicotte was the hurler in Game One of the 1919 Series. His confession to a Chicago grand jury in September 1920 opened the gates to the suspension and eventual expulsion of the eight implicated players.

The public uproar that greeted the September revelations finally prompted the owners to act. The stain of a fixed World Series could be permanent if decisive steps were not taken to restore the game's image. The National Commission was in a shambles. Garry Herrmann had resigned in February 1920 but no replacement had been named. Perhaps the owners had thought they could ride the postwar wave of baseball popularity without leadership. Reluctantly, they finally decided to call for help from someone outside the game, a hard concession for most of them to accept.

Ban Johnson was stubborn until the end, still hoping for another ruling triumvirate he could control. He was opposed to Judge Landis, whose name kept coming up because of his favorable disposition in the initial Federal League case. Johnson considered Landis a grandstander who should have thrown the Federal case out of court immediately, but he had only a fragment of loyal American League support behind him, and the Nationals were leaning heavily to Landis.

Landis seemed the ideal friend of baseball. In his final statements before the out-of-court settlement of the 1915 Federal League suit, Landis declared, "I want to say that . . . not the slightest evidence was presented to cause the most suspicious person to impugn the honor of the game, or of any of the individual players." Landis was an ardent baseball fan, and baseball craved his good image. One owner observed, "K. M. Landis, lawyer, means nothing to organized baseball, but K. M.

Landis, judge of the Federal Court of the United States, was worth any price he might wish to ask."

On November 12, 1920, major league baseball owners announced the appointment of Kenesaw Mountain Landis as the first Commissioner of Baseball. He exacted from them carte blanche dictatorial powers, and a new era was about to begin.

(right) James "Deacon" White, lifetime .303 hitter whose protest against the reserve clause spurred the formation of the Players League *(National Baseball Hall of Fame Library, Cooperstown, New York)*

James "Orator" O'Rourke, who played major league baseball in four decades and who fervently espoused early player causes *(National Baseball Hall of Fame Library, Cooperstown, New York)*

(left) Albert Goodwill Spalding, the first dominant figure in late 19th century baseball and leader of the National League against the Players League *(National Baseball Hall of Fame Library, Cooperstown, New York)*

(above) John Montgomery Ward, the first player-organizer *(National Baseball Hall of Fame Library, Cooperstown, New York)*

John Montgomery Ward, c. 1910 *(Mrs. Winifred Watson, Huntington Valley, Pennsylvania)*

(left) David Fultz, first president of the Professional Baseball Players Fraternity, in his playing days, c. 1904 (James Rowe, Berwyn, Illinois)

(below left) Charles "Chief" Zimmer, first president of the Protective Association of Professional Ballplayers, 1900 (National Baseball Hall of Fame Library, Cooperstown, New York)

Harry Leonard Taylor, legal adviser to the Players Protective Association, c. 1900 (National Baseball Hall of Fame Library, Cooperstown, New York)

(top) Clark Griffith, owner (National Baseball Hall of Fame Library, Cooperstown, New York)

(above) Ban Johnson, founder and first president of the American League (National Baseball Hall of Fame Library, Cooperstown, New York)

(right) Clark Griffith, while a pitcher for the New York Highlanders, c. 1903 (National Baseball Hall of Fame Library, Cooperstown, New York)

Bob Harris, St. Louis Browns pitcher, 1939-42 *(National Baseball Hall of Fame Library, Cooperstown, New York)*

Al Niemiec, Philadelphia Athletics, 1936 *(James Rowe)*

Seaman Second Class Tony Lupien with Commander Red Strader (famed football coach in peacetime), Sampson Naval Base, Lake Geneva, N.Y., Spring 1945 *(courtesy of Tony Lupien)*

(left) Outfielder Danny
Gardella, who filed a
potentially historic antitrust
suit against the reserve
clause, c. 1950 (courtesy
Danny Gardella)

Future author and future owner
(courtesy Carol Norton)

(above) First meeting of the Major League Baseball Players Association, Atlanta, Georgia, December 2, 1953—Standing: B. Feller, C. Erskine, B. Young, F. Fain, S. Hudson, B. Friend, W. Lockman, S. Musial, E. Yost, T. Gray, G. Hatton, R. Roberts. Seated: J.P. Durante, J.N. Lewis, A. Reynolds, R. Kiner, W. Spahn, E. Robinson. *(J. Norman Lewis, Miami Beach, Florida)*

Part III

The Age of Landis, 1921-1944

6

The Shield of Holmes
and the First Years of
Commissioner Landis

*"The players, it is true, travel from place to place in
interstate commerce, but they are not the game . . .
[which] is local in its beginning and in its end. . . .
The fact that the [owners] produce baseball games
as a source of profit, large or small, cannot change
the character of the games. They are still sport, not
trade."*
—*District of Columbia Court of Appeals, 1921 (269 Fed. 681)
upheld by the U.S. Supreme Court in 1922 (259 U.S. 200).*

*"The owners pledge themselves to loyally support
the Commissioner in his important and difficult
task, and we assure him that each of us will
acquiesce in his decisions, even when we believe
them mistaken; and that we will not discredit the
sport by criticism of him or one another."*
—*A clause insisted on by Kenesaw Mountain
Landis in his first contract from the major league
baseball owners, November 1920.*

In late June 1921, seven of the accused fixers of the 1919 World Series
went on trial in a Chicago courtroom. Public sympathy was rising for the
players—victims of Charles Comiskey's stinginess. "The magnates led
the public to believe that the ballplayers got about $10,000 a year . . .
when they got as little as $2,600," defense attorney Ben Short declared to
the jury. "At the end of the season, they have nothing left but a chew of
tobacco, a glove, and a few pairs of worn-out socks."

It was a strange trial. The owners recognized that airing the game's
dirty linen was not in their best interests. Therefore, they decided to
provide good attorneys to aid in the players' defense. Later, baseball
would punish its sinners by extra-legal weapons in its arsenal.

103

Powerful New York gambler Arnold Rothstein, deeply implicated in the scandal as the man who gave the go-ahead, greatly helped the owners' strategy by arranging for the theft of the players' confessions from the Chicago district attorney's office. Unable to use its most damning evidence in the trial, the prosecution was doomed. On August 2, 1921, the jury acquitted all the players.

Some of the Black Sox dreamed of reinstatement for the duration of the 1921 season. Commissioner Landis, in office since March, quickly crushed that hope. He pronounced, "Regardless of the verdict of juries, no player that entertains proposals or promises to throw a game; no player that sits in a conference with a bunch of crooked players and gamblers where the ways and means of throwing games are discussed, and does not promptly tell his club about it, will ever play professional baseball."

Landis's harsh ruling cemented his public image as a strong leader who would not allow baseball to be disgraced again. Landis told Chicago sportswriter Hugh Fullerton, who had played a major role in uncovering the scandal, "Baseball is something more than a game to an American boy; it is his training field for life work. Destroy his faith in its squareness and honesty and you have destroyed something more; you have planted suspicion of all things in his heart."

The owners did not take Landis's rhetoric seriously, and for his first years in office, they found most of his rulings compatible. He banned the Black Sox, but enabled Charles Comiskey to hold on to his franchise, although the White Sox would not contend for the pennant for the rest of Comiskey's life (he died in 1931). Ban Johnson had wanted Comiskey's hide, and Landis's tolerance of the Old Roman added to the feud between the new commissioner and baseball's former strongman.

Landis also made stern rulings against pitchers Dickie Kerr of the White Sox and Ray Fisher of the Cincinnati Reds. Kerr, one of the ablest and least paid of the "Clean" Sox of 1919, refused to accept a $4,500 salary offer from Comiskey for 1922. He had compiled 40 victories for the poor Chicago teams of 1920 and 1921, and felt he deserved more money. When Kerr accepted $5,000 from a semi-professional team in Texas, Landis suspended him upon Comiskey's request. Kerr returned to the big leagues briefly in 1925, but never won another game in the majors.

Fisher negotiated with an "outlaw" club in Pennsylvania after the

Reds had cut his salary. The pitcher had been offered the position of baseball coach at the University of Michigan, so he wasn't about to play for the Reds at a lowered salary. When he refused the higher offer from a Reds team desperate for pitching during the 1921 season, and accepted the Michigan post—which he held for over thirty years—the spiteful Reds reported to Landis that Fisher had considered joining an "outlaw" team. Although he never signed a contract with one, not going beyond the talking stage, the commissioner banned him from professional baseball for life.

At the end of May 1922 all of baseball's management heaved a giant sigh of relief when the Supreme Court of the United States unanimously disposed of the Baltimore Federal League suit. Speaking for the high Court, Justice Oliver Wendell Holmes justified an antitrust exemption for professional baseball which continues to exist into the 1990s.

Baltimore had pressed the suit because it had been left out of the peace settlement with the major leagues in 1915. Baltimore owners Ned Hanlon and Harry Goldman were angered because twice in the early twentieth century the port city had been robbed of major league baseball. The Orioles had become the New York Highlanders after 1902, and the Federal League Terrapins ceased to exist after 1915.

In April 1919 the Supreme Court of the District of Columbia had given Baltimore a victory when it awarded the plaintiffs triple damages of $240,000. The court accepted the Federals' argument that the major league monopoly in conjunction with the colluding former Federal leaders, Charles Weeghman and James Gilmore, had denied them a share of the baseball market.

In October 1920 organized baseball sent its chief lawyer, George Wharton Pepper, back to Washington to argue before an appellate court that baseball must not be subject to the antitrust laws. In the 1919 case, Pepper had insisted that baseball is "a spontaneous output of human activity . . . not in its nature commerce, that, therefore organized baseball cannot be interstate commerce." In his autobiography, aptly entitled *Philadelphia Lawyer,* Pepper recalled that his October mission in 1920 had coincided with the World Series: "While all of America was experiencing this annual thrill, a court was being called upon to decide whether these sporting events would have to be discontinued." Defenders of organized baseball never tired of predicting doom whenever their suspect practices were challenged.

Pepper based his argument before the appellate court on the theory that baseball was essentially a local enterprise. He drew the analogy between a Chautauqua lecture and a baseball game. Both baseball players and professional speakers crossed interstate boundaries to reach their destinations, Pepper argued, but both the lecture and the game were local activities.

In his discussion in the court, Pepper made a surprising admission. He said that the reserve clause was merely a "honorary obligation," not binding legally on the players. He also said that farm systems did not exist in baseball, each major league team claiming title to only forty players on its roster. In fact, farm systems would grow throughout the 1920s and into the future, and informal agreements between minors and majors had existed previously. But Pepper's job was to show the court that baseball was really a small local business.

Pepper also told the court that the antitrust laws could not apply to baseball because neither Senators Sherman nor Clayton had mentioned baseball or sport in their 1890 and 1914 bills. "No statute can be construed as applying to combinations to regulate sport unless Congress has plainly indicated an intention that this should happen," Pepper argued. Thus began organized baseball's traditional strategy of telling courts that Congress had the jurisdiction and, later, informing Congress that it did not have jurisdiction either.

Pepper's statements convinced the court. In April 1921 the District of Columbia Court of Appeals overruled the 1919 triple damages to the Baltimore Federal Leaguers. The notion that baseball was not interstate commerce was widely held at this time. Even Judge Bissell's ringing indictment of the baseball contract in the 1914 case involving Hal Chase had conceded that baseball was not an interstate commerce activity.

Still, the broad powers granted to baseball outside the law in the 1921 decision were startling. The court ruled: "The fact that the [owners] produce baseball games as a source of profit, large or small, cannot change the character of the games. They are still sport, not trade."

It was this decision that Justice Oliver Wendell Holmes upheld on May 29, 1922. Although Holmes did not say that baseball was a sport not a business, he was endorsing a verdict which said precisely that. Holmes, a former amateur player, spoke for a Court headed by former President William Howard Taft, who followed baseball closely at Yale University. Taft had even been rumored as a possible choice for Com-

106

missioner. The justices of the High Court had no desire to upset baseball's traditional practices.

Explaining the Court's unanimous verdict, Holmes wrote that, in baseball, "The business is the giving of exhibition games, which are purely state matters." He accepted Pepper's argument that the traveling to the games was purely "incidental."

Holmes's verdict also gave the owners' broad leeway on the reserve clause. Although Pepper had declared the owners only needed to reserve forty players, Holmes allowed for a far more generous interpretation of the controversial provision. "The reserve clause in baseball players' contracts under the National Agreement," Holmes ruled, "was intended to protect the rights of clubs operating under that agreement to retain the services of *sufficient* players" (italics added).

The news of the exemption brought jubilant acclaim from baseball officials. National League President John Heydler exclaimed, "It is a tribute to the foresight and the wisdom of the men who laid the foundations of the sport and who foresaw that the reserve clauses, the enforcement of strict discipline, with the restrictive provisions in the players' contracts, were all necessary essentials to properly conserve the game." George Wharton Pepper, elected senator from Pennsylvania in 1922, was hailed by the owners. Pepper wrote a new preamble to the player's contract which loftily exacted of players, and ostensibly of owners too, "a pledge of conformity to high standards of personal conduct, of fair play and good sportsmanship."

After the Holmes decision, there was scant chance of change for the next generation in the baseball system. The players were almost totally unorganized. Wisconsin attorney Raymond J. Cannon had failed in an effort to organize the players after the 1920 season. Cannon, who became a congressman later in the 1920s and tried unsuccessfully in 1937 to get the attorney general to investigate the "baseball trust," also failed when he went to court in 1924 in an effort to obtain back salary from the White Sox for his client, Shoeless Joe Jackson. The club used Jackson's confession of wrongdoing in the Black Sox scandal against him. Somehow, the document reappeared in the district attorney's office after its earlier theft.

The only organization the players formed for nearly thirty years after the failure of Dave Fultz's Fraternity was the Association of Professional Ballplayers in 1924. Chartered at a meeting in a Los Angeles barroom in 1924, the association was a purely charitable group, collecting dues for use only in emergencies.

With the Supreme Court giving baseball a virtual carte blanche, other agencies of government rarely tried to interfere. In 1923 some members of the Massachusetts legislature, undeterred by the Holmes judgment, tried to pass a bill which would license players and umpires because they participated in activities on state land for profit, but the bill was killed in committee.

Early in February 1925 New York City maverick congressman and later mayor, Fiorello LaGuardia, introduced a bill which would tax every ball club 90 percent of contract sales over $5,000 if the player did not receive half of his purchase price. LaGuardia may have been responding to a celebrated baseball controversy of 1923 when a Giants' pitcher, Jack Bentley, refused to report to New York unless he got a percentage of the $65,000 that Jack Dunn's Baltimore Orioles had received for his contract. Bentley held out through most of spring training in 1923 before he finally signed, perhaps receiving some of the sale price, in addition to a $5,000 salary, though the terms were never disclosed.

LaGuardia was angered by a baseball system where a player had to threaten retirement, as Bentley did, or to actually quit if he did not like his position. LaGuardia branded baseball the only business where "an individual failed to profit through improved ability and transfer of his services." After introducing the bill, LaGuardia confided, accurately, to his diary, "I am now wondering if I am up against the same kind of proposition as I am when I am fighting the steel trust, the railroad, or other interests." The bill was not even debated.

Perhaps the best commentary on the lack of concern for players' rights in this era was the bare mention that LaGuardia's bill received in the press. It was buried alongside the coverage of the National League's forty-ninth jubilee dinner in New York.

The dinner was a gala occasion on the evening of February 2, 1925. Former League President John Tener averred that his predecessors, William Hulbert, Nick Young, and Albert Spalding all were present in spirit and were enjoying "everlasting life." Arthur Soden, who had left baseball after 1905, cabled his best wishes. So did evangelist Billy Sunday, a former major league outfielder, who wrote, "Every time I see a grandstand of a baseball diamond the blood surges through my veins like a fire pressure." The audience sat intoxicated by these heady sentiments.

John Montgomery Ward also spoke. In probably his last public speech (he would die of pneumonia on a hunting trip in Georgia one month later), Ward was comfortable enough with his past to mention a "little known fact." The Players Brotherhood had revolted in 1889, he said, because the owners were conspiring to pay salaries based on what the cheapest of them wanted to spend.

Ward did not dwell on the Brotherhood. He wanted to assure the audience that baseball was undoubtedly an honest game. The only thing that could harm the game, Ward and others felt in the mid-1920s, was the lingering stain of scandal. Ward stressed that in his sixteen years of major league baseball, "I am proud that never in that time did I see a move that looked to be anything but straight."

Ward was trying to allay the fears of the baseball public, which had been disturbed by alarming reports in September 1924. Several members of the New York Giants had been suspected of involvement in a scheme to bribe other National Leaguers to throw games so that the Giants would win the pennant.

Commissioner Landis investigated the charges, and announced the lifetime expulsion of Giants' coach Jack Dolan and utility infielder Jimmy O'Connell. Many critics wondered if the commissioner had even touched the surface of the gambling problem. Ban Johnson, digging himself deeper into Landis's doghouse, urged that the 1924 Series between the Giants and the Washington Senators be postponed. Landis refused, which pleased the one-time Johnson loyalist, Clark Griffith, who did not want to lose a rare chance at World Series profits. Johnson refused to attend the big event, which sportswriter John Kieran in *The New York Times* wryly called "a magnificent gesture of disapproval."

With the memory of the Black Sox scandal fast fading, the last thing baseball needed was another gambling mess. Landis's visceral hatred of gamblers—"those wormy, crawly creatures who once befouled and almost ruined this great game we all love"—satisfied most of the public that the game was in good hands.

In addition to banning Dolan and O'Connell, Landis had earlier denied entry into the majors of the former Federal League batting champion Benny Kauff because of his questionable underworld connections. On the other hand, Landis allowed the former Giants' and Reds' pitcher Rube Benton, long suspected of betting machinations, back into baseball in 1923 after a year's absence. Landis also allowed old-time owner Frank Navin to keep his interests in racing stables, evidently using the argument that Navin had purchased his interests before Landis came on the job. But the commissioner insisted that the star infielder Rogers Hornsby, one of the most gifted and cantankerous individuals ever to play baseball, sell his racetrack stock. (Someone once commented that Will Rogers had never met Hornsby!) In one of his last decrees before his death in 1944, Landis forced Phillies' owner William D. Cox to sell his club because he had placed bets on his own team.

In late 1926 news of potentially the most damaging scandal of them all broke into the newspapers. Under suspicion were two of baseball's greatest idols, Ty Cobb of the Tigers and Tris Speaker of the Indians. Both player-managers had surprisingly announced their retirements at the end of the 1926 season, though both had batted over .300 and Speaker's Indians had given the Yankees a good battle for the pennant. Observers sensed there was more to the story, and they were right.

Sometime during 1926 Ban Johnson had received letters from former Tigers' pitcher Hubert "Dutch" Leonard, which incriminated Cobb, Speaker, and his teammate "Smokey" Joe Wood in a plot to throw the last game of the 1919 season, on September 25. The purpose of the alleged fix was to assure third-place money to the Tigers with the Indians already having clinched second and the White Sox first place. The Tigers won the game, 9-5, but Speaker, allegedly betting on a Tigers' victory, got two triples and a single. Joe Wood, the former Red Sox pitcher who had become an outfielder, did not even play in the game.

The letters had been written to Leonard by Cobb and Wood after the 1919 season, and indicated that bets of between $1,000 and $2,000 had been placed by all four parties and that discussions had taken place beneath the grandstand at Detroit's Navin Field during the last series of 1919. But there was no mention of baseball betting in the letters, and the Navin Field employee who actually placed the bets would claim that the money was actually wagered on a horse race. Dutch Leonard also had a vengeful motive for releasing the letters after several years. Cobb had sent him to the minors after the 1925 season although he had compiled a 11-4 record. Speaker, his onetime teammate in Boston, had not claimed him.

Despite these questionable circumstances, Ban Johnson accepted the evidence of Leonard's letters. He purchased them for the American League for $5,000, and in September 1926 he received the okay from league owners for what he hoped would be the star's quiet retirement from the game after 1926. Ban Johnson, no longer the strong man of his league, may well have taken some pleasure in the thought of having the obstreperous Ty Cobb at last out of his hair.

Landis saw things differently, not just because he and Ban Johnson could not agree on the time of day. Cobb and Speaker were national heroes, and the public rallied behind them as they denied any wrongdoing. Will Rogers spoke for most fans when he said, "I'd have liked to see them play when they wasn't selling." Moreover, Dutch Leonard refused to make his accusations directly to Cobb and Speaker in Landis's office in Chicago. He talked to Landis's investigators at his Fresno, California, home, but refused the commissioner's repeated requests to testify in person.

While Landis, in December 1926, delved into this latest scandal, Swede Risberg, one of the eight banned Black Sox, announced that betting schemes far more elaborate than the ones brought up by Leonard had been transpiring at the end of the 1917 season. This new can of worms caused Landis to moan, "Won't these goddamn things that happened before I came into baseball ever stop coming up?"

Early in January 1927 Landis dismissed Risberg's charges as the fabrication of a disgraced man, and reinstated Cobb and Speaker, absolving them of any wrongdoing. He did not discuss Joe Wood's alleged involvement because Wood had retired in 1922 to become Yale's baseball coach. But the Ivy League school exonerated Wood, who had been dragged into the affair much to the surprise of all concerned. Wood maintained a low profile on the whole matter. He would only say about Leonard's delayed accusations, "He had about seven years to frame a story around those two letters. In order to get at those two fellows he had to bring my letter in, and he had no concern about that."

In ruling that Cobb and Speaker were eligible to play once again, Landis further rubbed it in to Ban Johnson, who had banned them from his league. He decreed that only American League teams could bid for the stars' services. Navin was glad to be rid of Cobb and his $50,000 salary, which the player always saw as the owner's motive in supporting Johnson's ruling in the first place. Cobb went on to Philadelphia and Speaker to Washington for the 1927 season.

The public soon forgot the furor, but Ban Johnson changed his historic tune and announced his support of a congressional inquiry into baseball. "I am heartily in favor of any legislation which will make our national game clean and free from crookedness," he declared. He urged Congress to administer laws against baseball gambling, while assuring his colleagues that he still favored the owners' control over the "administration of the game."

Needless to say, Johnson's support of outside investigation was not shared by his colleagues. The tried-and-tested attitude of organized baseball had been to let the calls for reform subside. After the O'Connell-Dolan scandal, New York congressman Sol Bloom wanted baseball brought under the laws of interstate commerce, but nothing had happened. Similarly, after the Cobb-Speaker affair, Congressman Clyde Kelly of Pennsylvania and Senator Arthur Capper of Kansas wanted licensing regulation introduced into baseball; their requests fell on deaf ears. Ban Johnson's support of regulation succeeded only in producing an ultimatum from Landis to the American League that the earlier czar must go. Johnson resigned after the 1927 season, and was a lonely figure until his death in 1931.

The age of Landis in the 1920s was a happy one for baseball owners. Profits soared, and salaries were kept within strict boundaries. Babe Ruth's $80,000 salary by the end of the decade drew wide attention, but it was rarely reported that some of Ruth's teammates earned as little as $2,500 a year. It was "The Era of Wonderful Nonsense," as writer Paul Gallico dubbed the 1920s, and Babe Ruth's home-run heroics and gargantuan lifestyle set the tone. "He wasn't born, he dropped from a tree," a teammate said of Ruth. When a reporter asked him if he deserved a higher salary than President Hoover, Ruth replied, "Hell, I had a better year." As a reward for making it back into pennant contention, thanks largely to his purchases from Jack Dunn's Orioles, Connie Mack in 1929 became the first sports figure to win the prestigious $10,000 Edward Bok award for significant accomplishment in the Philadelphia area.

The emergence of radio as a national medium in the 1920s greatly enhanced baseball's image as a national game. Although some of the stodgy owners feared that broadcasts would cut down on the gate, the new medium served as a stimulus rather than a depressant. Fans throughout the country could listen to the World Series on radio and follow their favorite teams. Since the major sixteen teams had remained fixed since the 1903 National Agreement, it was common for boys in Oregon to know the entire Red Sox roster and baseball buffs in Virginia to know all about the Tigers.

In Commissioner Landis, baseball had a wonderful public spokesman. John Lardner, one of Ring Lardner's talented writer sons, called him "a sort of combination reformer, hangman, and symbol of integrity." His white mane was often photographed at the ball parks, and he seemed a pure fan. Landis also knew the value of a good press. When he left the bench in 1922, having held both the judgeship and the commissionership for fifteen months until he was persuaded to yield the judicial robes, Landis invited the reporters into his chambers for a party. He told them, "These people come in and say I'm a great man. But I know you fellows made me. You printed stuff about me and that's the reason I've got a fifty-thousand-dollar job. I don't kid myself."

Landis utilized his good press relations so well that by 1927 journalist-historian Henry Pringle could report that he was almost as recognizable to the American public as Charlie Chaplin. The grateful owners rewarded him with a salary increase to $65,000. The quiescent mood of the players, lacking organization, fitted the national temperament in a decade where the American Federation of Labor lost more than two million members. Landis was comfortable with a situation where players were not organized. Indeed, he had railed at an attorney in the 1915 Federal League case who called playing baseball "labor." In one of his last cases on the bench, a building trades dispute in September 1921, Landis had ordered a wage settlement less than what management was willing to offer.

Yet, by the end of the 1920s, Landis was preparing to go to war with the owners. Although the Depression of the 1930s was to stifle any organizational inclination of players, as they were happy to have major league jobs, Landis's rulings would attempt to eliminate the worst abuse of the reserve system, the denying of opportunity to deserving players. Landis would prove correct Will Rogers's prophecy at the time of the selection of the first commissioner:

> Baseball needed a touch of class and distinction. So somebody said: "Get that old boy who sits behind first base all the time. He's out there every day, anyhow." So they offered him a season's pass and he jumped at it. But don't kid yourself that that old judicial bird isn't going to make those baseball birds walk the chalkline.

7

A Czar Tries to Achieve Democracy

"Don't go to those owners if you get into trouble,
come to me. I'm your friend; they're no good."
—Bill Veeck, Jr.'s reminiscence of Landis's advice
to players. From The Hustler's Handbook.

Early in his reign as commissioner, Kenesaw Mountain Landis expressed a radical vision of a better baseball business. At the first meeting of the minor leagues he attended in December 1921, Landis called for a universal annual draft of minor leaguers.

He did not like the system of waivers and options of players that had developed. The procedures did not work because the owners did not want them to work. Landis told his minor league audience, "It cannot be a good thing for something calling itself sport that it is within the power of an individual in that sport to place a stone wall in the advancement of a ballplayer."

Landis had no illusions that the minor leagues would take the lead in pushing for reform. During his term, the minors increasingly came under the thumb of the major league farm system. It was a trend Landis decried but could not stop.

Under the National Agreement of 1921, the National Association, which had broken away from the National Commission's aegis in 1919, again came under the dictates of the major leagues. Appended to the Uniform Player's Contract throughout all of organized baseball was an ominous sounding "Important Notice" printed in red. It read, "No club shall make a contract different from the uniform contract or a contract containing a non-reserve clause, except with the written approval of [authorized bodies]."

The independently owned minor league clubs were Landis's favorites. Generally, local businessmen ran them and appealed to community pride in publicizing the team. The independents were throwbacks to the days at the turn of the twentieth century when every town had a team. The competition during minor league games was as fierce as it was in the majors.

The farm system clubs, on the other hand, usually were managed by major league employees. Their main interest was in providing talent for the parent clubs. The concerns of the local pennant race were secondary.

Farm teams became popularly known as "chain stores" and for the players, "chain gangs." The system enabled a major league club to sign innumerable recruits and farm them out to their minor league affiliates where they might stay indefinitely unless the parent club required their services. A player's progress was grooved into one channel, which irked Landis no end.

St. Louis Cardinals' boss Branch Rickey was the architect of the farm system. Rickey had left the St. Louis Browns in 1919, over the objections of owner Phil Ball, going across town to rebuild the Cardinals, a team without extensive financial resources. After paying $10,000 for ex-Reds' pitcher Jess Haines in 1919, Rickey vowed to never again make a major league player purchase. He signed hundreds of amateur players and farmed them out until as he liked to put it, "they ripened into money." At one time in his more than twenty-year reign with the Cardinals, Rickey controlled all the teams in one minor league.

His method did prove to be successful, as the Cardinals won five pennants and four World Series under his direction from 1919 to 1942, and were constantly contenders. Rickey himself earned the highest salary in baseball by the end of the 1930s, more than $80,000 a year.

With Ban Johnson removed from baseball in 1927, Branch Rickey took his leading place as Landis's special bête noire. But Landis could do little about the farm system for a variety of reasons. Veteran owners Barney Dreyfuss and Frank Navin advised Landis that ultimately the farm system would collapse under the weight of its expense. They underestimated Rickey's ability to pay his players cheaply throughout his vast system. They also forgot that success breeds imitation.

In the early 1930s, the Yankees, who had started to build their dynasty

116

on outright purchases from the Red Sox—like Carl Mays, Babe Ruth, and Herb Pennock—turned to developing a farm system. By the middle of the decade, the Yankees were producing future stars in outposts such as Kansas City and Newark, and in lower minor league farms.

The great economic depression initially hit the independent minors severely so that only twelve leagues existed by 1931. The standard excuse that the farm system propped up the minors was largely true during this time of economic stress. By 1941 the minor leagues numbered forty.

Another problem with Landis's endorsement of the independent minor club was the abuses which could occur when independent owners, too, held on to players and thwarted their natural advancement. Jack Dunn in Baltimore had been through the Federal League war and barely survived. Once he was readmitted into the International League, he made sure he would never be thrown so close to the precipice of extinction.

In June 1914 Dunn had been forced to sell Babe Ruth to the Red Sox for only $2,500. Secure again by the 1920s, and with the International League draft-exempt by the National Agreement of 1921, Dunn waited until the market price of his new Oriole stars soared. He got $65,000 for Jack Bentley from the Giants in 1923, and Bentley's demand for a percentage of that sale price was quietly settled.

Dunn also had a special arrangement with Connie Mack, who was too poor and too tight-fisted to invest in a farm system, and so purchased many of his finest stars from Dunn in the 1920s, including pitchers Lefty Grove and George Earnshaw, and infielders Joe Boley and Max Bishop. They brought Mack contending teams in the later 1920s, until he decided to sell them after the 1931 World Series for the same reason he broke up his 1914 champions: He did not want to pay them championship salaries.

Even with independent minor league clubs, the player's path to the top could be delayed if the minor league owner did not want to sell his contract. In 1928 Landis succeeded in getting the minor leagues to lift the draft exemption from the International League. The majors would have to pay a price increase from $6,000 to $7,500 to draft I. L. players, a far cry from the large amounts a draft-exempt club had received for its players. Regardless of these changes, the player still could be hidden by gentlemen's agreements among owners.

In March 1929 Commissioner Landis gave evidence that he was

prepared to take sharp preemptive measures in the name of player opportunity: He announced the freeing of ten minor leaguers who had been hidden illegally by the Senators, Pirates, Tigers, and Athletics. Catcher Rick Ferrell, buried in the Tigers' organization, was the most notable of the players freed to make their own deals. Phil Ball of the Browns gave Ferrell a $25,000 bonus to sign again. Rick Ferrell went on to enjoy an eighteen-year major league career, joined later in the American League by his pitcher brother, Wes.

In 1930 Landis turned the tables on Phil Ball. He ruled that outfielder Fred Bennett had been illegally shipped to the Browns' American Association farm at Milwaukee. Bennett had complained to Landis in a letter and the commissioner researched the story of Bennett's career. He had been signed in 1928 and shipped to a Browns' farm club in Wichita Falls, Texas. Bennett moved on to Tulsa, another Browns' club. Early in 1930 the Pittsburgh Pirates expressed an interest in Bennett's services, but Ball moved the player to his club in Milwaukee.

Landis ruled that Bennett should be free to deal with Pittsburgh or any other club. He had spent three years in the minors and according to the owners' rules, since he had not reached the highest AA classification by this time, he was subject to claim by other major league teams.

Phil Ball made the mistake of taking Landis to court. In April 1931 Federal Judge Walter C. Lindley of the Eastern District of Illinois upheld Landis's judgment. After studying the labyrinthine rules and codes of organized baseball, Lindley ruled, "No agreement is to be made between a Major club and a Minor club or between two Minor clubs for the purpose or with the effect of covering up a player from selection." Lindley did not say that Philip Ball or any other owner could not own farm clubs, but he did prohibit manipulations that allowed for "secret absolute control."

Judge Lindley upheld a very broad interpretation of the powers of the commissioner granted in the carte blanche clause Landis insisted on when he took the job. "The various agreements and rules . . . of Organized Baseball in America," declared Lindley, "describe a clear intent upon the part of the parties to endow the Commissioner with all the attributes of a benevolent but absolute despot and all the disciplinary powers of the proverbial pater familias." In 1977 Oakland Athletics' owner Charlie Finley ran into this same roadblock when another Illinois federal judge, Frank McGarr, refused to enjoin Commissioner Bowie

Kuhn from blocking Finley's million-dollar sales of his star players Joe Rudi, Rollie Fingers, and Vida Blue.

Commissioner Landis did not need another judge to endorse his powers. He knew that baseball needed someone to protect the owners from themselves. He was aware that the National Commission had collapsed when individuals like Ruppert and Mack had begun to take complaints to court. Landis had insisted that Ban Johnson be removed when he backed outside intervention in baseball. The commissioner informed American League owners that Phil Ball must go and so, in 1932, a year before his death, Ball sold the Browns.

As the 1930s progressed, the Depression began to affect baseball attendance. The total major league gate dropped to eight million fans in 1936, down two million from 1930. Player salaries remained low. Babe Ruth had drawn a lot of criticism for holding out for more money in the early 1930s. In 1935 he was sold to the Boston Braves, where he would hit three home runs in one game, but only .180 overall before he announced his retirement in June. It would be a long while before anyone commanded his fame and his salary.

A good example of tight salary practices could be seen in the case of Lou Gehrig, Ruth's overshadowed teammate, who won the Triple Crown in 1934, leading the league in home runs, runs batted in, and batting average. Yankee management informed Gehrig he should not expect a raise from $23,000. The Yankees were a profitable team, although in the largely National League town of New York, they did not draw exceptionally well. (Their 1920 attendance record stood until the postwar excitement of 1946.) Players on poorer teams suffered more. After Jimmie Foxx won the Triple Crown in 1932, Connie Mack asked him to take a $6,000 pay cut. A startled Foxx was finally traded to the Red Sox in 1933, where owner Tom Yawkey was wealthier and more generous.

The player climate in the 1930s was not militant not only because of the Depression. The athletes were lionized as the elite, baseball's "400," holders of coveted major league positions. Wisconsin Congressman Raymond Cannon, who had tried to organize the players after the 1920 season, talked of enlisting the miners' leader John L. Lewis, a national figure by 1937 for his role in organizing the Congress of Industrial Organizations, to unionize the players. It was just talk.

The incorruptible figure of Landis did much to allay possible discontent among the players. From 1931 to 1936 he took a pay cut to $40,000, and then his salary was restored to $65,000 in 1937 when the Depression momentarily seemed to end. Moreover, Landis never tired of investigating the owners' shenanigans. Two decisions in the winter of 1936-37 made national news.

In December 1936 Landis held a hearing which attracted attention because it involved alleged impropriety in Cleveland's signing a teenage Iowa farm boy, Bob Feller, to a secret minor league contract. Feller was a once-in-a-lifetime pitching prospect, whose exploits in high school and American Legion games made major league scouts drool in anticipation. In 1936 representatives from the Des Moines, Iowa, team in the Western League tried to sign Feller. They learned that since mid-1935, Feller's signature had been attached to a Fargo-Moorhead, North Dakota, club contract, although Feller was still in high school. Cleveland general manager C. C. "Cy" Slapnicka, briefly a major league pitcher in the 1910s, had an interest in the Fargo club and was hiding Feller on its roster.

Landis could very well have made the same kind of ruling the National Commission had when it freed George Sisler from Pittsburgh because he had been signed as a high schooler. One legend tells of Landis avoiding this decision because he was fearful of a bidding war for Feller's services which could severely disrupt the salary structure. This is reading too much of the present into the past. Landis allowed Feller to stay with Cleveland, largely because both the player and his father preferred that the son pitch for the Indians. Landis ordered Cleveland to pay Des Moines $7,500, which is what the Iowa club would have offered for Feller's contract.

In the middle of 1936 Feller arrived in the majors without spending a day in the minor leagues. He became an immediate star, fanning 15 batters in his first game. He went on to enjoy an outstanding career with Cleveland, setting many strikeout records, while winning 266 games, and earning election into the Hall of Fame in 1962. Feller was such a national hero in the 1930s that his high school graduation was broadcast live on national radio as was his induction into the navy after the attack on Pearl Harbor.

Within three months of his Feller decision, Landis faced another grievance against the Indians. Tommy Henrich was a promising minor league outfielder who had signed with Cleveland in 1934. After hitting over .330 for three years in the minor leagues, Henrich was no closer to

120

the majors than when he started. Henrich was unaware who actually controlled his contract, and so he wrote Landis a letter explaining his predicament. He had performed well at New Orleans in the Southern Association, Henrich related, but after the 1936 season, he discovered that he was headed for Milwaukee of the American Association. After Landis wrote back to Henrich that he must prove his contentions, Henrich cited chapter and verse from the story of his shuttled career throughout the minors. At a Landis-ordered hearing, Cleveland tried to claim it did not control Henrich's contract at all, but one of their scouts admitted that they had signed him originally. In mid-April 1937 Landis ruled that Cleveland had deliberately "covered up" Henrich in the minors, thereby depriving him of a legitimate opportunity to reach the big leagues, and declared Henrich a free agent.

Henrich sat home in Massillon, Ohio, and waited for the offers to roll in. The Tigers made a bid, but Henrich was wary of an organization that tried to sign him originally in 1934 by sending a contract with the terse note "Sign this and return immediately." Emissaries from Connie Mack came by but did not make a specific offer.

After mulling more than eight possibilities, Henrich chose to sign with the Yankees for a $20,000 bonus and a salary of $5,000. The winning tradition of the Yankees was their best selling point, as the Tigers actually offered more money. After a brief stint at Newark, Henrich joined the Yankees in June 1937. He hit a triple and a home run in his second game and, during his eleven-year career, became known as the Yankees' "Old Reliable."

Landis was criticized for evening up his decisions in the celebrated Cleveland cases of the mid-1930s. Henrich himself told Donald Honig in *Baseball Between the Lines* that he thought he was freed from the Indians because of Landis's dislike for Cy Slapnicka. Yet there can be no doubt that Landis possessed a genuine revulsion at the owners' hiding talent in the minor leagues. At the end of March 1938, he proved it dramatically by announcing the release of ninety-one free agents from Branch Rickey's St. Louis Cardinals' farm organization.

Landis's edict in baseball lore became known as the Cedar Rapids decision because the Iowa farm club was fined $588 by Landis for its part in covering up prospects. Landis also fined Springfield, Missouri, $1,000, and Sacramento, California, $588. All three clubs were part of Branch Rickey's vast farm empire.

In tangling with Rickey, Landis knew he had a formidable adversary.

Rickey had forged alliances with many minor league officials, including William Bramham, the North Carolina judge who headed the National Association throughout the age of Landis. Rickey was a lawyer, and knew that the idea of a farm system had been upheld in the Lindley decision of 1931. Landis did not fine Rickey personally. He also gave the players an opportunity to resign with the Cardinals, so long as they were clear on who controlled their contracts. Among the future stars who did get away from St. Louis was outfielder Pete Reiser who, though constantly hampered by injuries, went on to a fine career with Brooklyn. Ironically, Reiser was united with Rickey when the "Mahatma" took his services to Brooklyn after the 1942 season.

What Landis could do to Rickey was to publicly expose his machinations. He released the transcript of his Cedar Rapids hearing with the St. Louis boss. To Rickey's and owner Sam Breadon's protestations that their dealings had saved minor league baseball in Depression-hit towns, Landis retorted, "No club should contract away its right and obligation to get competitive playing strength as needed and whenever obtainable." He blasted Rickey's interference in pennant races not just in the higher minor leagues, but throughout his network of farms. Rickey's control of minor league players, clubs, and even leagues was "as big as the universe," Landis exclaimed.

Shortly before the 1940 season started, Landis struck again. He freed ninety-one farmhands of the Tigers. After the death of Frank Navin, a farm opponent, in 1935, the new Detroit ownership of Walter Briggs and Jack Zeller began to imitate the success of the Cardinals and the Yankees. Landis decreed that there were irregularities in the signing of ninety-one recruits. As before, most of the players re-signed with Detroit. Infielder Benny McCoy did not, accepting a $45,000 bonus from Connie Mack. A surprising gesture by the dormant Athletics, the bonus did not pan out as McCoy did not fulfill his promise.

Landis's actions in freeing minor leaguers, individually in the case of Henrich and collectively in the case of the Cardinals and the Tigers, did not revive the independent minor leagues as he hoped. Even a strong commissioner could not turn the tide of farm-controlled minors. All the teams who wanted to compete with the dominant forces had to build farms by the late 1930s. By contrast, Clark Griffith of doormat Washington, who did not want to spend money on a farm system, was reduced to railing regularly against the Yankees at league meetings. In 1939 he began to push for legislation that would curb the Yankees by reducing the number of farm teams within their control. What Griffith chose to ignore in his zest for twisting the Yankees' tail was the prevalence of the farms throughout baseball.

Landis's last years were relatively quiet. He was prepared to cut back on baseball after the attack on Pearl Harbor in December 1941, and refused to ask President Franklin D. Roosevelt for an exemption. A conservative Republican, Landis did not like the New Deal and "that man in the White House."

Landis approved National League President Ford Frick's effort to intercede with Roosevelt. In the company of Clark Griffith and New York Senator James Mead, who had been enlisted by John Stiglmeier, an influential Buffalo minor league owner, Frick met with Roosevelt early in 1942. The chief executive announced that it would be in the interest of the national morale for the national game to continue throughout the war. Although the draft took most of the stars, wartime baseball was played, and by 1944 attendance was climbing to near the prewar peaks.

Early in 1944 Landis was given another seven-year extension on his contract. The owners appreciated the clean image Landis had restored to baseball even if they had griped about his rulings. But Landis's health was frail and danger signs were apparent when he missed the 1944 World Series, the first time he had ever failed to attend the great event. Early in November 1944 he died of a coronary thrombosis. He left word that there should be no ceremony or funeral, only a quiet cremation.

Sporting News publisher J. G. Taylor Spink said it best, about his historic impact on the owners: "Landis put the fear of God into weak characters who otherwise might have been inclined to violate their trust." For the individual players, Landis left a legacy of concern for their advancement. He never had to face an organized players' constituency and his suspicion of labor unions might have caused problems. Yet on numerous times, privately, Landis warned owners that a perpetual reserve clause posed grave legal difficulties. Landis's secretary, Leslie O'Connor, averred regularly that any player who had asked for a contract without a reserve clause "would have been granted one instantly." Of course, no one ever requested one.

When Landis died, the owners decided to move slowly in naming a successor. They intended to choose a new leader who was more of a figurehead, preferably one with political connections in Washington to keep Congress in a benign, hands-off mood.

Branch Rickey, secretly preparing to risk controversy by hiring Negro Jackie Robinson for his Brooklyn organization in 1946, signaled the labor-management consensus of the owners. "The commissioner should represent the executive side of baseball. The club owners should constitute the legislative department," decreed Rickey in early 1945. "If the executive and the legislature are combined in one man, that is despotism." In retrospect, the despotic Landis had indeed saved the owners' legislature from much destruction.

Veteran *New York Telegram* sportswriter Joe Williams observed prophetically, "The tacit admission by club owners that the powers of the new Landis be curtailed, presumably at the expense of the players, would seem to give the unionists a strong talking point." It had been a generation since a fraternity of players existed. Ballplayers still were necessarily wary about sticking their necks out for improvements, given the dreadful past. Yet if the owners intended to turn back the clock, the players were not prepared to help wind the mechanism.

The shape of the post-Landis baseball world did not fully emerge at first. Early in 1945 the world war was far from won, and curtailment of the season seemed a possibility. By Opening Day 1945 the war prospects had brightened considerably. Peace came to Europe at the end of April. It would come to the Pacific in late August in the wake of the atom bombs dropped on the Japanese cities of Hiroshima and Nagasaki.

In late April 1945 the baseball world was surprised by the announcement of a new commissioner, Senator Albert Benjamin "Happy" Chandler of Kentucky. Most of the owners who came to a Cleveland meeting thought they were just screening candidates. The Yankees' new co-owner, Colonel Leland Stanford "Larry" MacPhail, masterminded the selection of Chandler, believing that the Kentuckian was the sort of political glad-hander baseball needed. MacPhail, who had introduced night baseball to the majors in Cincinnati during the 1930s and later rebuilt the Dodgers, was always a step ahead of his colleagues.

The early selection of Chandler did not change the master plan of the owners. Though he held out formal acceptance of the commissionership until he received the same carte blanche power Landis had insisted upon, Chandler lacked his predecessor's stature. He made so many gaffes in his first months in office that some owners were thinking of buying up the remaining years of his six-year contract. Chandler's first public pose was with baseball clown Nick Altrock, which struck many of the old guard as undignified. He tried to adopt Landis's stance against gambling, yet his family was frequently photographed at the Churchill Downs racetrack in Louisville. Within a year, even Larry McPhail soured on his choice when Chandler prevented a Yankee ticket price increase.

Chandler's early effort to show that he supported the most neglected group of baseball, the umpires, backfired. He mentioned to American League umpire Ernest Stewart that he was interested in hearing of the grievances of the men in blue. Stewart took that as an endorsement of efforts to start an umpires' union. American League President Will Harridge summarily fired Stewart for his activities. Harridge reminded a chastened Chandler that supervising the umpires was the jurisdiction of the league presidents, not the commissioner. When Chandler did nothing to reinstate Stewart, another lesson had been graphically given in the dangers of making waves in the baseball business.

Baseball owners had lived since World War I without a threat from organized players. By 1945 wartime fraternization had made the professionals more aware of their common problems. Regardless of teams, the players shared common grievances over travel, the rising number of night games, and the general indifference and pettiness of the front offices. As in earlier times of the twentieth century, many stars joined with the journeymen in expressing solidarity.

The returning servicemen and the older players who had remained at home did not underestimate the threat to their jobs. The owners looked forward to a favorable supply situation in 1946 spring training. The 1945 season had barely ended when the teams started cutting dozens of wartime ballplayers. They anticipated the return of the established major leaguers from the service. One estimate predicted that nearly one thousand big leaguers and more than three thousand minor leaguers would be demobilized by the start of 1946.

As the servicemen came home to the United States, they were rightfully hailed as deserving heroes. Newspapers and magazines were filled with stories about the need to welcome back and to reintegrate the returning soldiers. As part of the Selective Service legislation, a Veterans Act provision had been specifically added to ensure the returning soldier one year at his old job with at least his original salary.

The owners did not think that federal legislation applied to them, but

125

returning veterans like Tony Lupien intended to prove them wrong. Baseball officials thought they could continue to run their teams as feudal baronies. Harvard-trained labor organizer Robert Murphy made a valiant prophetic effort to right the wrongs. The major leagues thought their sixteen-team, two-circuit monopoly would last forever. A band of wealthy Mexican brothers, headed by flamboyant Jorge Pasquel, sought to revive the spirit of the Federal League. 1946 would become a year of great challenges to the entrenched baseball monopoly.

Part IV

1946: Year of the Great Challenges

8

A Tale of Three Veterans

*"Youth must be served, but not at the expense of
men who have worn the uniform and contrary to
law."*
*—Judge Lloyd Black, Washington State Federal
District Court, June 24, 1946, concluding his
verdict in behalf of Al Niemiec vs. Seattle Rainier
Baseball Club*

February 1946 found New England in the grip of a typically frigid winter. Tony Lupien warmed himself at his Lexington, Massachusetts, home with the thought that within days he would be off to spring training in Florida to resume his career as a Philadelphia Phillies first baseman.

Tony had enjoyed a fine year for the Phillies in 1944, arriving from the Boston Red Sox. Boston had signed him after his graduation from Harvard in 1939 and after seasoning in the minor leagues, Lupien had become the Red Sox' regular first baseman in 1942 and 1943. As a newcomer to the National League in 1944, Tony responded with impressive figures, a career high batting average of .283 with 81 runs scored. He shone defensively, ranking among the National League leaders in fielding percentage. When Tony had received his contract for the 1945 season from Philadelphia general manager Herbert Pennock, the former great Yankee pitcher, he was cheered to read his boss's assessment of his work: "I want you to know that your acquisition to our ball club last year was the outstanding achievement of my first year's operation."

Come Opening Day 1945, Tony was wearing a United States Navy instead of a Phillies' uniform. In January 1945 James Byrnes, National

Director of War Mobilization and Reconstruction, announced that men between the ages of 26 and 37, including those with families, would be eligible for the draft. Nearly 28, Tony Lupien had a wife and two small daughters to support. He should have been entering the prime of his baseball career. Instead, he was prime material for the military. In March 1945 he was inducted into the navy and spent most of the 1945 baseball season at the Sampson Naval Base in upstate New York.

Tony was fortunate enough to be discharged in early September. He immediately reported to the Phillies for the last weeks of the season. The 1945 Phillies were one of baseball's all-time terrible teams, winning only 46 games and finishing last in the league in hitting, fielding, and pitching. Although Tony did not fully regain his old form in the short time back on the job, he did hit .315 in 54 at-bats in 15 games.

Like most of the returning serviceman ballplayers, Tony Lupien looked forward to the first peacetime spring training in years. The competition for jobs would be stiff, Tony knew, but he was prepared for the challenge.

On the morning of February 8, 1946, Tony received a jolting phone call from Herb Pennock. He listened as Pennock told him, "Once we get waivers on you, Tony, we are selling your contract to Hollywood of the Pacific Coast League." The Phillies had just purchased the contract of 35-year-old first baseman Frank McCormick, formerly with the Cincinnati Reds. Though six years younger than McCormick, Tony was being victimized again by baseball's prejudice that a first baseman should be able to hit home runs consistently. "Power on the corners," first base and third base, is the goal of most general managers in building a baseball team. Tony had been sold by the Red Sox in 1944 because he lacked Jimmie Foxx's home run bat. Now he was being sold to the minor leagues for the same reason.

Lupien was not going to yield his major league status quietly. He paid a visit to Pennock in Philadelphia and reminded him of the Veterans Act. "Don't you know that a returned serviceman is allowed at least a year's grace at getting his old job back?" Tony demanded. With the haughty indifference that many baseball officials displayed toward the law, Pennock responded, "That doesn't apply to baseball." Tony retorted, "Who the hell are you to think that you're above the federal government?"

There was no point in continuing the meeting. Tony pondered the unpromising alternatives. He could accept his demotion quietly and try to work his way back to the major leagues, or he could try to earn his release by free agency in a special appeal to the commissioner. He decided on the latter option.

He returned to Massachusetts and drafted a letter to Commissioner Chandler's office in Cincinnati. He explained his case in the manner many a grieving player had done in the years of Landis. He had served his country willingly and not taken shelter in a civilian wartime job. He had paid his dues in the minor leagues from 1939 to 1941, and was now a proven major leaguer, who did not deserve such arbitrary shuttling back to the minors. Moreover, major league rules provided that servicemen should have at least thirty days in spring training before any decision was made on their future. Tony had spent less than a month with the Phillies in September 1945, and despite not being in baseball shape, hit over .300. He was not even invited to spring training, Tony went on, and this oversight alone was worth correcting. Tony concluded that he had no intention of dramatizing his story to the press, and pledged to keep his correspondence with the commissioner confidential.

There was not to be even a reply to Tony's letter. Within days, it was returned unopened to him in Massachusetts. The lame excuse offered was that Commissioner Chandler was out of town and no one in his office was authorized to receive registered mail. The contrast between a Landis eager to aid players and a Chandler not even accepting mail from them could not have been stronger.

With the internal gears of organized baseball meshed tightly against him, Tony Lupien now faced another hard choice. Should he fight baseball in the courts on the Veterans Act violation or give up the fight? Tony contacted his Selective Service Board office in Lexington, which informed him that he did have a valid case. Tony consulted his lawyer, Arthur Johns, a former Harvard classmate, and they mapped a strategy. They decided that since the moguls had treated him contemptuously, public exposure would now be a good ploy. Tony announced that he would fight to regain his job on grounds that the Veterans Act had not been applied to his case. He drew sympathy from many quarters. Dave Egan, the crusty and courageous sportswriter for the *Boston Record,* wrote, "Baseball players who are veterans did not fight for the dubious privilege of selling apples on street corners and in common justice are entitled to the same rights as all other citizens."

Tony's case promised to be costly and lengthy. The Massachusetts Selective Service Board told him that the Philadelphia office would have jurisdiction because the grievance was against the Phillies. Fighting the case in Pennsylvania would involve the expense of travel and the uncertainty the young family man could not afford.

In late February, Tony received a contract offer from Hollywood which both startled and annoyed him. The Stars were willing to pay him his expected Phillies' salary of $8,000, an unusually high figure even for a top minor league like the Pacific Coast circuit. Tony realized that the Phillies would be making up the difference between the $5,000 Hollywood normally would have offered and the $8,000. The major leagues were planning to circumvent the Veterans Act by paying the banished servicemen their prewar salaries, thereby meeting at least the provision that the former soldier received his previous salary. Tony was irked by this sleight-of-hand, and also grew angry at the violation of major-minor league rules involved in Philadelphia paying part of his salary. Tony's option had expired, and major league teams were supposedly prohibited from paying any part of the salary of a minor leaguer whose options had been used up.

Tony Lupien was enough of a realist to realize his chances for a victory over the moguls were slim. Lawyer Johns counseled, "These people will keep you in the courts for the rest of your life." Tony decided not to follow the path of litigation. Relenting, he received the Stars' permission to report at the end of spring training. Tony had never needed more than two weeks to get ready for a baseball season, and it always peeved him that the owners only paid major leaguers' transportation to the preseason camps and did not pay them salaries until after opening day.

The Lupien family started out on the long drive to Southern California. Unknown to him, Robert Murphy, the Harvard-trained labor organizer, was touring the Florida camps this very March trying to become the first man in three decades to organize major league players into a union. An unformed yet definite spirit of rebellion was in the air throughout baseball. The hard fact remained that there were so many qualified baseball players available that dissenters had to be careful lest they talked themselves "to Peoria."

When Tony arrived in Hollywood at the end of March, he resolved to play as well as he could in his effort to return to the majors. He also made it a point to inform other ex-servicemen of their rights in case they had the financial means to pursue their case to the bitter end.

A Tale of Three Veterans

The Pacific Coast League season traditionally began in early April with the Northwest teams, Seattle and Portland, playing series in Hollywood and Los Angeles, and then afterwards all four teams would return to the Northwest for the second half of home-and-home series. The PCL schedule was arranged in the same way as theater performances. During a huge season of 192 games, each of the eight clubs in the league played seven-game series with its rivals. Tuesday through Saturday there were night games, on Sunday there was a double-header, and Monday was a travel day. One of the unique joys of playing in the PCL was the train, the Pacific Coast Special, which took the two Northwest and the two Los Angeles area teams up the coast for the return engagements. The train was a nonstop ride except for a brief pause in Sacramento to change the bar car.

On the first run of the Pacific Coast Special in the 1946 season, Tony Lupien became reacquainted with an old friend in baseball, Al Niemiec, second baseman of the Seattle Rainiers. Though Niemiec was six years older than Tony, they shared similar backgrounds. Both came from New England and had starred in college, Tony at Harvard and Al at Holy Cross. Both had been signed originally by the Red Sox although Al only had a brief trial, "a cup of coffee" as the players call it, with the Red Sox in 1934. He did make the Philadelphia Athletics in 1936, but after hitting only .198 in 203 at-bats, Niemiec returned to the minors. He enjoyed his greatest success with Seattle in the late 1930s and early 1940s. In 1941 he starred on a championship team and was selected the all-star second baseman for the league.

In October 1942 the naval reserves activated Lieutenant Junior Grade Al Niemiec. During the war he attained a full lieutenancy and in January 1946, he was discharged. Niemiec eagerly awaited the chance to reclaim his old job. When he returned many changes had occurred in the Seattle organization. Bill Skiff had replaced Jack Lelivelt as manager. Skiff determined to build his own team. During 1946 spring training, Skiff cut two of Niemiec's 1941 teammates, retaining Niemiec, but only as a utility infielder.

Al Niemiec sensed his job was in jeopardy although he felt he never had a fair chance of proving himself. Tony Lupien was of course a sympathetic listener, and alerted Al to the provisions of the Veterans Act in case the ax fell. As the Pacific Coast Special rolled up the picturesque California coastline, they reminisced about old times. They shared a feeling that with Landis in the commissioner's chair, the players always felt they could get a hearing. Now they wondered what was happening in the baseball world. There was an evident sports boom, attendance records in the making all over the baseball map, and yet the players' traditional maltreatment continued. They sympathized with each other's problems: Al with Tony's being stuck with the label of the first baseman without home run power; Tony with Al's receiving the message he was "too old" to contribute.

When the Special pulled into Oregon, Tony got off with the Stars for a series in Portland. He wished Al well, and urged him not to forget the recourse he had in the Veterans Act in case he needed it.

The reminder proved timely, as on April 21, 1946, shortly after Seattle arrived for its first home stand of the season, Al Niemiec got word from Seattle management of his unconditional release. Niemiec was ready for action. He requested and received from manager Skiff a letter of introduction to other teams, in which Skiff assured Niemiec's future employers, "Al has quite a bit of good baseball left in him." Skiff explained that he simply felt he must go with younger players. Niemiec immediately took the letter and his release to his local draft board in Seattle. Not only did the board tell him that he had a legitimate grievance, but they offered Niemiec the services of a lawyer to test this violation of the Veterans Act. Federal Judge Lloyd Black of the Western District, State of Washington, heard the case and announced he would have a verdict by the end of June. Niemiec, meanwhile, paid his own way back East and found a job playing ball for Providence in the New England League.

Interestingly, the Rainiers' owner, brewer Emil Sick, wanted to reinstate Niemiec immediately. He had always liked the hustling second baseman. Rainier officials, however, had huddled with major league lawyers, who urged them to test the case. Baseball wanted to be free of the continual disruption of the Veterans Act plaintiffs. The majors had second thoughts about this strategy when Judge Black delivered his verdict on June 21, 1946.

Black ruled that Niemiec must be paid his entire 1946 salary by Seattle, minus what he had earned playing for Providence. Black reminded baseball management that the Veterans Act had been passed "to enable the serviceman to render the best he had for his country unworried by the specter of no payment during his first year after his return to civilian life." He stressed that the law did not prohibit baseball players from enjoying its benefits, nor were baseball owners "given the discretion to repeal an Act of Congress."

Turning to Niemiec's field record, he rejected management's argument that Niemiec was obviously declining. He had hit over .300 in the five games he played, made one error, and the team won three of the games. Black doubted whether anyone on the team could do better since the team's percentage was under .360. He conceded, "Baseball is a young man's game," and he stressed that the judiciary should not tell management who should play at any time. He asserted his right to inform Seattle that they must pay Niemiec his full salary. To Bill Skiff's argument that Niemiec would not have been able to complete the season, Judge Black rejoined, "He had no right to anticipate Mr. Niemiec's inability until it occurred." He added, "To allow the employer to decide that there will be cause in the future to discharge the employee presently is a far cry from the sportsmanship Americans the country over expect from baseball."

Judge Lloyd Black was far from finished. He gave a two-hour explanation of how he reached his judgment, leveling the strongest condemnation of baseball practices since Justice Bissell in the Hal Chase case. "We have heard the terms option and waiver. They are rather reminiscent of chattels," Black declared. The contract which the player must sign is "the contract of the employers," who demand "loyalty" of the players and order them to report to spring training on time but can terminate the contract at any time and do not pay them until the season starts.

There were few bases in the criticism of the baseball contract which Judge Black did not touch. He noted the dilemma of the option year salary for the player, which the employer could fix at will. He pointed out the absence of outside arbitration of grievances. As a jurist concerned about the Pacific Coast area, Black also raised the question of the authority of the Commissioner of Baseball to make decisions binding on clubs in the PCL who had no voice in his selection.

While he considered that the 1922 Holmes decision had been a correct ruling for its era, Black offered this ominous word of advice. "Professional baseball should not be too certain that some of the recent decisions by the United States Supreme Court," referring to interstate commerce affirmations of the insurance and news-gathering businesses, "would not be the basis for a reexamination of the interstate character of . . . professional baseball."

Al Niemiec received the news of his vindication gratefully. He returned to the Seattle area and was pleased to accept a job offer as a salesman for Emil Sick's brewery. Although he ended his career after playing at Providence, he had proven his point, thanks to Lupien's

135

encouragement. In 1948 he briefly returned to baseball as general manager for the Great Falls club in the Montana State League, and then he retired to private business. He still lives in the Seattle area, retains a fan's interest in baseball, and looks back content that his case contributed to some changes in the baseball player's condition.

The effect of Judge Black's ruling did not disrupt baseball's normal practices. *The Sporting News* estimated that more than one hundred forty major leaguers and more than nine hundred minor leaguers could qualify for payment due them because of illegal demotion. But the ballplayers were scattered across the country. Many of them had started new jobs, resigned to the fact that baseball had dismissed them at a time of surplus players. Most major league teams were carrying 30-man rosters in 1946, an increase from the usual 25, in deference to the returned serviceman. Still, this was only a token increase, which was rescinded when the 1946 season ended. For the ex-serviceman player cut without a fair tryout, he had to go to court to claim his back pay on the Black ruling. For many ballplayers, courtrooms were not pleasant places to contemplate. They were seen as places of travail instead of possible benefit. The story of pitcher Bob Harris's efforts at getting his back pay was perhaps typical.

Harris signed with the Detroit Tigers in 1938 and looked like a promising hurler. Having a roster abundant with pitchers in 1939, the Tigers traded him to St. Louis. He toiled there for three years, yielding, incidentally, Tony Lupien's first major league hit in 1940. In 1942 he came to the Philadelphia A's, the year following his career high of 12 victories. The next three years he spent in the navy.

In 1946 Harris reported to spring training with a lot of young and not-so-young hopefuls. Though Harris was not yet 30, management was concentrating on the younger players. Connie Mack could not have cared less that Bob Harris was a returning serviceman.

Like many players struggling to make a team, Harris injured himself in spring training. He hurt a heel, which led to a strained shoulder when he started compensating for the bad foot. He did not feel badly when Connie Mack released him at the end of the spring because he had heard that the Giants would look at him since they had been hard hit by losses to the Mexican League. But the Giants' call never came. Harris learned later that the New York team felt something must be wrong with him if Connie Mack had released an able-armed pitcher.

A Tale of Three Veterans

Harris spent 1946 in the minor leagues, pitching very well for Milwaukee of the American Association. When they offered him a 1947 contract without a raise, he decided to retire from baseball and to start a new life outside baseball.

One day in early 1947 he learned of the Veterans Act from an activist in the American Veterans Committee and, in particular, about the Black ruling in the Niemiec case. The activist told Bob that he should get restitution from the A's for his release during spring training of 1946. Bob exchanged letters with the Philadelphia club, and finally a meeting was arranged at a Philadelphia courthouse for late June 1947. Harris traveled at his own expense from his Nebraska home to Philadelphia where he and former A's Joe Gantenbein and Benny McCoy, the free agents Landis had liberated in 1940 from the Tigers, were eligible to receive settlements. Neither Gantenbein nor McCoy came to the meeting however.

In a 1978 letter from Nebraska, where he works as an insurance claims adjuster, Bob Harris reminisced about the meeting in Philadelphia in June 1947:

> When I arrived on the scene there was "Mr. Baseball" Connie Mack and the U.S. District Attorney, who was supposed to be representing me. I had a short consultation with the District Attorney at which time he informed me what a fine "Old Gentleman" Mr. Mack was and what he meant for baseball. It would be to everybody's benefit if I quietly took the settlement they offered. To top it off they asked me to stand in the corner of this large office and let them take a picture with me shaking hands with him. All of this I did because at this point in time I was ready to throw in the towel.

Not until the end of 1947 did Harris receive approximately $3,000 in back pay although his 1946 salary entitled him to at least $1,500 more.

The Veterans Act cases and Judge Black's ringing declaration had brought into the open the continuing operations outside the law of the baseball business. Until the players were organized into a permanent association, there was no assurance that management would not meet immediate crises with a temporary stopgap and then return to business as usual. It should be remembered that major leaguers had not raised collective grievances for thirty years, and only the presence of Landis had kept the owners from yielding totally to their most autocratic impulses.

On the Pacific Coast, Tony Lupien saw the need for an organization of players beyond the legitimate but limited interests of the ex-servicemen. He became active with a group of players who wanted to form a Players Guild in the Pacific Coast League. They targeted the San Francisco Seals for their first organizing drive because new owner Paul Fagan was sympathetic to the needs of the players and San Francisco was a strong union town. They drafted a model agreement which called for a minimum salary of $400 a month, payment for expenses during spring training and in-season road trips, improved lighting conditions on the field, and a reduction of night games, especially the elimination of the Saturday night game before the Sunday double-header. The Guild also asked for the outside arbitration of grievances and a player's share in a sale price. The spirit of Brotherhood and Fraternity past had been revived even in the minor leagues.

The Pacific Coast Leaguers realized that the fate of their Guild hinged on the developments on the major league level. If Tony Lupien had not heard of Robert Murphy during his somber journey to California in late March, all the baseball world was buzzing about him by the summer. Murphy's attempt to gain recognition for a Guild in Pittsburgh had been a model for the efforts on the Pacific Coast. How Murphy appeared and how his failure during the tumultuous year of 1946 nonetheless paved the way for the first changes in baseball's contract in nearly a half century is a fascinating and crucial episode in the history of baseball's labor relations.

9

A Prophetic Failure:
Robert Murphy and the
American Baseball Guild of 1946

*"The validity of the baseball contract makes me
laugh. A baseball owner can do as he wants with
a player on 10-day notice."*
*—Labor organizer Robert Francis Murphy, June
1946.*

*"It is extremely desirable that the players'
representatives recognize that the reserve rules are
for the benefit of players, as well as Club owners.
Consequently the Committee, in its meeting with
the representatives of the players, took the
initiative to secure such a statement."*
*—Report of Special Joint Committee chaired by
Yankee owner Larry MacPhail, August 27, 1946.*

Robert Francis Murphy sat reading the sports pages in his Boston
home one winter evening in early 1946. He had recently returned to his
birthplace after years as a labor relations man in Washington and New
York. Murphy had always loved baseball as a fan, but only played the
game a little. He ran track and did some boxing while at Harvard.
After he graduated in 1932, he went to Harvard Law School for two
years and then continued his law studies at night for two more years at
Northeastern University in Boston. He went to work in Washington as
an examiner for the National Labor Relations Board, which had been
established by the Wagner Act in 1935 to investigate and mediate
disputes involving labor unions in the turbulent and exciting era of the
late 1930s. Murphy had continued NLRB and other labor relations

work in New York City in the early 1940s. Never in his career had he ever directly represented the side of labor in his work.

The more he read the papers this winter, however, the more he considered undertaking one of the most quixotic crusades in baseball history: organizing on his own the major league baseball players into a modern union. Murphy read that some players were earning less than $3,500 in the big leagues. He noted the continuing contractual inequities, like the ten-day release clause and the failure to pay players during spring training. He understood why the freewheeling Pasquel brothers tempted many American players to join their refurbished league in Mexico. Ballplayers had to consider seriously the best opportunity at hand. Murphy understood, because no one, least of all the owners, cared about the players' tomorrow.

Murphy had been particularly moved by the case of Jimmie Foxx, the great slugger who ended a twenty-year career in 1945 and despite a .325 lifetime average and 534 career home runs, had not been able to save much from his salaries.

Murphy was casually acquainted with ballplayers who lived in the Boston area. He started talking to them to get their opinions about the situation in the baseball business. Though most of the players were fatalistic about the inequities in the game, they told him he would find out a lot about contemporary sentiment if he visited the spring training sites. During the season half of the players were always on the road, but now most of them could be located in Florida and they would have plenty to tell him. Murphy was between jobs, and he decided he would see for himself.

Jorge Pasquel and his recruiters were making the biggest headlines in the spring of 1946. The wealthy Mexican businessman reportedly went into Stan Musial's hotel room in Florida, and put five certified $10,000 checks on the star Cardinal outfielder's bed. Musial was earning $13,000 a year. Pasquel was also wooing the Yankees' outstanding shortstop, Phil Rizzuto, but neither of the stars was interested in leaving the country. Pasquel's people did sign up three other Cardinals and eight of the Giants, including pitcher Sal Maglie, who told the press that the $18,000 bonus and salary he received from Pasquel was more than he would make in five years with the Giants.

Robert Murphy was convinced that the Mexican League would not lure many American players if the baseball owners established basic reforms in their business, including minimum salaries and a contract not glaringly stacked against the player. He returned from his tour of the camps bubbling with ideas for a union of all the major leaguers. He would call it the American Baseball Guild. He hoped that after organizing one team successfully, other teams would quickly join. He wished, too, that a former ballplayer would head the Guild and he himself would only be responsible for the actual labor relations with management.

On April 17, 1946, Murphy formally established the American Baseball Guild as a labor organization, registering it in Suffolk County, Massachusetts. The next day he held a press conference explaining the Guild's purpose and program. He pledged his Guild to the cause of bringing "a square deal to the players, the men who make possible big dividends and high salaries for stockholders and club executives." The platform included a call for a minimum salary of $6,500, impartial arbitration of salary disputes and "other conditions of employment," and 50 percent of a sale price to the player. Murphy added that if the owners tried to avoid this demand by trading players, then he would ask that the bartered athlete receive four to five times his salary as a concession. He also called for the removal of the repugnant ten-day clause.

Unlike the previous labor spokesmen for the players, Murphy did not treat the reserve clause issue gingerly. He did not call for its outright abolition, but he did think it must be modified. He doubted the need for a perpetual restriction on players' services when he estimated that 95 percent of them were sold or traded at one point in their career. He observed that major leaguers lasted for barely four years on average, so a perpetual reserve denied logic.

Murphy followed up his press conference by sending a letter on Guild stationery to every major leaguer. He stressed that the program was not his invention but based on the discussions he had held with players. He told his potential constituency to talk with former major leaguers about their treatment. "Ask Babe Ruth and Jimmie Foxx what they think of the one-sidedness of the baseball set-up," he suggested. "If you think that you, like other professional men, doctors, lawyers and jockeys, should be a member of an association run by players for your benefit and protection, we should like to hear from you," Murphy concluded.

Murphy's Guild was definitely a news item, and the sporting press covered the story with interest but with the bias that thirty years of union inactivity in baseball had fostered. H. G. Salsinger, sports editor of the *Detroit News,* sounded like John Tener reborn when he declared, "Baseball is a profession not a trade." Vincent Flaherty of the *Los Angeles Herald Examiner* claimed that there was too much individualism in baseball for a union ever to work, and glory be for that fact. Dan Daniel of the *New York World-Telegram* found it "baffling" how Murphy expected the players to one day have modified reserve clauses with long-term contracts "renegotiated" at the end of each year, a prophetic desire of the organizer whose time had not yet come.

All the writers indulged in horrid fantasies where, under union rule, ballplayers would strike if the manager changed a popular pitcher or would not run out ground balls claiming a speed-up by management. But it is noteworthy that even the conservative sportswriters expressed sympathy to the players fighting the low salaries. Dan Daniel called the Cardinals' salary situation "a carbuncle on the major league body politic," and his editor, Joe Williams, felt "a player has the right to go wherever he gets the best offer," especially if the money is guaranteed.

The owners' response to the Guild was generally mute since Murphy was a one-man operation without visible means of support. But one of the most penurious of the owners, Washington's Clark Griffith, could not remain silent. He blasted Murphy's program. "What this organization calls 'freedom of contract,' giving a player the right to sign with any team of his choice, would be fatal to the life of baseball," carped Griffith. "If the reserve clause is killed, there won't be any big leagues or little leagues." Griffith of course had been Ban Johnson's most avid recruiter of National Leaguers when the American League was fighting to get established. That was ancient history now. Since he had become a full owner in Washington in 1920, Griffith had been able to prosper personally and to keep many of his family on the payroll while running a chronically noncontending franchise. He had maintained a team using many Latin American ballplayers whom he paid very little. Some observers though there was poetic justice in the Mexican League raids, given Griffith's past practices, which had drawn a rebuke from Commissioner Landis in 1943 after rising complaints from Latin American baseball officials.

Not about to change his ways, the recalcitrant Griffith warned that if

Murphy's Guild were recognized, "Eventually collective bargaining would put a ceiling on salaries and destroy initiative." Murphy did not appreciate Griffith's attacks and in late April 1946 he filed an unfair labor practice protest with the National Labor Relations Board regional office in Baltimore. He charged Senators' management with "intimidation" of players, preventing them from reading Guild literature and discussing the union in the clubhouse. The Baltimore office declined to take up the case because of the jurisdictional doubt given the continuing exemption of baseball from antitrust laws.

As Murphy continued his labor struggle, the Pasquel brothers continued their active search for American players. They were not having much more success than the Federal League had had in their search for stars. The Mexican League's biggest catch, shortstop Vern Stephens of the St. Louis Browns, had accepted a $15,000 bonus as part of a $175,000 five-year contract. After only a few games in Mexico, Stephens had returned to the United States in early April 1946. Knowing his departure would be unappreciated by his Mexican hosts, Stephens disguised himself in his father's suit and an old hat and made his way across the border.

The undeterred Jorge Pasquel swooped into New York in early May 1946 and announced, "I will not leave without taking a Yankee regular of the first rank." Although Pasquel did not succeed on his mission, Larry MacPhail went to court to get a temporary injunction against the Mexican entrepreneur, which was later rescinded.

Branch Rickey's low salary scale on the Cardinals, his old club, had contributed to player dissatisfaction in St. Louis. In 1946 Rickey even sued St. Louis sportswriter Ray Gillespie for acting as an agent of Pasquel in enticing his Dodger catcher, Mickey Owen, to Mexico. After much hesitation and waiting for Rickey to improve his salary offer, Owen left for Mexico in May, 1946. Like Vern Stephens, Owen soon changed his mind; he returned to the States within weeks by way of a $250 cab ride to El Paso. Rickey's suit against Gillespie was thrown out by Missouri Judge Rubey Hulen in early June 1946. Hulen ruled that Gillespie was merely trying to aid a friend, Owen, and to obtain a good story, both blameless motives.

In June 1946 the biggest story of the year was building in Pittsburgh. Robert Murphy had decided that the strong union town would be the ideal place to organize the first Guild chapter. Memories of the CIO steel union campaigns of the late 1930s were still fresh. Moreover, the Pirates had a collection of young players and returning servicemen who were receptive to the union idea. One of the Pirates, infielder Jimmy Russell, had a relative who had been injured in a mine accident. Reserve catcher Hank Camelli, a thirty-one-year-old ex G.I., also felt strongly about the need for an organization. Murphy had met with all the Pirates on their first trip into Boston in 1946. A sympathetic sportswriter, Al Abrams of the *Pittsburgh Post-Gazette,* described them as "avid" for the Guild.

By the end of May Murphy felt confident he had 90 percent of the team behind the Guild. He wrote Pittsburgh management requesting an election at the earliest convenience to see if the players wanted the Guild to be its collective bargaining representative. Pittsburgh's owners refused the request. The family of Barney Dreyfuss still ran the club, with the late Dreyfuss's son-in-law, William Benswanger, the chief owner. A union in baseball was a shocking idea, especially to an old-time baseball family. Before World War I, Dreyfuss had reportedly stifled a would-be players' strike by suggesting that his financier friend, Andrew Mellon, establish an impartial board to appraise the worth of the franchise. Dreyfuss then said he would let the players run the team so long as he received 6 percent profit. They backed off quickly, Dreyfuss cheerily recounted the story later.

The Pirates management of 1946 was not that condescending, but they did use all the traditional excuses in explaining their stance. Team lawyer Seward T. French, Jr., declared that the season was not the right time to discuss contracts and unions; it was like department-store workers asking for raises during the Christmas shopping season. French suggested a meeting after September to discuss whether the Guild was an "appropriate" union, whether unions in general were "appropriate" for baseball, and what conditions would be necessary for such an election. Murphy and many of the players resented French's talking down to them as though they were naughty schoolboys. The lawyer's call for a later meeting was quickly understood as the classic delaying tactic, waiting until the season ended when the players would be scattered across the country and would not be available.

William Benswanger's personal involvement, however, caused some players to waver in their commitment to Murphy. The owner announced that he had "never hurt" a player and he was always available to them for individual conferences. Benswanger was also known to be selling the team, which he did later in the summer of 1946. The pending sale may have raised some doubts in the minds of players who did not want to harm Benswanger's personal investment.

The stalemate between Murphy and the Pirates reached a boiling point on June 5. Murphy had set that day as the deadline for a decision on whether the Pirates would grant an election for the team to vote on Guild representation. Management announced that afternoon that they needed more time to study Murphy's request, claiming that they did not know if under major league rules one team could make such a concession without the consent of other clubs. They also criticized Murphy for alerting the NLRB about the Guild's readiness to organize, charging he was placing unfair pressure on them.

A majority of the players reacted angrily to the rejection. They wanted to strike immediately, but Murphy dissuaded them. Months later, he admitted he was overconfident and made a tactical error in not supporting the militant players. Murphy had been certain that if management continued to avoid an election, ultimately he would win his case before the NLRB and the public. On June 5, Murphy also felt a strike would be unfair to the more than 26,000 fans who had already gathered at Forbes Field for the night game. The Pirates lost the game and one newspaper headline the next day proclaimed "Strike-Minded Bucs Lose to Dodgers."

Murphy was now backed into a corner. Much of his constituency wanted to take strike action, and while Murphy had always been willing in the past to endorse "no-strike pledges" if management met him halfway, he had no choice now but to threaten a strike if not recognized. Friday, June 7, was the new deadline, and Murphy declared, "I guarantee that there will be a strike tomorrow night unless the clubs come across." He was immediately backed by city and state CIO leaders. "No red-blooded American man or woman carrying a union card will go to a ball game while there is a strike of players," promised regional CIO director Anthony J. Federoff at a June 6 luncheon where Murphy was feted.

The threatened strike was front-page news in Pittsburgh (and in Boston where Murphy had supporters as a local boy, though a somewhat notorious one). Memories of the Tigers' strike in 1912 were recalled, but Ty Cobb was quoted as opposed to a union in baseball because of "the impossible obstacles" to establishing the worth and the value of players. Manager Frankie Frisch, who had been through plenty of scrapes with John McGraw's Giants and the Cardinals' Gashouse Gang, prepared a lineup card with himself penciled in at second base and coach Honus Wagner at shortstop though these former great players were forty-eight and seventy-two years old, respectively.

When the players filed into the clubhouse two hours before game time, they discovered an unexpected visitor, William Benswanger. Owners rarely visited the players' quarters, and Benswanger had only been there once before. He told the players that he was available to them individually as always, and left unsaid what conclusion they should draw. Robert Murphy tried to get into the clubhouse for last words of advice, but he was barred by club lawyers and security officers. Murphy went outside and bought a general admission ticket, as he had done the previous Wednesday and awaited the results of the strike vote.

The players had agreed that a simple majority would not be sufficient but that two-thirds would be needed for a decision to walk out. Although Murphy had considered 90 percent of the team loyal to the Guild, the players realized the great risks they would incur if they struck. The fear of losing their jobs was understandably great. Management also had two strong advocates in veteran pitcher Eldon "Rip" Sewell and utility infielder Jimmy Brown, who happened to be the only two players on the Pirates earning over $10,000 a year. Murphy realized that on most clubs the highest paid players were the least union-minded, and Sewell and Brown managed to sway enough of the votes in this critical meeting to defeat a strike. The final tally was 20-16 in favor of a strike, not a two-thirds vote. The numbers were inflated; trainers and coaches could vote under Guild rules.

Less than a half hour before game time, Pirates' Public Relations Director Robert Rice opened the clubhouse door and told the expectant reporters, "No strike." *Pittsburgh Post-Gazette* reporter Vince Johnson described the scene: "Silently, even grimly, the Pirates made their way from the clubhouse to the field." Union member fans in the crowd of more than 15,000 greeted Rip Sewell and Jimmy Brown with boos. Sewell had been especially vocal against a union for baseball players. "I'm in favor of any union for men who can't help themselves," Sewell said, obviously referring to steelworkers and coal miners. "But I'd hate to see baseball unionized, as a player has no limit on what he can earn in this game." Sewell later received a gold watch from Commissioner Chandler as a reward for his efforts.

The Pirates thrashed the Giants in Friday's game, a contrast to their losses during the week when they had the potential strike on their minds, traditionalists observed. After the game, William Benswanger returned to the clubhouse to thank the players for their support.

Robert Murphy refused to call the vote a "repudiation" of the Guild. The next week, he filed an unfair labor practice protest with the Pennsylvania Labor Relations Board. After many delays the Board granted Murphy's wish for an election. The Board would reject the legal claim of Pirates management that a professional baseball club not only had an antitrust exemption but had a quasi-religious status outside the jurisdiction of state law. The election was not scheduled until August 21, which meant that the militancy of June 5 would have long passed. Undaunted, Murphy continued his crusade, filing similar protests in July against both Boston teams and all three New York clubs. He also made an effort to venture into the clubhouse of the Philadelphia A's. Alerted security men barred him from entering. Connie Mack had never been genteel in dealing with labor organizations.

Major league owners, given a reprieve in Pittsburgh, began to realize that the current situation in the sport could not be handled with the traditional methods of hauteur and indifference to player equity. By the end of June, the Black ruling in the Niemiec case made them further aware that swift managerial action would be necessary to forestall additional player activity and adverse legal judgments.

The summer of 1946 found big league management engaging in a remarkable series of meetings which led to the first changes in the player contract in several decades. The agency effecting these reforms was a special joint committee from the major leagues established in early July 1946. The so-called millionaires' wing of the owners, Phil Wrigley of the Cubs and Tom Yawkey of the Red Sox, was represented on the body along with Sam Breadon of the Cardinals and the league presidents, Will Harridge of the American and Ford Frick of the National.

The most vocal and active member of the committee was Leland Stanford "Larry" MacPhail of the Yankees. The tempestuous Mac-Phail, father of today's American League President Lee MacPhail, had been a pioneer baseball promoter. He had brought night baseball to Cincinnati in the mid-1930s and convinced many doubters among the owners (like Clark Griffith) that future prosperity depended on playing under the lights. He had moved to Brooklyn in the late 1930s and hired Leo Durocher as manager. In 1941 Durocher led the Dodgers to their first flag in over twenty years. It was Durocher who said of MacPhail, "He never took what he said about somebody else personally." After returning from the war in January 1945, Colonel MacPhail surprised the baseball world by joining forces with the more reserved new owners of the Yankees, construction magnate Del Webb and wealthy former Marine captain Dan Topping.

MacPhail's joint committee met seven times in slightly over a month from early July to early August 1946. To show their concern for making changes, they moved the meetings from Boston to Chicago to New York. Even more remarkably, given baseball's past indifference to player concerns, they invited representatives to speak to them and to express their concerns. Opening up carefully controlled lines of communication with the players was also a strategy of other owners, not just of the committee. In mid-July, the Boston Braves' owner, construction bigwig Louis Perini, met with an informal group of his players and heard their requests for a minimum salary, spring training expenses, and the prohibition of daytime doubleheaders after night games. That Murphy was still a presence in his home base of Boston undoubtedly influenced Perini's willingness to listen.

Three player representatives from each league convened with the joint committee twice during the last half of July. The American League players selected Yankees' relief pitcher Johnny Murphy as their spokesman. The Nationals chose Fred "Dixie" Walker, the Dodgers' outfielder. The committee assured the players that before the 1947 season began, a minimum salary and expenses for spring training would be approved by the full body of owners. They asked St. Louis Cardinals' shortstop Marty Marion to join preliminary discussions about creating a pension for major leaguers. Marion disclosed to the press that the goal for the first drawing on the pension was 1956.

The MacPhail committee was deeply worried about further court tests of the baseball contract. Its legal adviser was the long-time secretary to Judge Landis, lawyer Leslie O'Connor, who had bemoaned the owners' legal actions against Mexican League officials earlier in the year, reminding the moguls, "Judge Landis and I kept baseball out of the courts for twenty-five years." On O'Connor's advice and at MacPhail's urging, the committee told the players it would recommend the scrapping of the ten-day clause, substituting a more lenient thirty-day severance clause. It also decided to stipulate in the option clause of the contract a pay cut of no more than 25 percent upon renewal. Since the death of the Federal League, the iron-clad contract had been totally scrapped, and owners could cut players enormous amounts for the option year. Though the maximum 25 percent-cut paled in comparison to the 1888 contract in which John Montgomery Ward was assured that there would be no cut at all, the 1946 contract reform was still an improvement over the kind of arrangement the players had lived with for a generation.

In late July the terms of the recommendations of the joint committee became public. A minimum salary of $5,500 was announced, considerably lower than the Guild's requested $6,500, yet the principle of a floor beneath which no major leaguer should plunge had been established. Spring training expenses were set at $25 a week, a sum which players henceforth immortalized as "Murphy money." In a major innovation, the committee announced the establishment of a pension to be funded by the owners with player contributions. It would become available to all veterans over age fifty who had been in the major leagues for more than five full seasons. The idea of a pension was a breakthrough because it established a basic right for players, who then had something to fall back on after years of struggling to establish themselves as major leaguers. Because the pension was established by the owners as a sop to forestall player unionization, it would regularly become an area of great controversy every five years when it came up for renewal.

By August 1946 the owners could rest more comfortably. The announcement of a minimum salary, a cosmetic contract reform, and the introduction of a pension all combined to contain player discontent. The player representatives would have preferred a higher minimum salary, but after years of total neglect, they accepted what was given to them. They did not raise any fundamental questions about the baseball system. Ebullient Larry MacPhail crowed after one of the meetings, "The six player delegates reported to us that not even one percent of their constituencies had a crack about the reserve clause."

Most of the issues of Robert Murphy's Guild had thus been preempted. The Boston organizer went down bravely with his ship. The Pennsylvania Labor Relations Board had scheduled a Guild recognition election for August 21 in Pittsburgh. Murphy knew his position was weak, but he did his best. He confided to Tony Lupien in early August, in replying to Lupien's advice for the best wording on a Guild contract for the Pacific Coast League, "The efforts of the club owners are the most barefaced attempts to form a company dominated union that I have ever seen."

A clear sign of Murphy's declining influence came in mid-August when he deliberately stayed away from the clubhouse when the Pirates came to play in Chicago. He met them at their hotel because he did not want to "compromise their position with ownership." Although he betrayed no pessimism publicly, Murphy had little hopes for a positive vote with the pension program and minimum salary already announced. Moreover, one of his earliest supporters, Hank Camelli, had been shipped to the minor leagues.

On the morning of August 21, polling booths at a downtown Pittsburgh hotel were scheduled to open at 10:30 A.M. Not a Pirate showed up to cast a ballot for over three hours. The excitement of two months earlier had faded. The lingering fear of expressing union sentiments persisted. When the votes finally were registered, it was 15-3 against the Guild as a collective bargaining agent. More than a dozen Pirates abstained from voting. Murphy told *The Sporting News* he was not surprised by the outcome, and offered a prophecy:

> The players will eventually realize that the club owners who have had seventy years to change the one-sidedness of the baseball picture never acted until the American Baseball Guild threatened the very foundation—sometimes rotten—of their baseball empire.

Murphy faded from the scene almost as fast as he had appeared. He did continue pursuing unfair labor practice charges in many states, but when one hearing was scheduled in New York in January 1947, it had to be canceled. The labor board examiner admitted that deep in the off-season, the players were "relatively inaccessible."

Murphy flirted inconclusively with organizing hockey players in the

150

winter of 1946. Sometime early in 1947, he vanished as a baseball labor organizer. Before he disappeared, he passed on a vivid metaphor to one reporter: "The players have been offered an apple, but they could have had an orchard."

In a February 1947 conversation with Richard Armstrong, a Princeton undergraduate who was writing a thesis on baseball unionization, Murphy made some final trenchant comments. He noted that the overwhelming tradition of paternalism on one hand and naked autocracy on the other made action by the players against the owners extremely difficult. William Benswanger had neatly epitomized management's behavior. After the lost strike vote, when asked if the players would be punished, he replied, "Our power to fine and to suspend is automatic. Having that power and exercising it are two different things."

Murphy hoped that one day the fatalism of the players would be overcome. " 'Baseball is like that,' they say. They must be shown, taught that these things are not necessary conditions, that they are entitled to certain privileges and rights which are not theirs now," he declared. Nearly twenty years would pass before another man with strong union ties and far greater experience, Marvin Julian Miller from the United Steelworkers of America, would successfully apply collective bargaining principles to major league baseball.

Murphy had predicted that once the Guild threat passed, management would begin to take back some of the players' new rights. His words came true within days of the defeat of the Guild in Pittsburgh. On August 27, 1946, the joint major league committee headed by MacPhail issued its report to Commissioner Chandler. The minimum salary offer was now cut to $5,000, $500 less than the figure announced after the meeting with the player representatives in late July. A stiff clause to the contract was added, which intended to deny the player any recourse to legal action:

> The player agrees that he has exceptional and unique skill and ability as a baseball player; that his services to be rendered hereunder are of a special, unusual and extraordinary character which gives them peculiar value which cannot be reasonably or adequately compensated for in damages at law. . . . The player agrees that . . . the club shall be entitled to injunctive and other equitable relief to prevent a breach of this contract by the player.

Not content to merely immunize the owners from future legal

151

challenges, the MacPhail report proposed an extension of the major league schedule from 154 to 168 games effective in the 1947 season. MacPhail argued that 30 off-days in a season was unnecessary waste, and the new games would add needed revenue.

Baseball traditionalists, who agreed with the impulsive Yankee owner that collective bargaining should be forestalled by all means necessary, felt that the extended schedule was going too far. Except for the wartime curtailment in 1918, 154 games had been the established schedule for both leagues since 1905. After the Boston Americans won the first modern World Series in 1903, the embarrassed National League added 14 games to its log for 1904 to have a good excuse for not playing in postseason competition that year; in the winter of 1904, an agreement was reached to reestablish the World Series in 1905 after each circuit played 154 games. Many observers saw the 168-game schedule as a bald attempt to make the players pay for the concessions they had received. Arthur Daley, *New York Times* sport columnist, condemned it as a vindictive effort at "giving-an-inch-and-taking-a-yard."

In mid-September 1946, at yet another meeting in this season of high-level conclaves, the owners backed off from the extended schedule, which contributed to MacPhail's abrupt decision to resign from the executive council, major league baseball's newly created inner sanctum. The Yankee co-owner's peremptory manner had not won him many friends among his colleagues. He insisted on an Arthur Soden-like condescending word toward Robert Murphy in his committee's report: "Mr. Murphy would have been successful, in our opinion, if he had started with Minor League players. In that event we would have probably have awakened to what is known as a 'fait accompli.'" To even suggest such a strategy, hypothetically, rubbed traditional owners the wrong way. MacPhail had also taken to feuding with Commissioner Chandler when the Kentucky politician had rejected his plan for increase in ticket prices as being unfair to the average fan. During the post-World Series celebration of the 1947 Yankees, MacPhail upstaged his team to announce his retirement from baseball to lead the life of a Maryland rancher.

Though baseball's moguls by the 1940s were occasionally warring with each other, the climate seemed to favor their continued total monopolistic rule. In Commissioner Chandler, they had a leader of no great force or distinction which suited them perfectly. Murphy's Guild had been crushed and the Mexican League had failed to make significant inroads on players. The system of player representatives without voting power on any substantive issue, including labor relations, seemed to have established a workable, compliant company union for baseball.

As 1947 spring training rolled around, Dan Daniel, one of the writers especially favored by baseball's management, wrote, "Blessed are the magnates from whence all good comes." For a group of ballplayers who had played in Mexico and now were trying to earn a livelihood using their baseball skills, the magnates had been anything but beneficent. In June 1946 Commissioner Chandler had announced a five-year ban on all Americans who had left 1946 contracts to play in Mexico. He added a three-year ban on those players who had violated their reserve clause. As baseball turned back the challenges of the grieving ex-servicemen and the American Baseball Guild, it insisted on enforcing the blacklist against all professional players who dared to complete against the "outlaws" from the Mexican League.

1947 was not a congenial time to fight a battle for justice against an entrenched monopoly. The memory of wartime gallantry and sacrifice against international tyranny had been obscured by a growing national paranoia about Communism. Strict new measures against labor union abuses were passed in the Taft-Hartley Law during the summer of that year.

After having no chance to make a living playing baseball after a year in Mexico, Danny Gardella, a twenty-seven-year-old outfielder, was still willing to tackle the moguls. Constitutional lawyer Frederic Augustus Johnson, an attorney who knew baseball intimately, was eager to take his case. By the fall of 1947, they had teamed up to present the most direct legal challenge yet to the monopoly of organized baseball.

10

Gardella vs. Chandler:
The Case That Almost Toppled a Monopoly

"The only question raised by this appeal is whether Organized Baseball is trade or commerce within the Sherman and Clayton Acts."
—Attorney Frederic Johnson, before the United States Court of Appeals, Southern District, New York, November 26, 1948.

"I feel so relieved. If I were a drinking man, I'd get drunk."
—Baseball Commissioner Happy Chandler, October 8, 1949, after Gardella v. Chandler *had been settled out of court.*

Danny Gardella's love for baseball came naturally. He grew up in the Bronx, not far from Yankee Stadium, during the glamorous years of baseball after World War I. Danny was a Giant fan, and reflecting on the past one wintry day in early 1979, he said, "My destiny was with the Giants." He remembers how, at fourteen, he and some neighborhood buddies sneaked into the 1934 All-Star Game at the Polo Grounds. He saw one of his heroes, Carl Hubbell, memorably strike out Babe Ruth, Lou Gehrig, Jimmie Foxx, Al Simmons, and Joe Cronin in succession.

Danny began his career in organized baseball with a Tigers' farm club in Beckley, West Virginia, in 1939. The level of Class D ball was so high in this era that two of his teammates made the jump to the parent club directly—pitcher Johnny Gorsica and shortstop Murray Franklin. In 1940 Danny and his older brother Albert were two of the ninety-one Tigers' farmhands freed by Commissioner Landis's edict. They wound up in Class D ball in Pine Bluff, Arkansas, where Danny played through the 1941 season.

A punctured eardrum suffered in youth kept Danny out of the draft. In 1942 he went to work in a New York shipyard, building heavy tugboats. Two years later, Joe Birmingham, a former Cleveland player and manager, was on a scouting mission for the Giants whose roster had been hard hit by the military draft. Birmingham coaxed Gardella back into baseball, feeding him stories about Ty Cobb and appealing to the sense of tradition that had always made baseball attractive to Danny. Joe Birmingham was working for the Giants, which made the selling easier too. Danny signed and spent two weeks playing for manager Gabby Hartnett at the Giants' farm club in Jersey City, and then reported to the Polo Grounds. He hit six home runs in 112 at-bats in 1944. During the full season of 1945, Danny hit eighteen home runs and drove in seventy-one runs with a .272 batting average.

Danny Gardella loved the major league life. He enjoyed the travel and the celebrity. The only drawback was the low pay. He did not earn enough to buy a good suit, he recalls, but "though we weren't getting that much money out of it, we sure had our fun." Danny certainly did. He was (and still is) a physical fitness buff. Once he pulled a daring stunt on his roommate, Cuban infielder Napoleon Reyes. He left a suicide note on their hotel-room dresser and proceeded to climb outside the window, hanging onto the ledge, until the panicked Reyes ran over to see where the body had plunged.

Gardella also loved to sing. *New York Mirror* sportswriter and later Hall of Fame Director Ken Smith would play the accordion on road trips and Danny would bellow a resplendent "Babes in Toyland." Smith's *Mirror* colleague, Dan Parker, dubbed Danny "the opera singer."

When time came for the fateful 1946 spring training, Danny Gardella knew his position was very insecure. Many of the wartime major leaguers had not even been invited to spring training. Danny's chance of making a team with Willard Marshall and Whitey Lockman among the returning outfielders was not good. To make matters worse, he got off on the wrong foot by missing the train to spring training in Florida. He had to pay his own way South.

When Danny Gardella arrived, he found a troubled Giants' club owner Horace Stoneham, who had inherited the team from his father, Charles. Stoneham was a kindly man. He was known to take care of indigent ballplayers like Hans Lobert out of his own pocket. But Stoneham knew little about running a baseball organization which could compete with high-rollers like Larry MacPhail and brains like Branch Rickey. The Giants had fared well under John McGraw's field leadership. McGraw died in 1933, and his replacement, Bill Terry, an excellent first baseman and still the last National Leaguer to hit .400 (.401 in 1931), had less success.

Terry resigned late in 1941, complaining about the lack of money in the game for managers and players. He took a parting shot at baseball officialdom: "No business in the world has ever made more money with poorer management," he said. When asked if baseball could survive World War II, Terry declared, "It can survive anything." The Giants named outfield star Mel Ott as player-manager; it did not help the standings. As 1946 started, the Giants could scarcely hope to climb out of the second dividsion.

Danny Gardella balked at accepting an offer of $5,000 from the Giants. He felt he was deserving of a better offer after a promising year in 1945 despite wartime conditions and diluted quality of play. Gardella did not make it easier on himself when he arrived in Florida and walked into the team dining area without a jacket and a tie, violating a team rule of which he was unaware. When asked to leave the room, Danny decided he had taken enough. Unsigned and unlikely to make the team, Danny sensed his chances were shot already.

On February 18 Danny headed for Vera Cruz to join the Mexican League. He had met Alfonso Pasquel, one of the younger brothers, at a New York health club earlier that winter. Alfonso assured Danny that the Mexican circuit would more than double his wages. Gardella contacted a Mexican League agent in Florida and signed a contract for $8,000 plus a $5,000 bonus. It was a one-year contract with options for two more.

One month later, Gardella made his Mexican debut an auspicious one by homering in a 12 to 5 victory over Mexico City. In a stadium holding only 23,000 seats, 33,000 fans turned out for a gala opening. Before the National League season opened, seven of Danny's former teammates—including Nap Reyes, who fortunately would no longer be the butt of any further pranks on the part of Danny—joined him in Mexico City. Three prize St. Louis Cardinals also came to Mexico, infielder Lou Klein and pitchers Max Lanier and Fred Martin, the same man who in the early 1970s would teach the remarkable split-fingered fastball to Bruce Sutter of the Chicago Cubs.

Danny Gardella was one of those Americans who liked playing

baseball in Mexico. He appreciated the people, although many Mexican politicians resented the influx of the North Americans and passed a law forbidding more than 50 percent of foreigners on any team. Gardella hit over a dozen home runs for Vera Cruz. He continued to have his fielding problems. He lost more than his share of fly balls in the sun, which brought to mind the description of the New York writer, "He caught the ball—unassisted." Danny felt, and feels to this day, that "We should have been treated as ambassadors of goodwill to a friendly people."

The monopoly of organized baseball thought otherwise. In early June 1946 Mexican jumpers had been banned for up to five years. When Vern Stephens returned to the Browns before the edict took effect, he left the Mexicans angry and demanding his advance money be returned. U.S. government officials looked into the worsening relations between American and Mexican baseball moguls, but Happy Chandler snapped, "The State Department has enough to do without meddling in baseball." Stephens returned most of his advance money to Pasquel, and the incident was closed.

Mickey Owen was not so lucky. His expensive cab ride back to the U.S. had come too late. Owen was very repentant about leaving, and Branch Rickey declared, "I'd like to help that boy any way I can." But the moguls wanted to teach the players another lesson about the costs of defying the system. In July 1946 Cubs General Manager James Gallagher, another ex-sportswriter, wrote pointedly to Commissioner Chandler, "The spectacle of Mickey Owen languishing on a Missouri farm will do more to keep players from jumping this winter than anything Mr. Rickey or the rest of us could do."

By the end of the 1946 season the owners need not have feared the Mexican challenge. Like other third leagues, this one suffered from the lack of baseball brains and the extreme disparity in the size of its cities. Jorge Pasquel's ego dominated everything. He signed Mickey Owen for his Mexico City club, then sent him to Vera Cruz when he thought they needed a catcher. Always conspicuously in attendance at the games, Pasquel once overruled an official scorer to keep a no-hitter going in the sixth inning.

Although there were attractive aspects to the schedule, games three nights a week and only 98 in all, the stadium conditions were sometimes bizarre. In small Tampico, railroad tracks traversed the outfield. One American wit envisioned a sports bulletin one day, "Game called end of 8th. Slow freight." Poor lighting systems and the onerous bus travel during an especially rainy 1946 Mexican summer all added to the woes of the new circuit. The resentment of the Americans earning far more than the locals, also played a role in crushing the Pasquels' dream. The League survived only through the 1948 season. Seven years later Jorge Pasquel was killed in a plane crash in the Mexican hills.

Although by 1947 the Mexican League no longer posed a threat, the moguls continued to enforce the ban on the Americans. Their vindictiveness made life very hard on Danny Gardella and the other blacklisted players. After his one season in Mexico, Danny went to play winter ball in Cuba. He then hooked up with a barnstorming team called Max Lanier's All-Stars.

Max Lanier had been a starting pitcher for the Cardinals, a consistent winner for their three straight National League championship teams from 1942 to 1944. He left for Mexico in the middle of the 1946 season after winning his first six decisions. His barnstorming team won all 81 games it played in the winter of 1946/47, but it had a hard time making money or finding opponents. Word was out that organized baseball would enforce the blacklist against the former Mexican League players by banning anyone who played against them. No player with baseball ambition dared to go near these marked men, modern excommunicants from baseball's sacred church.

The Max Lanier All-Stars barnstormed their way North in the late winter and early spring of 1947 and then disbanded. Danny Gardella returned to New York where his wife, Katherine, was expecting the first of their nine children. He was only twenty-seven years old and had not lost his desire to play baseball. Gardella joined a semipro team, the Gulf Oilers, which played throughout the New York metropolitan area.

Early in the summer of 1947, the Oilers were scheduled to play a Negro team, the Cleveland Buckeyes, at Staten Island. Shortly before game time, the Buckeyes backed out when they learned that each player might lose his chance at making the white leagues if he played against Gardella. Jackie Robinson was on his way to Rookie-of-the-Year honors with the Dodgers, helping them to a pennant. The Cleveland black players did not want to jeopardize their own dreams of glory.

A few days later, a disgruntled fan told his dentist, Dr. Conrad Meibauer, the story of how he had missed seeing his nephew play for the Oilers because of the baseball blacklist. The dentist soon passed on this

159

tale of modern anathema to an interested patient, lawyer Frederic Augustus Johnson.

Frederic Johnson came from a well-established family in Cincinnati. His father had attended games of the original Cincinnati Reds franchise in 1869. His uncle, Edgar Johnson, had been counsel to the American Association Cincinnati club of the 1880s. Johnson's family knew Pirates owner Barney Dreyfuss intimately. Young Frederic kept up the friendship as he moved East to Yale, Harvard Law School, and then to work as a lawyer in New York City with close connections to Tammany Hall, the New York Democratic party organization. He had been legal secretary to Judge Joseph Crater at the time of his mysterious disappearance in 1930.

In 1939 Frederic Johnson wrote the first scholarly treatment of "Baseball Law" for the *United States Law Review*. He discussed the various cases disputing the baseball contract since John Montgomery Ward versus the Giants in 1890. Writing as a labor of love and as a baseball fan, Johnson had no harsh words for baseball management in 1939. He observed that when courts in the Lajoie case and the Killifer and Marsans disputes of the Federal League period had enjoined players from joining new leagues, they had upheld a fundamental baseball principle that players at central spots of the diamond were especially valuable: Bill Killifer was a catcher, Lajoie a second baseman, and Armando Marsans a center fielder. Johnson concluded his piece praising Commissioner Landis for presiding over the longest period of "uninterrupted peace" in baseball history. He also saluted John McGraw's charitable concern for old ballplayers, which brought credit to the industry.

In 1947, Frederic Johnson viewed the baseball business differently. He disliked the practice of American owners running to court to thwart Mexican competition. He agreed with Leslie O'Connor that Landis's great achievement had been keeping baseball out of the courts.

When Dr. Meibauer told Johnson about Danny Gardella's plight, the lawyer was angered. The dentist arranged a meeting between the ex-major leaguer and the well-informed attorney. Frederic Johnson listened as Danny Gardella explained the details of his story.

He had not jumped a Giant contract to play in Mexico. He had merely refused their 1946 offer and chose to peddle his wares in the Mexican marketplace. Unable to make a living as a ballplayer upon his return to

160

the United States in 1947, Danny had taken a job as a hospital orderly near Yonkers. His pay was $36 a week. As Frederic Johnson listened to Danny's story, he thought of how Landis might have handled the case. Johnson firmly believed that if Landis were alive, he would have told Gardella, "As soon as you have shown me that your contractual obligations are fulfilled in Mexico, you may apply for readmission to organized baseball." Danny had signed a one-year contract with no binding reserve so there was no legal reason he should not play American baseball again.

Frederic Johnson realized an epochal case could be made against the baseball monopoly, grinding a morally and legally blameless individual into the oblivion of a menial's existence. Johnson had only recently learned a vital fact unknown to him when he wrote his "Baseball Law" piece. Organized baseball had never argued that the reserve clause was legally binding on players. In the interminable Federal League cases, George Wharton Pepper had called it only an "honorary obligation" for the players, and Garry Herrmann in his testimony had stressed that the National Commission limited reserve lists to twenty-two players. Thirty years later the monopolistic controls of the moguls were far more pervasive with vast farm systems and forty players on each major league roster. The growth of radio revenue and the beginning of television investment in baseball made baseball's exemption from interstate commerce laws extremely vulnerable. Johnson advised Gardella to sue.

The case opened in New York before Southern District Federal Judge John Bright early in October 1947. Johnson asked for $100,000 in a civil suit, which under the antitrust laws would mean $300,000 because of the triple damages stipulation. He railed against the five-year suspension of Gardella, which "will destroy the ability of plaintiff as a professional player through the necessary absence from competitive play of the calibre to which he had become accustomed."

Johnson contended that the reserve clause had only been upheld historically in cases like Lajoie's, where he was deemed a "unique performer." Gardella was not in that category; still he was a professional ballplayer being denied a livelihood by a deliberate conspiracy against him.

Johnson concluded his affidavit with a ringing attack on the reserve clause as a weapon used "contrary to settled principles of equity and to further a conspiracy in restraint of trade and commerce." The reserve

161

clause had not equalized competition since 1920, as baseball officials insisted; it only served to perpetuate a monopoly which Johnson balefully pictured as "stretching from Hudson's Bay to the Equator."

Johnson added a parting shot at the farm systems which "allows . . . players to be signed during infancy without giving to them the common law right to repudiate such contracts upon attaining their majority or to exercise statutory rights for disavowing their contracts upon attaining their majority."

Baseball's lawyers responded with the kind of arguments expected from people who approved the blacklist in the first place. They disputed Johnson's contention that Gardella had committed no offense against the Giants baseball club. Mark Hughes, a Yankees' lawyer and one of a broad-based team representing baseball's united front, insisted that Gardella "violated his contractual obligations, playing in Mexico knowing he could be disciplined by the commissioner." He cited the Holmes decision at length, claiming that the Supreme Court exemption of 1922 was still valid. The expansion of the major league tentacles made no difference. "If sixteen clubs organized into two leagues are not engaged in interstate trade or commerce," Hughes said, "the addition of so-called 'farm clubs,' although increasing the number of clubs involved, does not convert the sport into trade or commerce." Baseball's case was built on the assumption that the reserve clause and the ineligible list were tried, tested, and necessary methods of what its lawyers called "preventing players from disregarding their obligations." The clause was an internal matter of "conservation of personnel," ownership claimed. Its restrictions had nothing whatever to do with interstate commerce.

Both the owners and Danny Gardella wanted a quick resolution. Gardella's enforced idleness from top caliber play had sapped his skills. He wanted to know soon if he could ever again play legally. The moguls wanted to go to bed at night secure in the knowledge their historic restrictions were safe.

Judge Bright died in February 1948 before he could render a verdict. It was not until July that his replacement, Judge Henry W. Goddard, ruled that it was outside his jurisdiction to overturn a Supreme Court decision and thus dismissed his case.

Danny was in a position similar to Deacon White and Jack Rowe in 1889. Only in 1947 there was no feeling of solidarity. The fear of winding up in Peoria kept the employed players from speaking their minds. Without an independent organization, there was little the athletes could do.

Public opinion was not friendly toward the case. The wartime players had been long forgotten once the regulars returned from service. Joe Williams of the *New York World-Telegram* criticized the blacklist as a dumb maneuver, yet he took a shot at Danny as "an exceptionally bad player," having some crude fun with the "exceptional player" defense management had used in the Lajoie case.

Frederic Johnson pressed on. In November 1948 he brought an appeal before the Second Circuit Appellate Federal Court in New York's Southern District. The eminent three-man panel consisted of Judges Learned Hand, Harrie W. Chase, and Jerome N. Frank, a former high-ranking New Deal official in Washington.

Fred Johnson made another forceful presentation before the appellate court. He insisted that organized baseball had become part of interstate commerce since the Holmes decision. The presence of radio and television revenues brought the transmission of baseball games into national business, he argued. He cited Garry Herrmann's revealing position in one of the Federal League appeals. "The reservation is not to monopolize the player market," the head of the National Commission had declared, "but rather to limit it to the extent that no club can have more players on its reservation list than are actually needed for its own purposes." If the reserve was limited to 22 players during Herrmann's tenure and chief lawyer George Wharton Pepper considered it only an "honorary obligation" upon the player, Johnson concluded, then the appellate court must find organized baseball guilty as charged with violating antitrust laws and Danny Gardella's Constitutional right to earn a living of his choice.

The court deliberated into early 1949. On February 10 it announced that by a two-to-one vote Gardella's case was strong enough to warrant a trial. Judge Chase was in the minority, considering the Holmes decision binding and calling radio and television revenue "incidental" to essentially local business of playing the games.

Jerome Frank joined the company of Herbert Bissell and Lloyd Black as a vehement judicial opponent of baseball's mode of business. Judge Frank called the Holmes decision "an impotent zombi" because recent Supreme Court decisions of the 1940s had far more broadly defined interstate commerce. Though insurance policies were written in one

163

locality, the high Court had ruled that they were matters of interstate commerce. So too were the activities of the International News Service, the journalistic wire service, and the American Medical Association.

Frank followed Lloyd Black in branding the baseball contract as a form of "peonage" which he found repellent in modern America. Many of baseball's spokesmen, including Commissioner Chandler, had said that if earning between $5,000 and $100,000 a year like ballplayers did is serfdom, most Americans would accept it gladly. Judge Frank tartly rebuked this attitude when he wrote, "Excusing virtual slavery because of high pay is only an excuse for the totalitarian-minded."

Learned Hand voted with Jerome Frank, issuing a milder opinion. He did not call the reserve clause a form of slavery. He did feel Gardella's case raised serious issues worthy of resolution by trial. He sympathized with the predicament Gardella faced, losing the opportunity to play baseball at the level he was accustomed to. Hand stated unequivocally that the antitrust laws banned "all restraints of trade which were unlawful at common law and one of the oldest and best established of these is a contract which unreasonably forbids anyone to practice his calling."

Newspapers on February 11, 1949, headlined the story of the court's ruling. A frontal challenge to the reserve clause was big news. Predictably, baseball's friends warned of the death of the game if Gardella pursued the case. Congressman A. S. "Syd" Herlong, a former player and executive in the Class D Florida State League, said that "a Gardella victory could well sound the death knell for the sport that has kindled the fires of ambition in the breasts of so many thousands of young Americans."

In April, Herlong and a rising young Congressman from Arkansas, Wilbur Mills, introduced a bill to legalize the reserve clause and to grant a legislative antitrust exemption to baseball. A new age of largely ritualistic but intense Congressional interest in the game was dawning. No fewer than sixty bills would be introduced within the next two decades concerning baseball's regulation or tacit deregulation, though legislative action would be taken on none of them.

The response of the players to the appellate court decision was especially disheartening to Gardella. Mickey Owen told the Associated Press that Gardella should drop his case. "Baseball didn't force us to go to Mexico; we went because of our weaknesses," Owen said. He had recently met with the commissioner. "I apologized for my actions and we had a long talk," Owen told the Associated Press. "We can see our mistakes now. I didn't know I had it so good until I was out of baseball."

Owen, Fred Martin, and Max Lanier actually paid a visit to Gardella in Yonkers shortly after the court's action. They urged him to drop the suit because Owen had the strong impression that Chandler would then reinstate all the blacklisted players. Danny served them wine and spaghetti and they reminisced a little about the old days, but his answer was no deal. Martin and Lanier decided then that they would sue Chandler on the same grounds Gardella had, although they had both walked out on signed contracts for 1946 when they left for Mexico.

Danny, with Max and Fred, went to federal court in mid-March to try to get an order which would force baseball to show cause why they should not be immediately reinstated. In mid-April another New York Southern District judge, Edward Conger, denied the plaintiffs' request because it "would restore them to positions they resigned voluntarily." With no immediate relief in sight, Gardella and Lanier headed for Canada to play in Drummondville, Quebec, for a Canadian league which organized baseball decided not to blacklist, having had enough troubles south of the American border.

The trial of *Gardella vs. Chandler* was now slated for November 1949. Meanwhile, Frederic Johnson had made a name for himself nationally and he was ready to take on all comers. In April Branch Rickey told a Baltimore advertising club luncheon that the reserve clause was opposed by people with "avowed Communistic tendencies." Johnson retorted, "Name calling is the last resort for a beaten man." He added some Landis-like shots at Rickey's farm system manipulations which "would have put Simon Legree to shame."

Occasionally, an independent voice in the sporting press like Dan Parker's expressed the hope that a court might clarify at last the controversy about the reserve clause "which has hung over baseball for seventy years like a sword of Damocles." Without naming names down the seaboard from New York, Parker observed, "If taking the reserve clause out of the contract would mean that the parasitic clubs that have been living off the richer ones would have to fold up, baseball would be much better off." It was a poorly kept secret that the American League partners had contributed as much as $250,000 a year to keep the weak St. Louis Browns franchise afloat in recent years.

On June 5 Happy Chandler surprised the baseball world by announcing an immediate amnesty to all the Mexican League veterans. Chandler phoned Mickey Owen and chortled, "Get your bag packed, boy, and get to your club right away." Owen now belonged to the Cubs to whom the Dodgers had sold him. Chandler explained that once Judge Conger had denied the petition of immediate reinstatement of the players, the commissioner could act freely and fairly. "The threat of compulsion by a court having been ended," Chandler said, "I feel justified in tempering justice with mercy in dealing with all of these players." Six weeks had passed, however, since Judge Conger's decision, which indicates that Chandler decided that dropping the blacklist would be less costly than risking the threat of future legal cases.

Sal Maglie returned to the Giants and was a key contributor in their pennant years of 1951 and 1954. He helped the Dodgers to a 1956 pennant and won the opening game of the World Series against the Yankees; his five-hitter in Game Five was overshadowed by Don Larsen's perfect game. Max Lanier and Fred Martin returned to the Cardinals, where they contributed to the club's gallant though unsuccessful 1949 pennant drive. Danny Gardella, playing in the wilds of Canada when Chandler issued his amnesty, still was without a major league contract. Frederic Johnson vowed, "We will fight this to the very end."

When Danny returned to New York in September 1949, he and Johnson took stock of the situation. There was no assurance that he would win his case in the trial court. Baseball would surely appeal a negative verdict all the way to the Supreme Court even if they won the first battle. Most importantly, damages might be hard to win in court because Danny had made more money in Mexico and Canada than he would have if he had stayed with the Giants at his old salary.

Johnson recommended an out-of-court settlement to his client. Gardella wished he could fight on "against an evil which afflicts all players, the reserve restriction." Like Tony Lupien a year earlier, economic necessity won out over an ideal of justice. Gardella could not afford a protracted court struggle.

Frederic Johnson did not let on publicly his willingness to settle. He interrogated Commissioner Chandler in pretrial hearings in late September. He arranged for the hearings to be held in a centrally located courtroom so reporters could hear the commissioner try to evade Johnson's questions about the extent of radio-television revenues in baseball.

Baseball's lawyers managed to keep the discussion to figures of 1947. Even then, before the age of television truly began, over $275,000 had been brought into baseball's coffers from the national media eager to broadcast the All-Star Game and the World Series. By 1949 the amount soared over $1 million, and would continue to rise.

Chandler took the familiar management line during examination by Johnson. Baseball had not tried to punish the blacklisted players, he said. It only "wanted them to live up to their obligations and responsibilities," which meant absolute obedience to the reserve clause and other rules of the owners. Chandler insisted on the inviolability of baseball's rules. He testified, "If a professional player plays against an ineligible player, he automatically makes himself ineligible."

Privately, baseball lawyers were urging settlement. The aged George Wharton Pepper, retired from the United States Senate, could not argue the case because Frederic Johnson had made well known his views that the reserve clause had no more binding effect on the player than an "honorary obligation." New chief lawyer, John Lord O'Brian, ironically a former federal government antitrust lawyer, told the major league owners to settle lest a scramble for talent occur if the reserve clause were ruled illegal.

On October 8, 1949, the World Series in progress between the Dodgers and the Yankees obscured the news that the Gardella case had been settled out of court a month before the trial was slated to begin. Fred Saigh, the new owner of the Cardinals, who within three years was sentenced to federal prison for income tax evasion, arranged for the purchase of Gardella's contract from the Giants. A cash settlement was arranged, which Danny Gardella in 1966 admitted to have been more than $60,000, an amount he split with Frederic Johnson.

Happy Chandler told the press, "I feel so relieved. If I were a drinking man I'd get drunk." The denouement of Danny Gardella's career was not happy. Not yet thirty, he reported to the Cardinals in spring training in 1950. His zest for the game had waned. The calumnies and the insults he had received since 1946 had taken their toll. He flied out in his only at-bat for the Cardinals in 1950. He then was sold to their Houston farm club in the Texas League. In 1951 he played for the Bushwicks, a well-known independent club in the New York area, and then hung up his spikes.

Gardella works today as a warehouseman in Queens, New York. He is glad that the players are earning better salaries and that the sons of the owners of his day are more generous, but he adds perceptively, "Maybe they pay more because they have to." (Gardella died in March 2005.)

After October 1949 the owners felt no pressure to improve the players' condition and they sat back and presided over business as usual. Yet slowly and hesitantly in the decade ahead, the players started to take steps to assure at last their equitable position in the business of organized baseball.

Part

*Seedlings of
Change in a
Quiet Decade*

11

The Celler Sub-Committee Hearings of 1951

"You show me anybody that has come up in the movies such as Ty Cobb or Joe DiMaggio or any of those men. . . . You can't take men like Red Skelton or those kind of men and put them on a par. These fellows are clowns. Men in baseball represent a symbol."
—Sporting News *publisher and editor J. G. Taylor Spink, testifying before the Celler Sub-Committee, October 1951.*

The baseball owners entered the 1950s supremely confident that their mode of operations would stand perpetually unfettered. Other businesses might have thought about the judicial warnings uttered by the appellate court, particularly Judge Jerome Frank, in early 1949. For the vast majority of the owners, the out-of-court settlement of the Gardella case meant the problem had been removed. They rested proudly in the knowledge that all the threats of the year of the great challenges, 1946, had been dissipated: Robert Murphy's Guild had disappeared, the competition from the Mexican League had faded away, and the direct challenge to the reserve clause in the Gardella case had been settled.

In December 1950 the owners gave notice that they wanted to run the show totally when they refused to give Commissioner Chandler an early extension of his seven-year contract. The Kentuckian's pact was not due to expire until mid-1952, but he felt he should be rewarded for his role in presiding over the restoration of the unchallenged baseball monopoly.

While owners' meetings then and now are highly secret affairs, it seems that Chandler's folksy ways had especially irritated the New York owners. A commissioner willing to sing "My Old Kentucky Home" at a moment's notice embarrassed the urbanites. More crucial than this difference over style was the desire of the owners to find a more pliable leader from the baseball family. Although Chandler did not have the innate suspicion of the owners that Landis had, he did act occasionally against their traditional interests. He freed ten Detroit Tiger farmhands in 1948 because of signing-irregularities. In 1947 he fined Leslie O'Connor, who was serving briefly as vice-president of the White Sox, for signing a prospect who was still in high school. Chandler also was concerned that the new players' pensions be administered fairly. Many of the owners were quite willing to put the pension on the back burner, now that the Guild threat had abated.

Although Chandler knew by the end of 1950 he would be a lame-duck commissioner, his term of office was not slated to end until July 1952. He remained through the first portion of the 1951 season. Some owners were embarrassed by Chandler's staying on, but most did not want an executive officer anyway.

In the late spring of 1951 Chandler's lawyer John Lord O'Brian made him aware of other lawsuits pending against baseball's monopoly. Though none was as dramatic as the Gardella case, O'Brian advised his client that he could be legally liable in case baseball lost in the courts. O'Brian warned that baseball might find Chandler a convenient scapegoat in case of legal troubles. He suggested Chandler should resign sooner rather than later. In mid-June 1951 Chandler announced that he would leave office on July 15, 1951. One of his last statements was an exercise in wishful thinking: "I always regarded baseball as our National Game that belongs to 150 million men, women, and children, not to sixteen special people who happen to own big league teams."

Rhetorical excesses would not be a trait of Chandler's successor, National League President Ford C. Frick. Frick was chosen after a long deadlock with Cincinnati Reds' President Warren Giles. Giles had surprising support among American League owners, probably because his administrative skills reminded them of their able executives from Ban Johnson to Johnson's former secretary, reigning American League president William Harridge.

On labor relations, there was little choice between Giles and Frick. Both agreed that the situation of submissive players was just fine. Giles ultimately withdrew from consideration to break the stalemate. He succeeded Frick as National League president. The rearrangement of the baseball family had been completed without the need to call on a political outsider.

Ford Frick was probably the ultimate expression of the gee-whiz sportswriter turned compliant baseball executive. He had been both a radio announcer and a sportswriter during the "Era of Wonderful Nonsense" after World War I. He had been Babe Ruth's ghostwriter, which accounted for Frick's insistence in 1961 that Roger Maris's sixty-one home run record be entered into the record book with an asterisk (because Maris had needed 162 games instead of the 154 games Ruth needed for sixty home runs in 1927).

Frick had been National League president since November 1934. He succeeded the late John Heydler after only nine months as public relations director of the senior league. Many owners had wanted to name Frick commissioner after Landis's death, but Larry MacPhail had brought in Chandler before many knew what was happening. After his 1951 appointment, Frick showed his gratitude immediately. He said, "I am the commissioner of the owners who elected me."

In his reign through 1965, Frick would skirt many controversial issues such as expansion and franchise shifting by calling them "league matters." The always-maverick Bill Veeck said Frick's autobiography should be called *Armageddon Is a League Matter*. When Frick did publish his autobiography in 1973, its title was an apt description of his awed outlook on baseball: *Games, Asterisks, and People: Memoirs of a Lucky Fan*.

The owners entered the 1950s confident and set in their ways. Yet the problems of the sport were mounting. The post-World War II attendance boom had ended. With the outbreak of the Korean War in June 1950, there was some fear that another world war could again reduce baseball business.

Hardest hit were the minor leagues, which were suffering drastic cutbacks. Each year from 1946 to 1949, minor league total attendance had set a new high. 1949 saw nearly 42 million total attendance and an all-time record of fifty-nine minor leagues participating in baseball. By 1951 the number of leagues had plunged to 50, and by 1953 it was down to 38. Attendance plummeted to 21 million.

Much of the problem could be laid at television's doorstep. More than 60 percent of major league games were televised in the vicinity of minor league teams, sharply cutting into attendance. Major league owners, trying to stem the tide, passed a rule that prohibited television into minor league areas on the day of a minor league game.

In 1951 baseball's officials were warned by Justice Department sources that the rule could be considered in restraint of broadcast trade. Gordon McLendon, a Liberty Broadcasting Company executive, was preparing a suit for $12 million, charging baseball with blocking his "Game of the Day" from major league cities. Other suits were feared, and the owners dropped their rule. Instead of trying to establish guidelines for proper subsidy of the minor leagues and for judicious exposure of the big league product to a wide television audience, the owners ran away from the threat of legal action while carrying the handsome sums of the television stations to the bank.

Three especially noteworthy cases still were pending against organized baseball, two of them brought by frustrated minor league pitchers. Jim Prendergast had appeared briefly for the Boston Braves in 1948, but then was farmed out to Syracuse of the International League. In 1950 he balked at a trade to Beaumont of the lower classification Texas League; Prendergast did not feel like relocating his wife and three children. George Toolson was a Yankee farmhand who refused to report to Binghamton in the Eastern League after he had been demoted from the International League Newark club. Both pitchers charged in their suits that the reserve clause and the farm system had kept them bound indefinitely to one club, denying them the chance to improve their livelihood.

The third case was brought by Jack Corbett, a minor league owner in El Paso, Texas, who had tried to sign former players in the Mexican League. Corbett discovered that as part of the 1949 settlement, which removed the "outlaw" stigma from the Mexican League, the American moguls had promised to respect the reserve clauses of players who had remained in the Mexican circuit. Corbett wanted $300,000 damages for being denied access to the player market.

The specter of baseball in the courts and the lingering bad taste of the Gardella case prompted some members of Congress to start looking into the baseball business. Brooklyn Democratic Congressman Emanuel Celler was an ardent baseball fan. He was well placed in Congress on the Judiciary Committee, chairman of the Sub-Committee on Monopoly Power. He had been sensitized by the Gardella case and was aware that eight antitrust cases still pended against organized baseball. In May 1951 Celler observed, "If baseball is illegal, then we must prosecute the owners or change the law." After many delays, he finally opened an investigation of baseball in late July 1951.

Celler announced at the start of his investigation:
> Organized baseball affords this sub-committee with almost a text-book example of what might happen to an industry which is governed by rules and regulations among its members rather than by the free play of competitive forces.

Armed with subpoena power, the Celler Committee pledged itself to decide whether the thirty-year-old antitrust exemption was still valid for baseball. It planned to consider legislation which would either specifically overturn that exemption or, as many baseball men hoped, expressly grant baseball immunity for its unique provisions like the reserve clause.

From the very first day of the hearings, with venerable Ty Cobb called as the first witness, it was evident that the Committee had no desire to upset baseball's applecart. Cobb had been trotted out during the tumult over Robert Murphy's American Baseball Guild in 1946 to insist that baseball unionization would be impossible to achieve. Cobb now told the legislators that baseball needed no outside interference. The reserve clause was necessary, he declared.

A long list of management pooh-bahs came before the Celler Committee to sing the praises of the national game and its wise organization. Very few players testified openly before the Committee because the memory of Murphy's defeat was still fresh. As a retired minor leaguer, Cy Block, who later became a prominent New York City insurance executive, told the Committee, "A ballplayer cannot afford to put himself in the limelight." Block hoped that baseball could be persuaded to adopt a system of irrevocable waivers so players did not have to lose valuable years stuck in an uninterested farm system.

The Celler Committee did make baseball officials put on the public record under oath their unchanging defenses of the status quo. Branch Rickey conceded that the reserve clause might be a "harmless illegality." He admitted that exclusive territorial rights for baseball clubs might also infringe on other businessmen's trade and commerce. If so, Rickey suggested he would be happy if the Committee decided to give baseball immunity.

Pacific Coast League attorney Leslie O'Connor repeated his statement that if anybody had ever asked his former boss, Commissioner Landis, for a contract without a reserve clause, "it would have been granted instantly." O'Connor's argument was purely hupothetical because nobody during Landis's reign had ever requested such a con-

175

tract. It was a rather unlikely conjecture; as if an admiral would tell a career naval man that he could become a civilian at any time.

O'Connor suggested to the legislators that certain of baseball's practices such as the assignability clause could use specific legal exemption. "We all know that a personal-service contract is not assignable at common law without the person's consent," he testified. Later in the 1950s, O'Connor gave evidence that he had inherited some of his former boss's concern for player opportunity when he told a reconvened Celler hearing in 1957 that he hoped baseball would never develop the kind of draft which professional football had introduced for amateur talent. O'Connor considered a draft of labor "un-American," but as the owners sailed along into the 1960s without fear of legal restraint, they would introduce such a draft in 1965.

Democratic Senator Edwin Carl Johnson of Colorado, the nonsalaried president of the Class A Western League, headquartered in Denver, was probably management's most insistent witness about the need for legalizing the reserve clause. He decried the "apathy" of baseball officials to the threat of legal tests of the standard contract. Speaking to Dan Daniel in *The Sporting News* in early May 1951, Johnson had warned of "the tremendous chances" baseball took if it allowed its contract to be ruled upon by judges. He suggested the different approach of protective legislation: "Baseball has a lot of friends in Congress. It has a lot of friends in the Department of Justice. I am confident we could work something out."

Some writers suspected Johnson harbored ambitions for the commissionership, a goal he did not come close to, although his son-in-law, Robert Howsam, became a highly successful baseball executive, a key architect of the Cincinnati Reds' 1970s' champions. Testifying before the Celler Committee in October 1951, Johnson really poured it on in defense of the system. "Baseball has adopted itself a code of ethics worthy of emulation by any God-fearing group," including the churches and Congress, he declared. He noted how fierce and honest the competition was on the field of his Class A Western League. By that strange logic which stressed the heroic confrontations on the playing field as a defense for collusive practices in the front office, Johnson deplored the notion that the antitrust laws might be "used to threaten the very existence of the great American game." He warned the legislators, "Chiselers, blackmailers and ambulance-chasing lawyers could be expected to take full advantage of the chaos which an adverse report by this committee would touch off."

The legislators were interested in Johnson's opinions on the survival of minor leagues in an age of expanding television and rising national rather than local identifications. Johnson blasted the Liberty Broadcasting Network of Gordon McLendon for his "Game of the Day" radio coverage in Western League areas. Yet some of the very friends of baseball in the Justice Department Johnson had hoped would exempt baseball's questionable practices had urged the owners to drop any restrictions on television into minor league areas. Johnson would protest, but minor league officials were too much a part of baseball's closed family to threaten action against big league policy in any area. As one wit put it, "They were afraid to sue because they might win." As for Gordon McLendon, he accepted a $200,000 out-of-court settlement and the owners once more had finessed their way out of trouble.

National Association President George Trautman revealed the minor leagues' full acceptance of subordination before the big leagues. He told the Committee that outside interference in baseball's operations was not necessary.

If the minor leagues were totally beholden to their major counterparts, they had the consolation of total control over their players. Nearly forty years earlier Dave Fultz had fought for the right of minor leaguers to get five-day notice before their release. In the 1950s minor leaguers could be dropped without any notification. Trautman defended the practice, claiming it "inspires the player to hustle a little all the time."

Octogenarian Clark Griffith also appeared as a witness to give an apologia for his operations. Congressman Celler and Griffith had engaged in a little parrying before he testified. Celler had sent Griffith a small check for the players' pension fund. Griffith had the check returned with a note explaining that only players and owners could contribute to the benefit plan. Griffith offered Celler a season's pass, which the Congressman refused.

In the witness chair, Griffith gave a succinct explanation of the purpose of the reserve clause: "It is to give a man the right to hold what he had." He denied that he had joined an "outlaw" league when he became an American Leaguer in 1901 and actively recruited for Ban Johnson. His logic was that the American League had not raided the minor leagues, which was not entirely true. His real justification was that only 56 people had come to see him pitch in 1900 when the Chicago Nationals played in Cleveland. Although he had not suffered any penalty for leaving the National League, Griffith testified that he felt Danny Gardella's five-year suspension had been justified.

In 1950 Griffith had turned back a potential challenge to his thirty-year ownership of the Senators' franchise. Pennsylvanian John Jachym of the Kendall Oil Company had bought 30 percent of the Senators' stock and hoped to gain control of the franchise and pump energy and money into the chronic noncontender. "First in war, first in peace, and last in the American League," was the old saying about the Senators. It was not exactly true, but the Senators had been mired in the second division since their last pennant in 1933, except for two second-place finishes during the diluted conditions of World War II competition. Griffith excelled at wrapping up baseball in the flag; he had regularly invited U.S. Presidents to throw out the first ball at the season's openers, beginning with William Howard Taft in 1912, but he did not want to spend money on farm teams or on major league player salaries.

Nonetheless, Griffith was able to turn back Jachym's challenge and bought out the oil man's stock. After Griffith's death in 1955, his adopted son, Calvin Griffith, took control of the team and after the 1960 season moved it to Minnesota. To placate congressional critics, the American League voted Washington an expansion franchise, a guaranteed tail-ender, which itself was moved to Texas after the 1971 season.

If the players did not speak out during the 1951 Hearings, there was little that the Celler Committee critics could do to assist them. The fear of winding up in Peoria was still very great. The failure of Murphy's Guild had reinforced in many players a fatalism that the system could never be changed. In 1948 the owners capitalized on the players' passivity by enlisting the first league player representatives of 1946, Johnny Murphy (later a New York Mets general manager) and Dixie Walker, to testify before a Massachusetts legislative committee about the necessity of the reserve clause. Not surprisingly, when the time came for player testimony before the Celler Committee, even the most outspoken athletes muted their criticism.

Fred Hutchinson, an outstanding Tigers pitcher and the American League player representative, was a good case in point. A fierce competitor and a man of insistent principle, Hutchinson and National League pension representative Marty Marion, the St. Louis Cardinals' renowned shortstop, had forced their way into an owners' meeting during the 1950 World Series to demand the right to consultation on the funding and the administration of the pension plan. In March 1951 Hutchinson had blasted the owners for firing Happy Chandler without giving a reason. He even suggested that the players might rehire Chandler as their own representative since he was known to be sympathetic to their interests in maintaining a good pension.

When Celler Committee investigators asked Hutchinson for his views on the pension, he would only say it was "a fine step in the right direction for major league baseball." He did hope that minor leaguers would receive higher pay and that the major league minimum, frozen at $5,000 since 1946, would be raised. But as far as the reserve clause was concerned, Hutchinson testified that most players were "well satisfied. There are a few that are disgruntled, but usually they are the players who would be disgruntled at any time."

Ned Garver, who had won twenty games for the lowly Browns in 1951 and who had received public sympathy, as had Walter Johnson, for the plight of being stuck on a poor team, offered one of the rare critical comments. He suggested that good players on teams stuck in the second division should be allowed to earn a fair salary. He suggested that the leagues should institute blind bidding on every player who had toiled for three consecutive years on a second division club. If the player did not receive from his original club at least the average of those bids, the league should either make up the difference or allow the player to become a free agent. Very roughly, Garver's idea was an anticipation of salary arbitration which the players won in 1973. It should be noted that Garver did not testify in person but sent his suggestion by mail from a barnstorming tour where he hoped to augment his $18,000 salary with an additional $1,200 if the weather cooperated.

Garver's constructive suggestion was isolated. More typical and perhaps the saddest example of the fear inbred in professional ballplayers was the abortive attempt of a minor leaguer's wife to inform Congressman Celler of organized baseball's duplicities. She wrote him that the official line that baseball was sport and not commerce was ludicrous: "If baseball is not a business, why does every team have a business manager?" She urged him to listen to the story of her husband, who like so many players was trapped in a farm system without chance for advancement in his chosen profession.

The very next day the minor league wife hastily wrote Celler again, imploring him to tear up her letter lest her husband become a "laughing stock" among his peers for publicizing his problems. She resigned herself to his finishing his career wherever fate took him. Undoubtedly, the distraught woman had never heard of John Montgomery Ward but how apt and unresolved was Ward's lament of 1887 about the ballplayer's condition: "He goes where he is sent, takes what is given him, and thanks the Lord for life."

The one achievement of the 1951 Celler hearings into organized baseball was the indirect pressure it placed on major league owners to invite other cities into their exclusive club, which had remained unchanged in membership since 1903. Put into the record of the hearings were embarrassing facts about the St. Louis Browns' inferior attendance—many minor league cities drew more fans—and the loans other American League owners gave to the Browns to keep the franchise afloat. Maverick owner Bill Veeck, who tried to revive the Browns after great success in Cleveland in the late 1940s, considered moving his club to Milwaukee or Los Angeles, but it was the Boston Braves who won the right to Milwaukee beginning with the 1953 season. The Browns finally left St. Louis for Baltimore in 1954, but the price of American League approval of the shift was Veeck's selling of the team to Baltimore interests. (His autobiography *Veeck—As In Wreck* tellingly recounts this story.)

If the solons did prod baseball to consider other areas of the country for big league franchises, they steered away from any action to bring baseball practices into the legal mainstream. *Sporting News* publisher and editor J. G. Taylor Spink had branded critics of the reserve system as "Communistic" and Celler himself was very sensitive. "I discovered I could match the wrath of any one single sportswriter against the wrath of Mr. Benjamin Fairless," whose United States Steel Corporation had earlier been investigated by Celler's Committee. The Committee's May 1952 report did not favor the adoption of legislation to exempt the reserve clause from litigation, as Senator Edwin Johnson had hoped, but the report clearly accepted management's traditional defense of the reserve when it stated, "Experience points to no feasible substitute to protect the integrity of the game or to guarantee a comparatively even competitive struggle."

The legislators further suggested that it was up to the courts, which had granted to baseball the antitrust exemption in the first place, to review its continued applicability. Thus continued the game of volleyball about jurisdiction over baseball which the Congress and the courts would play until this very day, and which organized baseball's lawyers cleverly capitalized upon, suggesting to each body that the other had the proper authority.

Needless to say, the players remained powerless through these maneuverings and the disinclination of the Celler Committee to aid them. As the 1950s began, it soon became a time of hot war in Korea and cold war at home with a domestic paranoia fed by the sensational charges of Senator Joseph McCarthy about Communist treason in the government. Despite this unfavorable climate, at the end of 1953 the roots for the most important development in the history of baseball's labor relations would be planted in the formation of the Major League Baseball Players Association, the first players' interest group since the decimated Players Fraternity before World War I. Although 1953 would also see the courts uphold the 1922 Holmes decision, progressive forces had slowly been set in motion.

12

The Birth of the Major League Baseball Players Association

"Whenever we tried to discuss anything with the owners, they were always stuffing lunch into us."
—Bob Feller, remembering the early 1950s in testimony before the Celler Committee, June 1957.

In September 1949 ten-year-veteran major league pitcher Ernie "Tiny" Bonham died at age 36. There was not enough money in the pension program to fund his widow. Faced with a crisis, Commissioner Chandler hastily sold the TV-radio rights for the World Series and the All-Star Game to the Gillette Safety Razor Company for $1 million a year over the next six years.

Chandler did not get a good price. The Mutual Broadcasting System, to whom Gillette had given broadcast rights, sold its package to NBC the next year for $4 million per year. Since the money was designed for the pension fund, the players understandably were concerned about the maneuvers.

By the middle of 1953 the players still had not received an accounting on the pension. With no organization of the players in existence, the magnates felt they could avoid the players' questions. Commissioner Frick brushed them aside by insisting that he was taking care of the fund for the good of all concerned.

During the All-Star Game of 1953, the new league player representatives, Allie Reynolds of the Yankees and Ralph Kiner of the Cubs, took stock of the situation. Both were star players. Reynolds was an outstanding starting pitcher who also performed key relief chores for the champion Yankees. Kiner had been a premier home run hitter for the cellar-dwelling Pittsburgh Pirates. Early in the 1953 season he was traded to the Cubs. Branch Rickey, in charge of the Pirates since 1950, had not wanted to pay Kiner what a slugger of his prowess deserved because, in Rickey's logic, "We could have finished last without you."

Kiner and Reynolds were moderate and cautious. They requested permission to raise some questions before the owners' meeting at the All-Star Game. They wanted the minimum salary raised, they wanted accountability on the pension, and they wanted ballplayers earning less than $10,000 a year to have the opportunity to play Latin American baseball during the winter.

Although the owners listened to the players, Frederic Lieb reported the establishment's skepticism in *The Sporting News*: "With baseball going through a trying period, and with attendance declining in most cities, this is a poor time for the players to request new concessions." Lieb added, without a trace of irony or sarcasm, "Despite their failure to gain any definite concessions, they did get a luncheon from the magnates."

Kiner and Reynolds decided that they had done all they could by themselves to establish some workable relations with the owners. Upon consultation with the team player representatives, they went out in August 1953 to hire a lawyer to serve as liaison between the players and the owners. They selected a New York lawyer, Jonas Norman Lewis. Lewis and his associate, James P. Durante, had written a series of articles on "Baseball Law" for the *New York Law Journal* in 1945.

Lewis had been with a law firm which represented the New York Giants for years. He also served as the lawyer for the Harry Stevens concessionaires, which operated a lucrative business at ball parks and racetracks around the country. In an article penned for the *Labor Law Journal* in April 1954, Lewis criticized picketing as an unfair labor practice, and described himself as "a lawyer primarily interested in labor cases from management's side."

Lewis's 1945 articles had fully supported the reserve system and the antitrust exemption granted by the "beloved Oliver Wendell Holmes, a former ballplayer." Lewis accepted the thesis that the ballplayer should be happy to earn good money playing baseball when otherwise he would likely be working in a factory. He said the average salary of $5,000 a year in 1945 placed the player in an "enviable position" compared to workers of comparable age.

184

After decades of turning back, indeed crushing, all independent organizations of the ballplayers, the owners responded to the hiring of Lewis as if he were young Harry Taylor or Robert Murphy revisited. Yankee General Manager George Weiss greeted the news with disbelief. "It certainly does not sound like something Allie Reynolds would do," the Yankee boss said.

Boston owner Tom Yawkey, one of the more personally generous of the magnates, decried the hiring of an "outsider." He suggested the names of a couple of ballplayers, including his own Dominic DiMaggio, whom the players should have selected as their representative. Yawkey resented the inference that the players thought Ford Frick did not represent them, though Frick had bluntly said he was "the commissioner of the owners." National League president Warren Giles stated best the paternalistic monopoly's viewpoint when he declared:

> The players can do more for themselves than any outside representative, no matter how able that outsider may be. By delegating someone else to negotiate for them, the players are surrendering a privilege that has been very valuable to them.

Ralph Kiner, well aware of baseball's traditional hostility toward outside organizers, conceded that the hiring of a lawyer was a "drastic step." Kiner had been a rookie on the 1946 Pirates and had seen firsthand the rise and decimation of Murphy's Guild. He tried to put a modest face on the players' action, explaining, "Ballplayers are the worst businessmen in the land and they feel they are entitled to representation." Dom DiMaggio was more outspoken. He defended the hiring of a lawyer because of the owners' continued "evasion" of the questions about the pension.

The executive council of the owners was due for a meeting in late August 1953. J. Norman Lewis requested an invitation so he could present the players' grievances about the pension and the need for a rise in a minimum salary to $8,000 to account for cost-of-living increases since 1946. Commissioner Frick responded that Lewis was not welcome at the meeting. The owners would entertain the league representatives; their lawyer could wait in the hall. Reynolds and Kiner did not take kindly to Frick's hostility, but they attended the meeting and reported to Lewis.

Shortly thereafter, Lewis made public the demands of the players. He told the press that Frick had wanted him to keep silent on the issues;

Lewis felt it his duty to serve his clients by publicizing their reasonable demands. Although Lewis was very conservative in his attitude toward the business, he was a fighter for his clients. Walter O'Malley of the Dodgers had tried to talk him out of his new job, saying, "Norman, you're an owners' man." Once he was impressed by the sincerity and legitimacy of Reynolds and Kiner and their grievances, he became an ardent advocate; perhaps too abrasive, thought many owners.

No action came immediately. Baseball was waiting for the denouement of the Toolson case before the Supreme Court. Interestingly, Cubs' owner Philip K. Wrigley had averred earlier in 1953 that he expected baseball to lose the case and thought it would work out better for the game if the farm system controls were loosened up.

Wrigley, who occasionally would let slip out the word "monopoly" in describing the baseball business, was, of course, in a lonely minority in his opinion. Most of the owners hoped that the Holmes exemption would stand. Commissioner Frick refused public comment until the Court made its ruling. Congressman Celler, whose baseball investigation had expired with his committee's report of 1952, tried to pressure Frick to support an outside committee of eminent citizens that would try to propose an alternative to the perpetual reserve system and a fairer organization of major and minor league operations. *Sporting News* publisher J. G. Taylor Spink supported the idea, but Frick refused to consider it. He did not want to appear to succumb to outside pressure.

On November 9, 1953, Frick and the baseball monopoly rejoiced with the news of the Supreme Court's upholding the 1922 antitrust exemption. The *Sporting News* story was headlined, "Organized Baseball Wins the Big One, 7-2." The majority of the high Court had tersely decided that after thirty years of legislative inaction on the exemption, it was not the Court's place to change baseball practice; Congress must decide, said the justices. Not only did Toolson lose but so did a former Dodger farmhand Walter J. Kowalski, pressing a similar grievance (Jim Prendergast had dropped his case), and Jack Corbett; their complaints had been combined into one legal action against the monopoly.

Baseball's lawyers had succeeded once again in deflecting the issue back and forth from the courts to Congress. Washington sportswriter Shirley Povich supported the antitrust exemption, but he questioned the logic of the Supreme Court. The decision reminded him of Yankee pitcher Lefty Gomez's explanation of why, with the bases loaded, he had thrown a perfect bunt to second baseman Tony Lazzeri without a chance of making an out: "You have the reputation for being the smartest player on the team, so I threw it to you. I didn't know what to do with it."

Associate Justice Harold H. Burton did issue a 2,700-word dissent, concurred in by Justice Stanley T. Reed. Burton felt the Toolson case should stand trial because he could not believe that as vast a national business as organized baseball did not fall under interstate commerce statutes. Burton cited the 1952 Celler Report which, though it had recommended no legislation against baseball, had admitted, "Inherently, professional baseball is intercity, intersectional, and interstate." With three-quarters of the minor leagues extending beyond state lines, and of course the major leagues too, Burton asserted the importance of baseball's "compliance with standards of reasonableness comparable with those required by law of interstate trade or commerce."

In 1955 Burton's reasoning would be followed when the Court ruled that the International Boxing Club was a monopoly in restraint of trade for dominating the television fights with its contracted boxers. In 1957 the Court extended antitrust coverage to professional football. It ruled in behalf of a football player, William Radovich, who had refused to play for the National Football League which had drafted him. Later, he was blacklisted from a minor league team which had a working agreement with the NFL. Radovich's case was nearly identical to Danny Gardella's. The high Court conceded in 1957 that baseball's continued antitrust exemption was "unreasonable, illogical, and inconsistent."

Yet the shield remained, and it made the baseball owners more set in their ways. After the Toolson verdict, an anonymous Washington lawyer told *The Sporting News* presciently, "The temptation will be to follow the easy, complacent path."

Despite Toolson's lost case, players were intent on receiving satisfaction on the pension problem. In early December 1953 the owners' annual winter meeting was scheduled for Atlanta. They invited the players to send representatives. They pointedly reminded them not to bring their lawyer, J. Norman Lewis.

The players were miffed, and decided to hold their own meeting in Atlanta. Some players phoned ex-Commissioner Chandler for advice. He told them that hiring a lawyer for pension consultation was a good idea.

Lewis informed the press that the owners refused to budge on providing accountability on pension monies. "What business is it of the players? It is not their money," Lewis reported the owners' line. He disagreed. He declared that the players wanted a permanent pension program with monies provided by two-thirds of the television receipts from the World Series and the All-Star Game. The players wanted eligibility for the pension reduced from the six years established in 1946.

The players representatives paid their own way to Atlanta in early December 1953 and held a meeting separate from the owners. They voted to start a new organization, the Major League Baseball Players Association. J. Norman Lewis took out a charter for it in New York in the spring of 1954. Bob Feller, in the twilight of his great career, was elected the first president of the new association.

The owners' response to the players' defiance was bitter. Edgar Munzel, veteran Chicago sportswriter, wrote in *The Sporting News* that the squabble over the pension had left the magnates "ready to throw up their hands and junk the whole thing." Veteran executive Frank Lane, known as "Trader" for his willingness to swap players recklessly, warned that the players are "trying to shoot Santa Claus." Dixie Walker and Johnny Murphy, the retired player representatives of 1946, were called upon to tell the players, "There is no need for a lawyer."

The hand-wringing and the ritualistic poor-mouth cries of the owners subsided in early 1954. They agreed to meet with Lewis. A pension committee was established, headed by wealthy horse breeder John W. Galbreath, owner of the Pirates, and Cleveland general manager Hank Greenberg, one of the rare players who had made it into management. Galbreath and Greenberg met with J. Norman Lewis and they worked out a compromise on pension funding. Sixty percent of the national radio-TV revenues from the Series and the All-Star Game would henceforth go into the pension fund.

In May 1955 Lewis issued his first *Report to Major League Baseball Players*. In addition to the substantial gains on the pension, Lewis announced that the minimum salary had been increased to $6,000. He had wanted $7,200 as the base, which would be the equivalent of $5,000 in 1947, but the owners refused.

Lewis achieved some minor advances which revealed how laggard the industry had been toward its employees. He bargained the time down from ten to eight years, after which a major leaguer could earn free agency if assigned to the minor leagues. The player now would receive

188

his seasonal contract on January 15 instead of February 1, giving him a little more time to prepare for the year.

Lewis also announced in his report to the players that a joint study had started to devise "some possible formula which may be acceptable to the owners and which would provide that a player would get a percentage of the price received for his sale to another Major League club." The sale price issue was as old as the Players League rebellion, but the study proved fruitless as the owners were not about to concede such a privilege to their still loosely organized chattels.

Nothing in Lewis's 1955 report mentioned anything about the reserve clause. If extensive congressional hearings in 1951 had resulted in no recommendations for reform, the players on their own could hardly have expected to push for change. A 1956 scholarly study by economics professor Paul Gregory, *The Baseball Player*, summed up the mood of the age when it described the reserve clause as "a harmless and inevitable exploitation." Discontent among the players still seethed beneath the surface, but they knew too well the price paid if one was labeled a "clubhouse lawyer" or a "chronic malcontent."

Though Norman Lewis had achieved a breakthrough in establishing regular funding of the pension, the perennial problems of players' groups remained. There was still no permanent office or officer. Like David Fultz, J. Norman Lewis allowed the player representatives to meet in a room in his New York law office, but no sense of stability and permanence could be achieved that way. The age-old problem of losing communications during the off-season had not been solved either.

J. Norman Lewis had been promised a retainer of $15,000 a year if all the players contributed dues. But it had been so long since there was an independent organization that many skeptical ballplayers did not contribute. Lewis concerned himself more with his other clients, who included a TV entertainer who brought home $25,000 a week. It did not occur to him or others in this decade that ballplayers, too, were TV entertainers, deserving of high pay in an enormously profitable industry.

The ballplayers demonstrated their acceptance of the reserve clause and its restrictions in testimony before the reconvened Celler hearings in June 1957. The Radovich decision in February 1957 had prompted Congressman Celler to question some more witnesses. Ford Frick's surly opinion on Radovich, "I am not commenting on it and I don't think anyone else should either," was an indication to Celler that someone should inquire further. The Brooklyn legislator was also peeved that the Dodgers were likely to head for Los Angeles after the 1957 season.

Once again, the hearings reached no conclusion. The players were cautious again on speaking out. Even Massachusetts' Congressman Torbert MacDonald's idea for a definite, renewable four-year reserve was not enthusiastically greeted by the players. When Bob Feller boldly called for a five-year limitation on the reserve clause, he experienced immediate retaliation. He was locked out from a clinic he was scheduled to hold in Los Angeles' Wrigley Field.

In 1958 Congressman Celler introduced a bill that would bring all professional sports under antitrust laws except where "reasonably necessary" to preserve "competitive practices." The bill got nowhere as few legislators wanted to grapple with the thorny question of whether a reserve clause was "reasonably necessary."

More in keeping with the age was a statement that a group of sports-loving congressmen entered into a 1958 House Judiciary Committee report on antitrust applicability to professional athletics. Faced with the contradiction in legal policy toward baseball and football and boxing, these solons maintained:

> Constant intervention in [sports] affairs by paternalistic do-gooders will lead to nothing but trouble for all concerned. In our view the policy of decisions of sports should be made by people in sports— the owners and players alike. They should not be made by men in black robes who may never have been to a ball park.

With little fear of either judicial or legislative restriction, the major league owners had turned the middle 1950s into a bonanza of franchise-shifting, with the culmination coming after 1957 when the historic New York teams, the Giants and Dodgers, were whisked away to San Francisco and Los Angeles. One anonymous baseball official talked brazenly about a forthcoming age of "roving franchises" that would move every few years in search of a bigger buck.

The odds were against the Players Association in such a climate. Norman Lewis sensed that the players had legitimate grievances, but he doubted their commitment as measured by their delinquent paying of dues. He did broach the radical idea in late 1958 that the owners contribute 20 percent of their revenues to player salaries, which prompted Tom Yawkey to comment that he would sell his Red Sox before such a state of affairs arose.

190

The players were surprised at Lewis' proposal, an indication of the lack of close communication within the Association. In February 1959 the player representatives decided to oust him, giving no clear reason except that they wished he would devote more time to them. He had refused to tour the spring training camps each year because of the time involved. A month earlier, Lewis had fallen into further disfavor when his associate, James P. Durante, undertook an ill-advised effort to organize the International League players in behalf of a pension; a threatened strike quickly fizzled.

As Lewis's successor the players chose Robert C. Cannon, the son of former Wisconsin Congressman Raymond J. Cannon, who had unsuccessfully tried to form a players union in 1920. The elder Cannon had represented Shoeless Joe Jackson in his back-salary case, and had tried without success to get the attorney general to investigate baseball during the 1930s.

Judge Cannon lacked his father's maverick qualities. He was a great baseball fan who dreamed of replacing Ford Frick as commissioner when the latter's retirement was due in the mid-1960s. His job as players' counsel was simply to advise them in matters of "baseball law." Cannon felt ceremonies such as having each owner sit with one player at a meeting would advance labor relations.

Early in the 1960s the players' minimum salary crawled to $7,000, yet other grievances piled up. The expansion of each major league to ten teams by 1962 had not brought increased pension benefits. The change of the schedule to 162 games, breaking with the tradition of 154 games in effect since 1905, had brought increased travel without significantly improved salaries. The growth of national television weekly broadcasts had brought increased money into the owners' coffers, as had the fee for expansion teams to join the exclusive leagues, but neither of these new sources of revenue was being shared with the players. A sense was growing that the players were not getting a rightful share of the industry's profits. Meanwhile, in 1965, the owners adopted an amateur free-agent draft, which ended baseball's long tradition of competitive scouting. It limited a recruit to one team to bargain with, and further extended the tentacles of the baseball monopoly.

Some of the players who had founded the Association in 1953 decided to assert themselves. A search began for a permanent director who would end the frustrations of the past. There was only $5,400 in the

Association treasury, barely half of what David Fultz's Fraternity had raised a half-century earlier. A beat-up old file cabinet was the only property in the Association's name. Yet the major league baseball players stood on the threshold of dramatic, even unimagined, gains.

(left) Curt Flood in his prime with the St. Louis Cardinals of the 1960s *(National Baseball Hall of Fame Library, Cooperstown, New York)*

(below) Bowie Kuhn, Fifth Commissioner of Baseball (1969-1984). Kuhn won the legal battle of *Flood v. Kuhn*, but ultimately lost the war when the perpetual reserve system crumbled in 1976 *(National Baseball Hall of Fame Library, Cooperstown, New York)*

Andy Messersmith as a Los Angeles Dodger shortly before he brought his historic grievance *(National Baseball Hall of Fame Library, Cooperstown, New York)*

Dave McNally as a Baltimore Oriole, years before his grievance *(National Baseball Hall of Fame Library, Cooperstown, New York)*

Baseball's sixth commissioner Peter Ueberroth (October 1984-March 1989); will be best remembered for bringing modern marketing to baseball and orchestrating the disastrous collusion against free agents *(Office of Commissioner of Baseball)*

A. Bartlett Giamatti, baseball's seventh commissioner, who made his presence felt in only four months on the job *(Roy Gumpel, courtesy Office of Commissioner of Baseball)*

Francis T. "Fay" Vincent, Jr., baseball's eighth commissioner (April 1989-) *(Office of Commissioner of Baseball)*

Part VI

*The Coming-of-Age
of the Major League
Baseball Players Association*

13

The Arrival of Marvin Miller

*"The essential dignity of equals sitting down
together just can't be overemphasized."
—Marvin Miller, shortly after taking office as the
first Executive Director of the Major League
Baseball Players Association.*

It was the fall of 1965 and Robin Roberts was worried. His anxieties had nothing to do with the coming end of his great pitching career. He would leave the major leagues in 1966 with 286 victories, mostly with the noncontending Philadelphia Phillies, and in 1976 he would be elected to the Baseball Hall of Fame.

Roberts's concern in 1965 centered on the drift in the affairs of the Major League Baseball Players Association. He had been a founding member at the December 1953 Atlanta meeting, and later in the 1950s, he had been elected the National League's player representative. But he realized that without a permanent office and a full-time director, the players' interests would never be adequately served. In 1962 Roberts had even invited J. Norman Lewis back to serve the association, but the lawyer no longer wanted to be bothered.

Phillies' pitcher Jim Bunning shared Roberts's concern. Another outstanding moundsman who would amass 224 victories in his career (and become one of very few pitchers to win a hundred games in each major league), Bunning had been active for many years in the players' group. He had been the American League player pension representative in the late 1950s during his years with the Detroit Tigers for whom in 1958 he had pitched a no-hitter. In 1959 Bunning had supported the addition of a second All-Star Game because it would generate extra money for the pension fund. When the owners agreed in 1962 to devote 95 percent instead of 60 percent of All-Star gate and television revenues to the fund, the second game was dropped by mutual agreement of the owners and the players.

In 1964 Bunning had pitched the first perfect game by a National Leaguer in the twentieth century and joined Cy Young and Tom Hughes as the only hurlers in baseball history to throw no-hitters in each major league. In the glow of his fame, he authored an autobiography in 1965, *The Story of Jim Bunning*, in which he articulated the rising business sense of the modern ballplayer. "We're an entertainment providing relaxation for people," declared the pitcher. *Sporting News* publisher J.G. Taylor Spink had expressed a traditional view when he called the players "symbols" before the Celler Committee in 1951, but the modern player was beginning to understand that he was in fact an entertainer in an extremely profitable industry who was consistently being short-changed. Bunning (who since his retirement in 1971 has become a prominent player agent and a state senator in Kentucky) and Roberts (since 1977 coaching baseball at the University of South Florida in Tampa) were determined to find an individual who shared this evaluation, would serve them permanently, and would not be a spokesman for the owners.

The star players, along with Bob Friend, another ace pitcher with the Pirates, and Harvey Kuenn of the Giants, a former American League batting champion, set up a search committee. Roberts, who lived in the Philadelphia area in the off-season, phoned George William Taylor, a Wharton School of Finance professor, to ask for some recommendations. Taylor had never met Roberts, but he recognized his famous name. One of his first suggestions was a man named Marvin Julian Miller, a high official since the early 1950s of the United Steelworkers of America, a union based in Pittsburgh.

Taylor had served with Miller on the War Labor Board in the 1940s. In the early 1960s he had worked with Miller again as one of the public representatives on an unusual tripartite panel which established, in 1963, an unprecedented profit-sharing plan for the workers of the Kaiser Steel Company. Four years earlier, Kaiser had been wracked by a bitter 116-day strike. Miller had impressed Taylor with his mediating skills, which he had honed in Washington as a member of the federal conciliation service in the late 1940s. His experience in the area of pensions also suggested him as a person the players should definitely seek out.

For years the owners had drummed into their chattels a fear, "Beware the labor boss!" When the Roberts committee first interviewed Marvin Miller, they were impressed by a soft-spoken, well-groomed man who did not look the part of the caricatured labor dictator. He did not smoke a big cigar nor did he sprinkle his speech with "dese" and "dem" and "dose," although he was born in Brooklyn and educated primarily in New York.

Yet Miller had an iron belief in the principles of unionism. His father had been a worker in the New York City garment industry and a strong supporter of his union. The elder Miller had, in Brooklyn, rooted for the Giants, and may have transmitted to his son a legacy of courage against great odds. Marvin's ability to lead an active life—including vigorous tennis despite a slight deformity in his right arm—revealed the kind of determination at the core of his character.

Though the players were favorably impressed by Miller, the committee's first choice for the permanent directorship was Judge Cannon. Fear of rousing the owners' hostility was still ingrained.

A snag developed when Cannon hedged on taking the job. He did not want to set up an office in New York, which the Association had suggested. The players compromised and offered him an office and the $50,000-job in Chicago. Cannon again turned them down, perhaps miffed that he had lost out on the job he really wanted—Commissioner of Baseball.

The committee turned to its second choice, Marvin Miller. Miller accepted the offer, contingent on approval from the full membership of the Association. He consented to tour the training camps in 1966 to meet his constituency. J. Norman Lewis had never been willing to take the time to meet the players when they were gathered together closely.

Not surprisingly, J. Norman Lewis, Judge Cannon, and Bob Feller, the original Association president, all warned the players about choosing Miller. None of the three had been willing to serve the athletes on a full-time basis, however, which made their cautionary words less credible.

Marvin Miller arrived in Florida during the sensational holdout of Los Angeles Dodger pitchers Don Drysdale and Sandy Koufax. Not since Ty Cobb had held out with some teammates before World War I had players banded together collectively for more salary. Koufax and Drysdale were asking for $1 million spread over three years. They had even taken the audacious step of hiring a Hollywood agent, J. William Hayes, to represent them.

Owner Walter O'Malley was outraged at this breach of etiquette in the Dodger family. "I never have discussed a player contract with an agent," he bellowed, "and I like to think I never will." Dodger General Manager Emil J. "Buzzy" Bavasi urged the "boys" to report to camp immediately. He told the press that if he granted their wishes, "I'd have to tear up thirty-eight other contracts" for the rest of the Dodger roster. Another Dodger official offered the advice, "As you go through life, beware of a guy who has an initial for his front name."

Drysdale and Koufax had exceptionally strong bargaining points. In 1963 and 1965, the Dodgers had won the World Series and the hurlers had accounted for six of the eight victories. The Dodgers were a light-hitting team relying heavily on pitching and the speed of Maury Wills. Without Drysdale and Koufax they would undoubtedly fall from contention.

The pitchers had been irked over the years at how management played them off in negotiations, telling each one that he would get substantial raises in alternate years. They decided that if they held out together, management would have to pay them what they were worth.

They were armed with statistics about how their pitching starts had attracted fans in far greater numbers than the average attendance. They cited a California law, designed to keep Hollywood studios from indefinite claim to their actors, which prohibited any personal service contract from extending for more than seven years. As Koufax wrote in his autobiography after he retired at the end of 1966, "The goal was to convince them that they would have to approach us not as indentured servants but as coequal parties to a contract, with as much dignity and bargaining power as themselves."

Agent Hayes announced that the pair would soon star in a made-for-television movie. The players, using the one option they had under the reserve system, "retired" and waited to see management's response. In late March, the holdout ended when the Dodgers agreed to meet with them and increase sizably the salary offer. Neither player received a multiyear contract, but Koufax got $130,000 for 1966 and Drysdale $115,000.

The Arrival of Marvin Miller

As the Drysdale-Koufax holdout drew the headlines, Marvin Miller began his tour of the spring training camps in Florida and Arizona. He faced with his characteristic calm the predictable barrage of warnings about the "labor boss" who would in the words of a *Sporting News* editorial turn baseball teams into "faceless organizations." The influential weekly insisted, "Ballplayers are members of teams, but they win recognition as individuals."

The time had come, however, for the players to opt for labor organization; nothing else had worked previously. Miller received a resounding vote of approval, 489-136, a margin even more impressive when considering that the bulk of the 136 nay votes came from trainers, coaches, and managers who were eligible to vote and some of whom had tried to disrupt Miller's earliest meetings. (As late as spring training 1973, Leo Durocher, then Houston Astros' manager, ordered his coaches to hit fungoes into the outfield where Miller was trying to meet with the players.)

Shortly after the 1966 season began, Miller established an office on Park Avenue in New York City for the Major League Baseball Players Association, the first permanent address for a players organization in baseball history.

The business Miller entered in 1966 was stagnating. Professional football seemingly had become the nation's favorite sport as baseball attendance remained static. Twenty-one million fans attended major league games in 1948; in 1965, despite franchise expansion and population growth, the attendance in the majors had barely increased by one million.

When Ford Frick retired in 1965, the owners had selected an obscure air force general, William D. Eckert, to become baseball's fourth commissioner. New York sportswriter Larry Fox quipped, "They've done it. They've chosen the Unknown Soldier." John Underwood observed in *Sports Illustrated* that Eckert's moods had been known to run from "stoicism to constraint."

The new commissioner did not begin impressively. He was well into his acceptance speech before he realized he was delivering a talk prepared for aircraft industry executives. Eckert would be cut from the same passive mold as Frick. Unlike Landis, who treated his role as the guardian of the game's integrity and stability seriously, Eckert saw his job as ceremonial. He refused to get involved in the controversial move of the Braves from Milwaukee to Atlanta. He said, "I think that in this great democracy we live in, if a man wants to take his property somewhere else and can do it legally, then I could not stop him."

After a lame duck year in Wisconsin, the Braves moved to Atlanta in 1966 because the new owners coveted the Southeastern area television market. So much for the Wisconsin fans who had turned the Milwaukee Braves into an exciting franchise in the 1950s. A Wisconsin state court refused to enjoin the Braves' departure, accepting baseball's lawyers' contention that state antitrust laws did not apply to the baseball business. Federal antitrust laws held, claimed baseball, knowing well that the antitrust exemption of 1922 remained. A Wisconsin lawyer was particularly frustrated by one of the National League attorneys, Bowie Kent Kuhn. "I don't get answers. I get platitudes," he moaned.

Marvin Miller quickly discovered how widely "baseball law" differed from real law. He studied the executive director's contract drawn up for him by Judge Cannon. He saw there a clause that stated he could be fired for moral turpitude. Cannon told Miller, "You can always prove you're innocent." A shocked Miller replied, "Prove I'm innocent? Judge, have you ever heard of the Constitution of the United States?" The clause was stricken, Miller recalled in a March 1974 interview with Robert H. Boyle of *Sports Illustrated.*

The funding of Miller's office then became a thorny point of controversy. During the early 1960s, when serving as an unofficial adviser to the players, Judge Cannon had received a stipend from the commissioner's office. This practice was a violation of both the Taft-Hartley and the Landrum-Griffin Acts, which forbade employers to contribute to the funding of unions. In March 1966, expecting that Judge Cannon would represent the players officially, the owners voted to establish a salary for the Players Association director. They planned to devote 35 percent of All-Star Game proceeds—95 percent of which was already going to the players' pension fund—to fund the Association office.

Faced with Marvin Miller as their unexpected adversary, the owners hedged on their commitment. They professed a desire to avoid "diluting the pension fund," and noted the hitherto blithely ignored fact that they could not legally fund a labor organization.

Miller suggested a way out of the impasse that was finally approved at the December 1966 winter meetings. The owners would guarantee the pension without the players contributing the $2-a-day or $344-a-year that had been the prior practice. Miller would have the right to a voluntary dues check-off to fund his office to the amount of $344 a year per player. The owners evidently thought that the players would not fund Miller's office once their pension was guaranteed. They expected him to remain underfinanced and ineffective like previous players' leaders. But with the exception of one aging ballplayer, the Association reported full membership and a soundly financed office by the end of 1966.

Another important agreement was reached in December 1966. The players agreed to scrap the 60-40 division of All-Star Game and World Series radio-television revenues in exchange for a lump sum of $4.2 million annually. The figure was computed with the prior funding formula taken into consideration, but the Association expressed a preference for a lump sum because it suspected that the owners were not accurately applying the 60 percent of the television revenues from the World Series and All-Star Game to the pension fund. Moreover, none of the television "Game of the Week" revenue went to the players. Since the early 1960s, owners such as the calculating Walter O'Malley had been seeking ways of diluting the player TV revenue, so in late 1966 Miller advised the acceptance of a lump sum.

By 1969 Miller estimated that the pension fund lump sum contributions had surpassed the original 60-40 breakdown, but many retired players were doubtful. Allie Reynolds, represented by J. Norman Lewis, went as far as suing the Players Association for the return to the old method, but the case never reached trial. A summary judgment was granted to the Players Association against the complaint because there was nothing in the original percentage agreement which indicated a perpetual 60-40 split.

In less than a year upon taking office, Marvin Miller had established himself as a formidable leader. He was not a lawyer. but his strong advocate's skill made many suspect that he was. He probably did not mind the misconception because it was not lost on him that the baseball owners had a historic fear of legal entanglements. As the counsel to the Association, Miller hired Richard M. Moss, a Harvard Law School graduate and a former colleague from the Steelworkers Union.

The ballplayers now had a permanent office; they no longer would be inconvenienced by the lack of communication during the off-season.

They had a leader in Miller who was impervious to the barbs of management and the sporting press. There was no patronage the owners could offer him such as the league and club presidencies which David Fultz and John Montgomery Ward had accepted in their later years. Miller's dedication was to the players alone and he vowed to make their relationship with management "dignified and mutually respectful."

He took aim at the standard baseball contract, which he compared in its one-sidedness to the tenant's lease in a typical apartment building: The only right a party had was to play ball or to pay rent. He assured the players that if they stuck together behind a strong Association, great gains would be won. He proclaimed, "I never before have seen a group of people who are so irreplaceable in relation to their work."

He devoted himself to the players' cause as no one had ever done before. He did not lose patience with them like J. Norman Lewis or deliver moral lectures like David Fultz. The experienced unionist considered ballplayers as talented workers in a particularly unique form of entertainment industry—major league baseball.

Miller was not strident or ideological, which appealed to an Association membership largely apolitical or politically conservative. He did not consider it important that the players traditionally did not like the term "union" to describe their organization. Under the law, the Players Association was chartered as a labor group. Miller convinced the players that if they stuck together on the collective bargaining of a minimum salary and basic working conditions, the baseball industry was healthy enough to provide them all—individually—with substantial economic gains. Miller was forceful, even eloquent, in educating the players about their hidden strengths. He once said, "The player should be paid as a man, not for a job."

The Topps Chewing Gum Company was one of the first organizations to discover the new pride and strength of the Players Association. For years, Topps had been making millions of dollars selling the famed bubble gum cards of the players while paying them minimally. Topps would sign up the minor leaguers for $5 a year and pay major leaguers only a $125 lump sum with no royalties. Miller organized a boycott of the players from signing releases to Topps. In early 1968 Topps conceded the new muscle of the players and negotiated a lucrative contract with the Association. It provided royalties of several million dollars to the players with increments for expanded sales.

In February 1968 a milestone in baseball's labor relations was

202

reached: the announcement of the first Basic Agreement. In 1967 the owners had hired John J. Gaherin, the president of the New York City Newspaper Publishers Association and an experienced industrial relations man, to head a new group, the Major League Baseball Player Relations Committee. The two league presidents, three owners from each circuit, and Gaherin comprised the new group, which would serve as major league baseball's first formal negotiating link with the players. In naming Gaherin to represent them opposite Miller, the owners seemed to be facing modern realities of give-and-take in industry. No longer could organized baseball think that labor relations might be smoothed over with minor concessions on "baseball law."

The creation of a Basic Agreement was a big event in the history of baseball's labor relations. The players were granted, for the first time, an input into the standard contract by which they had been governed for nearly a century. An "Important Note" was attached to the front of the Major League Rules which announced that in any conflict between the old rules and the Basic Agreement, the latter document would take precedence. A previous "Important Note" had been owner-inspired: the red warning on the top of contracts between 1920 and 1946 which promised penalties to parties involved in nonreserve clause contracts.

The 1968 Agreement also established a formal grievance procedure for the players. Although the ultimate arbiter remained the employee of the owners, the commissioner, a step had been taken toward lifting the heavy cloud of fear from the player. The players also received a substantial increase in the minimum salary to $10,000; it had only moved from $5,000 to $7,000 in the two decades before Marvin Miller's arrival.

The Agreement provided for a joint labor-management study of the reserve clause. Miller's thorough understanding of the economics of monopoly emboldened the players to oppose the reserve system more forcefully. He reminded them how their bargaining power was depressed because they faced only one buyer and thus received only one market price; the technical word for this buyers' monopoly was monopsony.

The owners were not about to loosen up the reserve system. They had conceded more rights in the first Basic Agreement than in all the previous decades of the sport. They had agreed to "study" the reserve clause, thinking the dissent would subside once the grieving players retired or were sold. They did not use the word "core" to describe their perpetual system until the last-ditch defense in the Messersmith case. Management simply assumed its monopolistic control would last forever. They were unprepared for the kind of sustained professional bargaining at which Marvin Miller excelled.

Shortly before 1969 spring training was due to start, a crisis in baseball's labor relations erupted. The owners were balking at the Association's proposal for increased health care, life insurance, and pension benefits, including lowering the eligibility requirement to major leaguers with four years' service. Management was enraged that the players had dared to turn down their "final" offer. The adamant players responded by refusing to sign their contracts for the upcoming season, a tactic as old as the century in baseball's labor disputes. A delay in spring training loomed as a distinct possibility.

To the rescue rode one of the National League's lawyers, Bowie Kent Kuhn, a descendant of the famed Western hero Jim Bowie. Kuhn counseled calm and compromise to the owners, and the crisis was averted. The players received what they wanted and peace was restored.

Kuhn was rewarded with the position of interim commissioner, the job having been vacated when General Eckert was fired by the owners in December 1968. Baseball's general stagnation—epitomized by a punchless 1-0 All-star Game at the new Houston Astrodome in 1967 and Carl Yastrzemski's anemic .301 to win the American League batting championship in 1968—amid football's continuing surge had not been halted by this silent, reluctant leader.

The appointment of Kuhn, a dignified lawyer instead of an unknown soldier, was widely hailed. By the middle of 1969 he had been voted a full eight-year term by the owners. Knowledgeable Roger Angell in *The New Yorker* expressed the hope, "He may be the best thing that has happened to baseball since the catcher's mitt."

In 1969 baseball also embarked on its most dramatic structure change of the twentieth century. Each league expanded to twelve teams and then split into two six-team divisions. The division winners were to meet in a five-game postseason Championship Series for the right to enter the World Series.

The playoff system proved lucrative to baseball because television was willing to pay postseason prices for the right to broadcast the contests. But the owners had little time to celebrate. Before 1969 ended, baseball's refusal to liberalize its autocratic labor relations would send the sport back to the courts. The creation of the Players Relations Committee had not eased baseball management's enduring hostility to player organizations. The same problem persisted: the humane owners could or would not do anything to control the abuses of their more intractable partners.

It was Curt Flood of the St. Louis Cardinals who forced the issue. He filed a suit in the same New York federal court where Danny Gardella had initiated his litigation nearly a quarter century earlier. Flood protested the perpetual reserve clause which would force him either to accept a trade to Philadelphia or retire from the game. Although ultimately he would lose in the Supreme Court, his daring step accelerated the movement which, by the mid-1970s, would end the historic reserve restrictions.

14

Curt Flood and the End to
the Perpetual Reserve Clause

"After twelve years of being in the major leagues, I
do not feel I am a piece of property to be bought
and sold irrespective of my wishes."
—*Curt Flood, letter to Commissioner Bowie*
Kuhn, December 24, 1969: in Flood's
autobiography, The Way It Is *(New York: 1971).*

"Most lawyers are paid to get people out of
trouble. Our lawyers are paid to get us into
trouble."
—*Calvin Griffith, July 1976, shortly before the*
announcement of the Basic Agreement which
ended the perpetual reserve clause.

In 1967 and 1968 the baseball world toasted the St. Louis Cardinals.
They won the World Series in 1967 and repeated as National League
champions in 1968 before losing the World Series in seven games to the
Detroit Tigers.

Co-captain of the St. Louis champions was its lithe, compact center
fielder, Curt Flood. Flood graduated from the same McClymonds High
School in Oakland, California, which produced such baseball stars as
Frank Robinson, Vada Pinson, and Tommy Harper, and basketball
great Bill Russell. In 1968 *Sports Illustrated* hailed Flood in a cover story
as "Baseball's Best Centerfielder."

1969 would prove a troublesome year for the Cardinals. Even before
the season started, owner August "Gussie" Busch, baron of the beer
fortune, was disgruntled over the players' continuing protests about the
pension. Busch paid the greatest salaries in the National League as

befitting his two-time pennant winners. Albert Spalding had said, "Championship players deserve championship salaries." Spalding doubtlessly would have been upset like Busch if he believed the players were not properly submissive to the wisdom of management.

Busch tore into his players at an unusual spring training meeting in 1969. He lumped the rebellion of the Players Association with the general spirit of protest erupting in American society in the 1960s. He urged his players to remember, "It takes hundreds of people, working every day, to make it possible for eighteen men to play a game of baseball that lasts for about two hours." He asserted that the players took few risks and could qualify for a pension which would make most Americans envious. He added sarcastically, "I am not going to talk about such corny things as 'hustle.' That's supposed to be old-fashioned." Busch sounded like Joe Vila, a spokesman for the old order waging ideological war on the players.

If Busch's speech had constructive purposes instead of serving as a mere outlet for his rage, it did not work. The Cardinals slumped to fourth in 1969. Shortly after the season ended, Flood was informed by phone by a low-level Cardinals' official that he had been traded to Philadelphia. In this major transaction, slugger Richie Allen would be coming to the Cardinals.

Flood balked. He felt that after twelve years in the big leagues, he deserved something more dignified than an impersonal phone call and a little card in the mail which told him he had been traded. He wanted to make his own deal.

Flood did not want to play in Philadelphia with its reputation of hostility to black people. The black power movement had asserted itself in the 1960s. While Flood was not politically active, he was sympathetic to the goals of the activists. In March 1969 Flood had been distressed when his younger brother Carl, a more gifted athlete than Curt, had been arrested for larceny. A combination of unhappy events left Flood aggrieved and angry.

As he recounted in his fascinating autobiography, *The Way It Is*, he turned to Marvin Miller for advice. Miller had always been repulsed by the indignities of the reserve clause which left the player with the option of retiring or reporting. A realist, Miller knew that to condemn an injustice was not to remove it. He sympathized with Flood's dilemma, but advised him to rethink what could be drastic consequences if he desired to tackle the powerful baseball monopoly.

208

In early December 1969 Flood returned to Miller, convinced he wanted to sue for his freedom. Miller invited Flood to attend the executive board meeting of the Players Association, which was scheduled for Puerto Rico in mid-December.

The player representatives heard Flood and fired hard questions at him. "Are you simply suing to earn more money from the Phillies?" was a question frequently asked. Most Association members, Marvin Miller, and Richard Moss, Association counsel, believed a frontal test of the reserve clause would be best brought by a bench warmer. Constitutional infringements on the right to employment would look most violated if a player was stuck in the minors or on the bench behind a star athlete.

Curt Flood's sincerity of motive compelled the player representatives to back his case unanimously. They would accept all legal fees. None of the players raised the issue that the death of the traditional reserve clause would ruin baseball, which gratified Flood. The Association's only doubts had been tactical, and these were dispelled by Flood's genuineness of purpose.

Hopes were high in December 1969 for a legal victory. Many neutral observers believed that the case ultimately would be decided in the Supreme Court, which needed to face honestly its anomalous 1922 antitrust exemption. This was especially true because Burton's dissent in the Toolson case had become law in the Radovich and International Boxing Club cases of the mid-1950s.

To serve as Flood's lawyer, Marvin Miller recruited his former colleague on the Steelworkers Union "brain trust," Arthur J. Goldberg, former associate justice on the United States Supreme Court. Goldberg's choice looked prestigious and it thrilled Curt Flood. Unfortunately, Goldberg did not have the grasp of baseball practice and its historic machinations that Danny Gardella's lawyer, Frederic A. Johnson, had possessed.

On Christmas Eve 1969 Flood made his first gambit, a letter to Commissioner Kuhn. As Flood recalled in *The Way It Is*, he informed the commissioner that he was not a piece of property to be traded like livestock. Flood made a prophetic request of Kuhn:

> I believe I have the right to consider offers from other clubs before making any decisions. I, therefore, request that you make known to all Major League clubs my feelings in this matter, and advise them of my availability for the 1970 season.

By the end of 1976 most major league veterans would have these

209

rights. In 1969 organized baseball was not prepared to relinquish its historic control. Kuhn replied to Flood:

> I certainly agree with you that you, as a human being, are not a piece of property to be bought and sold. That is fundamental to our society and I think obvious.

Demonstrating the fundamental gap in communication, Kuhn insisted, "I cannot see its applicability to the situation at hand."

Arthur Goldberg searched for some sign of conciliation from the owners. He did not want Flood at a critical baseball age, thirty-two, to have to sit out a year. His skills might well erode by not playing, a terrible penalty for a ballplayer to pay.

Paul Porter, baseball's chief Washington lawyer, told Goldberg that the owners did not plan to yield to Flood's presumptuous requests. The hard-line stance became clear at a meeting of the Players Association representatives and the Player Relations Committee in early 1970. When the question of modifying the reserve clause came up, management refused to consider the topic. Seattle player rep Jim Bouton asked if the owners would consider terminating the reserve restriction when the player reached his sixty-fifth birthday. The Association members guffawed, but National League attorney Louis Carroll replied in all seriousness, "No, next thing you'll be asking for is a fifty-five limit."

In late February 1970 Judge Irving Ben Cooper heard preliminary arguments in the Federal Court, Southern District of New York. He refused to grant Flood a preliminary injunction which would have enabled him to play in 1970 for somebody. Judge Cooper believed the issue of the antitrust exemption must be discussed in a trial. A danger sign for the Flood cause came when Cooper did not announce a recess in the hearing. He called it "a seventh inning stretch." Once arguments were completed in early March, Cooper announced, "Now you have thrown the ball to me and I hope I don't muff it." Cooper would not be the last judge to let his awe of baseball affect his judicial demeanor.

Shortly before the trial was scheduled to begin in May 1970, Curt Flood received a telephone call from one of Commissioner Kuhn's assistants, Monte Irvin, a former star player for the Giants and in the Negro leagues. Irvin informed Flood that the commissioner was willing to concede to Flood half of his December request. He was free to attempt to arrange a deal with any National League club and not damage his litigation.

210

Flood realized that if he accepted the offer, his case would likely end. A federal court was not likely to hear the grievance of a player who had earned unprecedented freedom of contract for baseball. Flood turned down the last-minute offer, cheered by the obvious concern the owners must have had to make such a concession.

He recalled his mood: "I now knew that someday the owners of baseball would instruct Kuhn to issue a similar invitation to Marvin Miller and the leadership of the Major League Baseball Players Association . . . to discuss revisions in the reserve clause." Flood's prophecy proved accurate, though fulfilled too late to help him.

Early in May 1970, shortly before the Flood trial was to start, the Second Basic Agreement was announced. The product of bitter bargaining with the litigation pending, the Agreement, retroactive to January 1, 1970, brought more substantial gains for the players.

The Players Association received recognition as "the sole and exclusive collective bargaining agent for all Major League Players." The minimum salary was raised to $12,000 for 1970 and would increase to $15,000 by 1972. The owners consented to reduce the maximum cut in salary to 20 percent a year or 30 percent over two years. It had been 30 percent and 44 percent for decades. The players received a written guarantee of the right to utilize an agent in negotiations with management. Four years after the Drysdale-Koufax cause célèbre, with Walter O'Malley moaning about agents, all the players had obtained the right to representation.

Most significantly, the 1970 Agreement achieved Harry Taylor's and Dave Fultz's futilely sought goal, arbitration of grievances outside the commissioner's office. Bowie Kuhn said it was a "valid assertion" that many players might feel uncomfortable with a former National League attorney judging their fate in a sensitive grievance. Lewis Gill of Philadelphia became baseball's first outside arbitrator. At the end of his contract term in 1972, Gabriel Alexander of Detroit replaced him, and in 1974, Peter Seitz of New York, originally considered for the position in 1970, became baseball's third and most historic arbitrator.

Article XIV of the 1970 Basic Agreement reflected the Association's continuing disapproval of the reserve system and its displeasure that the study of the controversial control mechanism had proven so fruitless. "Regardless of any provision herein," XIV read, "this Agreement does not deal with the reserve system." The Association wanted to go on record as opposing the reserve as a creation of the Major League Rules and not of the players. It also wanted to avoid implication in any future litigation against the reserve system. The owners would later claim in the fateful Messersmith-McNally case that the Association was actually accepting the reserve by omitting it from the Basic Agreement, as if the players and their representatives had been agitating for the exercise.

In 1970 the Association of course hoped that the Flood trial would at last force changes in the perpetual reserve system. A few former players like Jackie Robinson and Hank Greenberg came to testify in Flood's behalf. So did the irrepressible Bill Veeck, in the middle of a fifteen-year exile from the game. Veeck insisted that baseball could survive a loosened reserve. While studying law at night in the late 1930s, Veeck had suggested to Leslie O'Connor that the reserve clause was illegal. O'Connor, later fond of quoting Landis's willingness to approve nonreserve clause contracts, gave Veeck an answer that was more typical of baseball's resistance to change: "A little knowledge is a dangerous thing."

Baseball lawyers, old hands at deflecting challenges, reminded Judge Cooper of the unbreached 1922 antitrust exemption. They cited the Celler Committee report of 1952, which had recommended no legislation against the reserve clause. They stressed that Congress had never passed a bill against baseball despite dozens of attempts at drafting measures.

The owners added a new twist to their strategy. It may have saved the Flood case, yet laid them open to the ploy that ultimately killed the perpetual reserve system.

Flood's grievance was not an antitrust issue, they argued. It was "only a labor dispute over a mandatory collective bargaining issue." Though they had never proposed serious revisions of the system to the Association, the owners professed a flexible stance in the trial.

Judge Cooper sided with management. He cited the reasons that had kept the Holmes decision in effect for nearly fifty years. "Decisions of the Supreme Court are not lightly overruled," he announced on August 12, 1970. "Prior to trial we gained the impression that there was a view, held by many, that baseball's reserve system had occasioned rampant abuse and that it should be abolished."

After the testimony Cooper decided, "We find no general or widespread disregard of the extremely important position the player occupies. . . . Clearly the preponderance of credible proof does not favor elimination of the reserve clause." He added that "negotiation" and "arbitration" would be well advised for modifying the controversial feature.

Arthur Goldberg immediately appealed the verdict to the circuit court, hoping for the kind of vindication Danny Gardella had won in his case before the same courts. Ultimately, the Supreme Court would probably decide, Goldberg and Flood realized.

Of course, the process was time-consuming. Flood had fled the country for Denmark before the Cooper verdict had even been announced. An extremely sensitive man, whose hobby and off-season business had been portrait painting, Flood was unprepared for the calumnies he had received. A friend said of Flood, "He wore his nerves on edge." He was emotionally unprepared for the taunts of sportswriters and fans whom Flood sensed considered him the "little black bitch trying to destroy baseball." The centerfielder had felt all alone on trial. No active player came to see the proceedings in court; they were still afraid of repercussions for too great a curiosity, he later realized.

In October 1970, Robert Short, owner of the Washington Senators, contacted Flood and offered him a job in 1971. Goldberg gave him assurance that his litigation would not be damaged because he had suffered severe damages from missing the 1970 season. Goldberg's point was unfortunately true physically as well as legally. Flood lasted less than a month of the 1971 season, his skills greatly eroded during his unwanted layoff. He left for the Spanish island of Majorca, where he opened a tavern and hoped for vindication in the Supreme Court. In October 1971, after the second circuit court in New York had refused Flood's appeal, the High Court heard arguments in *Flood* v. *Kuhn*.

On June 18, 1972, the verdict came down, 5-3 in favor of continuing the 1922 exemption. It was a decision that puzzled many mainstream sportswriters. Arthur Daley, sports editor of *The New York Times*, said it revealed "a total lack of logic."

The narrow doctrine, *stare decisis*, or let the old doctrine stand, was employed to justify the continuing exemption of baseball from the strictures of interstate commerce. Woodward and Armstrong's 1979 book on the Supreme Court, *The Brethren*, has disclosed the embarrassment many of the Court felt about the decision and in particular, Justice Harry Blackmun's litany of baseball greats from the past which introduced the decision.

Even Blackmun in the substance of his verdict conceded that base-ball's continued exemption was "an aberration," in the light of the other professional sports' antitrust liabilities. Chief Justice Warren Burger admitted to "grave reservations" about continuing the exemption. In the buck-passing style which had allowed the admittedly illogical privilege to exist for decades, Burger declared, "It is time Congress acted to solve this problem."

For the minority, Justice William Douglas went on record as having erred in the Toolson case when he supported the 1922 decision. Justice Thurgood Marshall issued an eloquent plea for taking responsibility for the helpless position in which the High Court had placed the baseball player:

> Whatever muscle they might have been able to muster by combin-ing forces with other athletes has been greatly impaired by the manner in which this Court has isolated them. It is this Court that has made them impotent, and this Court should correct its errors.

To the baseball establishment, a victory, even a lucky squeaker, was a vindication of their past practices. Whatever joy the verdict brought was tempered by the reality of the growing strength, even the militancy, of the Players Association. Public opinion had strikingly changed against the reserve system in baseball. Some polls showed as many as 8:1 in favor of Flood's position in the trial. By contrast, Robert Murphy had tried to organize players in 1946 at a time when one public opinion poll showed only 12 percent of a sampling in favor of a baseball union.

By the 1970s there was a growing critical spirit against the stubborn standpattism of the baseball establishment. Although Congress had not come close to passing a bill about reserve practices, there were many legislators concerned and outspoken about professional sports' monop-olies. Democratic North Carolina Senator Sam Ervin, long before he became a national figure in the Watergate hearings, opposed mergers of the warring football and basketball leagues because they would impair the athletes' bargaining power. "Even if I believed the solemn predictions of the pro sports industry spokesmen, and I don't," raged Ervin, "I would still oppose a system that demands lordlike control over the serflike hired hands."

Although the Supreme Court gave the owners a narrow and almost unexpected victory in the Flood case, the tide of player assertiveness was not receding. Before the start of the 1972 season, the major league players went out on strike, the first industrywide work stoppage in baseball history.

The immediate issue was familiar: the owners' unwillingness to add what the players thought was a fair cost-of-living increase to their pension and medical benefits. But as in all heated labor disputes, the issue took on symbolic importance. Ruly Carpenter, scion of the DuPont family and inheritor of the Phillies from his father, Robert, declared, "If we had taken this stand three years ago, we wouldn't be in this position today." Irascible Gussie Busch added, "Let them strike." California Angels' owner Gene Autry broke up an owners' meeting with an avowal, "If I have to, I can still back that horse out of the barn and make it that way." With that bit of symbolic nonsense from the wealthy radio entrepreneur the owners vowed to stand united.

The players had decided to strike after an extraordinary late March meeting of the player representatives in Dallas, located between the training camps in Florida and Arizona. The delegates were angry, but Marvin Miller and his counsel, Richard Moss, urged caution. They warned that twenty-four big league publicity departments would be arrayed against them if they struck. So would undoubtedly all of the sporting press.

After six hours of intense argument with every representative speaking at least once, they voted with one abstention (Wes Parker of Walter O'Malley's Los Angeles Dodgers) to recommend a strike vote to the full membership. Miller accepted the will of the overwhelming majority, realizing that these professional competitors had decided that they must fight just as vigorously in behalf of their off-field interests. Chicago White Sox player representative Jay Johnstone later commented, "There was so much enthusiasm generated in there by those guys. I honestly think that a bunch of them wanted to get up and fight somebody."

A last-minute averting of the strike suddenly seemed possible. Miller calculated that the extra money for medical benefits could come from the interest from securities in the players' pension fund. The owners refused the suggestion, determined to show the players who was boss.

The walkout from spring training occurred on April Fool's Day, which *The Sporting News* called "the darkest day in sports history."

Managements told players to take their equipment from the clubhouses. Many clubs wrote out one-way tickets for the players to their permanent homes.

Press opinion was of course hostile. *The St. Louis Globe Democrat* declared, "Marvin Miller has struck out. He would do the game of baseball a great favor if he disappeared, got lost, or found the nearest hole and jumped into it." Dick Young in the *New York Daily News* portrayed Miller as a Svengali who "runs the players through a high-pressure spray the way an auto goes through a car wash, and that's how they come out, brainwashed." C. C. Johnson Spink, the latest in the family of *Sporting News* publishers, averred that the pension had been a bad idea in the first place because baseball would only be a "secondary career" in the life span of the players.

That venerable expert on labor relations in baseball, Rip Sewell, told the *Wall Street Journal* that he was glad the owners had finally told their ungrateful employees where to get off:

> First the players wanted a hamburger and the owners gave them a hamburger. Then they wanted a filet mignon and they gave them a filet mignon. Then they wanted the whole damn cow and now that they got the cow they want a pasture to put him [*sic*] in.

Despite the rage of management and its traditional allies in the sporting press, the Players Association did not break. No one this time would qualify for a gold watch from the commissioner's office. Sensing that his constituency was united on principle, Marvin Miller declared at the fever pitch of the strike, "Money is not the issue. The real issue is the owners' attempt to punish the players for having the audacity not to settle and for having the audacity not to crawl."

Calmer heads finally prevailed, with Miller and federal mediators trying to impress upon the owners an understanding that nobody really wins a strike. The pension increase was funded from surpluses in the fund's securities, which Miller had suggested before the confrontation. The thorniest problem remained what to do about 86 games that had been canceled during the strike. Some owners astonished Miller by suggesting that all games be played without overtime for the players. The ultimate solution left some teams playing three less games than others, which cost the Boston Red Sox a shot at the American League East pennant because they lost the same number of games as winner Detroit but won one less.

216

The Players Association felt prouder than ever after the strike. Though Curt Flood had lost his lonely individual fight, the reserve clause had been exposed to much public criticism and the players understood that if they stuck together, changes would have to come.

On the other hand, the owners' divisions were becoming obvious. In 1969 and in 1972, the hard-line owners had failed to break the players' group with their traditional bluster. In January 1973 another obvious disagreement broke into the open when the American League voted to adopt a designated hitter for the pitcher in all league games. The idea was not new; in the early 1930s the National League had been for it with the American League opposed and Commissioner Landis tabled any further discussion. That one league in 1973 would make such an arbitrary change in the rules and not be stopped by the commissioner was further evidence to the players of bitter internal divisions, which a united player organization could capitalize upon. In fact, the resplendent Players Association paid its negotiator Marvin Miller $75,000—$25,000 a year more than the owners paid John Gaherin, the beleaguered head of the Players Relations Committee who never had received substantial bargaining authority from his bosses.

The Basic Agreement signed in late March 1973 brought the greatest advances yet to the players, though not before a protracted struggle that left the opening of spring training in doubt well into February. Fresh from the Flood victory, the owners wanted no changes in the reserve system, only another three-year study, which the players found unacceptable. In less than ten years, the mystique of the reserve clause had evaporated and the players asked openly for freedom from the reserve after seven years of service and again after twelve years and then seventeen years.

The players won no concession on the reserve system in 1973, Article XV of the Basic Agreement reflecting this fact, "Except as herein modified, this agreement does not deal with the reserve system." But the minimum salary was bargained upward again to reach $16,000 by 1975. A "Curt Flood rule" was added, which gave a veteran of ten major league seasons with at least five years on his current club the right to veto any trade.

Most importantly, the players earned the right to salary arbitration. After six years of tangling, Marvin Miller and John Gaherin, both experienced labor relations men, had worked out a respectful adversary relationship. Their salary arbitration mechanism was hailed in a *New*

York Times editorial as a "Home Run in Baseball" worthy of copying in other industries.

The key to the procedure was the submitting to an impartial arbitrator a best bid by both the owner and the player locked in a salary dispute. The arbitrator would choose one or the other; there would be no compromising on figures so each contestant had to be realistic in his appraisal. The system worked well in its first years, with the arbitrators' decisions made on a case-by-case basis with each side winning approximately half of the time.

The significant factor in salary arbitration was that, by law now, salaries had to be made public. Players had always discussed earning power and there was envy as in any professional group. (Remember that Napoleon Lajoie had left the Phillies in 1901 because of his peeve that teammate Ed Delahanty had received $200 more!) By 1973 there no longer was any doubt about what the salaries were; they had to be divulged, which prompted one executive to moan that the reserve clause could be modified but baseball could not survive salary arbitration.

As usual, the cries of doom proved groundless as baseball made a great comeback in popularity throughout the 1970s. The end of the Vietnamese war brought a calmer era to the country. Youngsters found and older fans rediscovered the quiet yet taut charms of baseball. It was also a period of franchise stability, a time when fans could develop attachments to teams and players without worrying about the imminent departure of a club to dollar-greener pastures.

The 1973 Agreement did not augur improved labor relations, however. For the first time, Commissioner Kuhn had publicly endorsed the stand of the owners during negotiations, which only made the players more convinced of the importance of a strong Association. The winning of salary arbitration had not been easy. It had only occurred after Marvin Miller adamantly refused to accept a proposal that would have allowed arbitration only in alternate years and would have deleted the maximum salary cut of 20 percent. Knowing his baseball history, Miller warned that the owners would likely take any gain "out of the player's hide" in the alternate year and he refused to accept it; finally, management dropped the idea.

The owners persisted in believing that Congress and the courts had sanctified their business, especially the reserve system, but the players were increasingly emboldened to test the restrictive mechanism. As early as 1969, Yankee pitcher Al Downing had asked the Association: What would happen if a player refused to sign his contract and therefore not the renewal clause either? Miller said that it was his judgment the player would be free to go elsewhere at the end of the year. Always the realist, however, Miller cautioned Downing that "simply asserting what your rights were wasn't necessarily going to solve the problem." Indeed, Yankee player personnel director Johnny Johnson, who has since become the president of the National Association, told Downing that if he did not sign his contract, he should not bother to report to spring training (precisely what the Giants had told Jack Bentley in 1923 when he refused to report from Baltimore without receiving a percentage of his purchase price).

Downing complied in 1969, but other players soon got the same idea about testing the renewal clause. Ted Simmons, the Cardinals' valuable catcher, refused to sign a contract in 1972, realizing that a hard-hitting defensively skilled backstop was one of baseball's rarest commodities. The Cardinals let Simmons report and play in spring training, the owners perhaps wary of enforcing one of "baseball's laws" more draconian provisions while the Flood case was still undecided. Simmons even started the championship season unsigned, the first player in baseball history to appear with a renewed (unsigned) contract.

Marvin Miller and Richard Moss felt confident that Simmons could play out his renewal year and become a free agent. They felt as John Montgomery Ward must have felt when he advised Deacon White and Jack Rowe in June 1889 to report unsigned to Pittsburgh so they could join the Players League the next season. There was no rival league in baseball of course, but court decisions during the basketball and hockey trade wars of the 1960s and early 1970s had concluded without exception that a renewal of a contract could not be perpetual but valid only for a period of one year.

In Ted Simmons's case the point became moot because he signed a two-year contract with the Cardinals during the middle of the 1972 season. In the next three seasons, however, seventeen major leaguers threatened to play out their options; each began a championship season unsigned. All but Andy Messersmith and Dave McNally eventually agreed to terms. It should have come as no surprise to the owners that eventually some player would insist on testing the controversial renewal clause, Section 10(a), of the uniform baseball contract. Yet organized baseball clung to the belief that the old reserve system would never change and they scorned the efforts of Player Association officials to modify it.

When the Messersmith-McNally case came to Peter Seitz's arbitration panel in November 1975, the owners shunted aside John Gaherin and his Players Relations Committee counsel, Barry Rona, and brought in the veteran League lawyers who had won the Flood case. Baseball's barristers concocted a defense that the Players Association had agreed not to dispute basic "core" issues of the reserve system when, in fact, the issues had been raised constantly by the Association since the late 1960s; and never had management used the term "core" to describe the reserve system until this grievance.

Time had run out on the clever game of avoiding jurisdictions which organized baseball and its lawyers had been playing for decades. It had told Congress that the judiciary must rule on baseball, and then told the courts that it was a legislative function. But when baseball in the Flood case said that the reserve system was a subject for mandatory collective bargaining, they were almost suggesting a route of recourse for the players. As if Marvin Miller needed any coaching! By refusing to yield a few inches, the owners lost yards. Yet the Players Association, given wide latitude by Seitz's rejection of the renewal mechanism in every contract, showed a spirit of compromise by negotiating a limited free agency. Only veterans of six years in the major leagues would be eligible for free agency, according to the Basic Agreement ratified in July 1976.

It was poetic justice that the players, after a century of inequity, turned to their advantage one of the little homilies of Albert Spalding, that archmonopolist of baseball's formative days: "Baseball in youth has the effect in later years of making the player think and act a little quicker than the other fellow." Thanks to the strength of the Players Association, the modern player announced to the owners that he was already a sharp businessman. He expected competitive salary and treatment as a human not as a chattel. The new system allowed the player to take his wares elsewhere if he was not satisfied.

But there were inklings of a major showdown as negotiations neared for a renewal of the historic 1976 Basic Agreement expiring on December 31, 1979. Economically, baseball had never prospered more than during the first years of free agency. Attendance, television money, and "competitive balance" in the form of close pennant

220

races had all increased. Yet the element of the irrational and the vindictive had always been great in the history of the imperfect diamond.

The owners' extension of a bitter major league umpires' strike in 1979 was a case in point. Though the umpires, always hailed as the guardians of the game's integrity, were asking for far less money than journeymen ball players recently received, some owners declared that delaying a settlement until late May 1979 was intended to teach the players a lesson for 1980. The owners had been trying to dictate the same lesson to the players since the emergence of a strong Players Association, and they had proven poor teachers.

The introduction of a $500,000 fine on any owner discussing the negotiations for 1980, a suggestion by new Player Relations Committee director C. Raymond Grebey, Jr. who replaced John Gaherin in 1978, suggested that a ban on private discussion might also reveal a lack of constructive private thought. In a society where the press is active, indeed ceaseless, in its search for news, plans for a rigid salary-limitation scale and a harsh compensation provision were discovered by enterprising reporters in January 1980. If the owners wanted to turn back the clock and refuse to engage in good faith arms-length bargaining, it was clear that the players would fight vigorously against them.

Part VII

The Wars of the Monopolies:
Players Versus Owners,
1980-1990

15

THE SHOWDOWN OF 1981:
THE UNPRECEDENTED 51-DAY STRIKE

*"With nearly three-fourths of increased revenues
going to players' salaries, it seems apparent that
the rapidly rising trend in salaries should be
slowed down."*
— *C. Raymond Grebey, Jr., chief management
negotiator, shortly before the averted 1980 baseball strike.*

*"The players are getting too much money for
their own damned good. Sure, we know who bid
the contracts up to where they are now, but now
it's got to stop."*
— *Writer Roger Angell explaining management
thinking at the start of the 1981 baseball strike.*

A March 3, 1980 issue of *Sports Illustrated* prefigured the first
crisis of the 1980s with a graphic photo of an empty ballpark cap-
tioned, "Yankee Stadium, Opening Day, 1980?" In the story, senior
writer Ron Fimrite warned that both sides were heading towards
a major confrontation as they tried to hammer out a renewal of
the historic 1976 Basic Agreement.

Management was determined to win two significant givebacks.
First, it wanted the players to agree to a scuttling of salary arbitration by accepting a system of salary maximums for players with
less than six years of major league experience. The second change

225

involved a significant modification in the free agent system. The owners asked the players to agree to the substitution of a major league player for an amateur draft pick as compensation to the team that had lost the free agent. "If you lose a starting pitcher," American League President Lee MacPhail told Fimrite, "you don't want a high schooler."

The Players Association saw no reason for change. After a century of reserve system restrictions, they felt that salaries had at last grown towards justifiable levels. If the game was prosperous, why shouldn't the players, the stars of "The Show," as minor leaguers enviously called the big leagues, earn a fair share of the proceeds? Not only had the average salary jumped to nearly $150,000 a year, but such superstars as Reggie Jackson, Pete Rose and Nolan Ryan had been able to sell their wares for millions of dollars in long-term contracts on the open market. A rising tide lifts all boats and the players were not inclined to return to the shore of salary stagnation at a time when baseball was setting attendance records year after year.

Even if some players had an inclination to be flexible on changes in the system, their leader, Marvin Miller, would be sure to correct them. At 63, Miller had announced his retirement after the conclusion of the 1980 negotiation, but Fimrite warned management, "The heavy sighs, the shrugging shoulders, the mirthless laugh are all deceptive. . . . [Miller's] dedication to the organization he virtually created is unflagging."

One by one, Miller dismissed management's positions in the current bargaining. As for the salary maximum proposal (an idea that went back a hundred years and had indeed provoked the Players League war of 1890), Miller declared, "They are saying that the Players Association should assume the responsibility for policing what an owner might want to pay." He dismissed the idea as "radical," going against baseball's long history of individual negotiation of salary on the basis of performance. He also argued that salary maximums would only serve as an excuse for under-the-table payments. (The owners' stated maximum of over $153,000 a year for a six-year player was itself far lower than what many veterans were already making.)

226

As for the idea of major league compensation for lost free agents, Miller opposed it because the bargaining power of the free agent would obviously be reduced if the team that signed him stood to lose a major league player in the transaction. Miller said that he preferred the term "taking hostages" for the owners' proposal, chuckling, "They get furious when I compare compensation to hostages." (Jimmy Carter's single-term Presidency was unraveling at the time because of the Iranian seizure of American hostages.)

A major key to Marvin Miller's success was his undivided support from baseball's stars and superstars. "The key word about Marvin is that he is essential," said Ted Simmons, the Cardinals' articulate catcher (who in 1989 became St. Louis' director of player development). "Without him, strong and intelligent as he is, we might not have that bright light that serves us as a beacon." Simmons contrasted Miller's success to the failures of Ed Garvey, the beleaguered head of the pro football players union who had never won the support of the football stars and who had accepted a system of compensation that kept free agency from coming to football.

"[Garvey] stood out as one who represented a bunch of lost sheep, so to speak," Simmons explained to Fimrite, and the football owners "finally turned his light out. But nobody's turned Marvin Miller's light out ever." Simmons concluded, "All I need to know is what he wants done." Above a caption describing him as "one of his most vocal supporters," Reggie Jackson was photographed sitting on the arm of his leader's couch in Miller's New York apartment. When once asked to describe the seriousness of the budding dispute in baseball, Reggie replied, "As serious as death."

Yet many owners still craved a "victory" over Marvin Miller before the staunch unionist retired undefeated. In 1978, C. Raymond Grebey, Jr. had replaced John J. Gaherin as director of the owners' labor relations arm, the Player Relations Committee. The change supposedly gave a signal to the union that a tough negotiator was replacing the more conciliatory and avuncular Gaherin whom many owners believed "had given away the store." In Grebey, management could not have found a more ideological opposite to Miller. Grebey had come to baseball from the General Electric Company, which was known for its labor relations policy of Boulwarism.

Named after the theorist Lemuel Boulware, Boulwarism essentially told the workers at the bargaining table, "Take it or leave it."

Sports Illustrated photographed Grebey in his office with two baseball bats standing in the corner. "With nearly three-fourths of increased revenues going to players' salaries," Grebey wrote in a recent management memo, "it seems apparent that the rapidly rising trend in salaries should be slowed down." As for the controversial compensation proposal, Grebey told reporter Fimrite, "I hate the word 'compensation'. I prefer 'improved player selection rights'."

The lines were thus drawn for another major baseball confrontation as spring training camps opened. On March 4, 1980, the executive board of the Players Association authorized a strike on or after April 1st if no satisfactory contract had been signed. Some progress was made in the middle of the month when the owners withdrew their salary maximum proposal from the table, but they still were holding fast to their insistence on improved compensation for free agents.

"60 Minutes," the popular Sunday night program on the CBS television network, devoted a segment of a late March show to the dispute. Ray Grebey insisted that 21 out of 26 clubs were losing money and something had to be done about it, but Marvin Miller expressed extreme skepticism about baseball's fiscal woes. "The newspaperman has no statutory authority to ask for the data," he intoned, "and simply prints what they say."

On April 1st, eight years to the day from the beginning of the last baseball strike, the players walked out of their training camps. 92 exhibition games were canceled, including some lucrative cross-city rivalries in Los Angeles and the San Francisco Bay area. The vote was reported as 967-1, the lone dissenter being Jerry Terrell, a Kansas City Royals infielder who voted no out of religious convictions.

The players then threw a curveball at the owners by announcing that they would resume the regular season on time, but would strike again on May 23rd if no agreement had been reached. Minnesota Twins pitcher Mike Marshall, the brilliant reliever who had won the Cy Young award while a member of the Los Angeles

Dodgers in 1974, explained that postponing the strike would hit the owners hardest in their pocket books because attendance traditionally did not pick up until around the Memorial Day weekend. Marshall was unimpressed when told that two-thirds of the public favored the owners in the dispute. "The players know what the baseball industry needs," snapped the stubborn individualist who had argued in 1976 that the players had given the owners too much by allowing as many as six years before free agency. "If we were another union, and we had been insulted like the owners have insulted us at the bargaining table, we would be out bombing cars by now."

Few of the players were as vocal as the combative Marshall. In fact, slugging outfielder/designated hitter Don Baylor of the California Angels, the 1979 American League Most Valuable Player, tried to placate his owner, Gene Autry, who was one of the big spenders in the free agent market. Baylor urged that Autry should not take the action personally, but understand it as a union response to owners in general. In one of his more restrained replies, Autry declared, "I've been a member of unions almost all my life and I know that once they get their foot in the door, they're never happy." He sighed, "For an owner who is trying to do the right things, it's all very frustrating."

The 1980 baseball season began without disruption, and early attendance returns indicated another banner year in the making. Yet the clock was ticking towards the midnight hour of May 23, and neither side was blinking. Hard-line owners interpreted the mini-strike of spring training as a sign that the players would not risk losing fat paychecks during the season. The players, on the other hand, expected a break in ownership ranks before the deadline. It had always happened since they had been led by Marvin Miller.

There was slight progress on the compensation question as both sides tried to reach a mutual agreement on what constituted a "ranking" free agent that would require major league compensation. It all depended on how the free agent's "performance" should be defined. The players argued that wins and earned run average for pitchers and batting average and runs batted in for everyday players should be the measure of performance, but Ray Grebey insisted that rankings should be based only on appearances in games.

There were also preliminary discussions about the idea of "pooled compensation" for ranking free agents. Each team might protect a given number of its most prized players, and then put the other players into a pool from which the team that lost a free agent could select a replacement. There was a precedent for such a pool in the expansion drafts that had stocked the new major league teams in 1960, 1961, and 1976. If the owners insisted on the "warm body" of a major leaguer for compensation, the players argued that they might accept this indirect kind of compensation. They insisted, however, that there was no way that they would allow a free agent transaction to become a straight man-for-man trade.

No substantial progress was made in either the area of defining performance or establishing the pool. It looked like the strike was on when the wire services began reporting on the evening of Thursday May 22, 1980, that the San Francisco Giants players were not boarding their plane from Pittsburgh to Montreal, their next destination on a long road trip. Then, at 4 A.M. on May 23, 1980, the players' faith in Marvin Miller was vindicated once again. After marathon bargaining sessions in New York City, a compromise settlement was announced.

The players won increases in the minimum salary for the next four years from $30,000 to $35,000. They also won an important reduction in salary arbitration eligibility from three years to two years. The free agent system remained the same as in 1976, but a four-man committee was established to study the question of increased compensation for owners and to report no later than January 1981. If the committee failed to reach agreement on modifications in the system, the owners had the right to implement their last proposal on compensation which was included as Attachment 9 at the back of the 1980 agreement.

The key section of the attachment read, "If the free agent Player is within the top 1/3 of his performance category, the signing Club shall be entitled to protect 15 players from the total number of players under contract to or controlled by the Club." If a player ranked only in the top half of performance, then the signing club could protect 18 players. If the committee failed to find a compromise on compensation, the settlement gave the players the choice of accepting Attachment 9 or informing the owners no later than March 1981 of their intention to strike no later than June 1981. The players also had the option of accepting the proposal for 1981 with the right to strike in 1982.

Many observers wondered if the agreement had only postponed the strike for one year, considering that joint study committees in baseball had usually proven ineffectual. Yet, in a baseball world where "history" is yesterday's game and "futurism" is next season, there was a general sigh of relief. Peace and a complete season were assured for 1980.

It was a year that turned out to be another artistically and financially successful one. The Yankees won 103 games to the Orioles' 100 in the American League East, but they lost the league championship series in three straight games to the Kansas City Royals, who avenged their three straight post-season losses of 1976 through 1978 to the New Yorkers. The Philadelphia Phillies, aided by free agent acquisition Pete Rose (who had joined the club in 1979 after he hawked his services in a highly publicized off-season caravan), won a thrilling five-game playoff from the Houston Astros. Then, 97 years after they entered the National League, the Phillies won their first World Series championship, beating the Royals in six games.

The only discordant note in Philadelphia's long-awaited triumph was a joint decision by the Phillies' management and the city government to protect the field and players from rampaging fans by any means necessary. Dick Kaegel described the scene in *The Sporting News* as the Phillies' triumphal moment neared: "Black-helmeted riot police wielding nightsticks, snarling attack dogs straining at the leash, [and] mounted cops astride pawing steeds." Tug McGraw, the Phillies' irrepressible ace reliever, was on the mound trying to save the final victory in Game 6 with the bases loaded and the potential go-ahead run at the plate in Willie Wilson. Looking up at the massed show of force around the ballpark, McGraw thought, "That's weird, this doesn't happen on a baseball field."

But the sight of canines made him think of K-9, a strikeout of the hitter, and he proceeded to fan Wilson and clinch the series for Philadelphia.

Growling police dogs poised to attack served as a good symbol for the state of baseball labor-management relations. The worst situation in a normally contentious labor-management environment is a one-issue negotiation; there is no room to trade-off or maneuver. Given that the one issue on baseball's bitter labor relations scene was the most controversial one, changes in the new free agent system, baseball seemed headed inexorably towards a 1981 cataclysm.

I personally experienced the vast gulf in views of the world on both sides of the labor front when I met the principals during the 1980 season after mailing them complimentary copies of the first edition of this book. Because of the owners' ban on discussing the issues during the negotiations, I had been unable to interview Ray Grebey in the preparation of the first edition.

Grebey greeted me very cordially in his Players Relations Committee office where I noticed on the wall a signed photograph of Bill Veeck, the maverick baseball owner who, like Grebey, had attended Kenyon College in Ohio. Grebey exuded genial baseball paternalism. "What a warm human being!" he exclaimed about entertainer Danny Kaye, at the time a part-owner of the Seattle Mariners. Grebey volunteered that he had recently seen to it that one of the underpaid infielders in baseball had gotten a raise from his owner.

When I asked him what he thought of my book, he replied, "I wish you had been nicer to the owners. You know the players don't really have any longterm interest in the game. They are really like long-distance truckdrivers." (A variant of the old management saw, "The players come and go, but the owners last forever.") He then offered a surprising interpretation of baseball's labor history. "From reading your book," he said, "it shows me that sportswriters have always had a left-wing bias."

When I subsequently shared Grebey's last comment with Marvin Miller, I was startled when Miller reacted with sustained hilarity.

It was the "mirthless laugh" of an advocate chortling at his opponent's misunderstanding of history.

The personal animosity between Miller and Grebey left many people in baseball utterly pessimistic about a compromise settlement. "They're both so straight out of the politics of the Great Depression that it's scary," one insider told Thomas Boswell of the *Washington Post.* "Romantic left-wing steel worker organizer against brilliant, tough capitalist. Each one thinks the other just might be the devil."

The countdown to the 1981 confrontation began shortly after the new year when it was announced that the joint study committee had been unable to reach a compromise on the question of free agent compensation. It was not a surprising development but nonetheless a disappointing one because all four members of the committee were genuinely respected throughout baseball. Management had been represented by Harry Dalton and Frank Cashen, two experienced general managers who had both worked for the Baltimore Orioles and now had similar jobs with the Milwaukee Brewers and New York Mets, respectively. The players were third baseman Sal Bando of the Brewers, who had been the glue on Oakland's world champion teams of the early 70's, and catcher Bob Boone of the Philadelphia Phillies, an experienced veteran and son of former American League infielder and current Boston Red Sox scout, Ray Boone.

Years later, both Dalton and Cashen lamented that the committee had not been allowed the authority to make compromises. "We understood the players' concerns and they were listening to our side," Cashen recalled in a 1990 interview. "It was the best committee I had ever been on in baseball." Dalton recalled in 1988, "We tried to get something done, but we were sandbagged." In his 1989 memoirs, *My Nine Innings,* Lee MacPhail recalled that whenever the committee seemed to be making progress, the warring principals, Miller and Grebey, would enter the discussions and their antagonisms made progress impossible.

Federal mediator Kenneth Moffett had received an early signal that his services would be needed again in 1981. After the study committee sessions ended, he and his mediation service counsel,

233

David Vaughn, received a co-signed letter from Lee MacPhail and Chub Feeney, American and National League presidents, thanking the mediators for saving the 1980 season. Included with the letter were "Lifetime Passes" to all major league games. "Both Vaughn and myself returned the passes, and let them know that it was against the law for us to accept any gratuities for over $50.00 in value," Moffett recollected in 1990 from his office as special assistant to the president of the National Association of Broadcasters, Engineers, and Technicians (NABET).

Events in the off-season free agent market and arbitration hearings had hardened the owners' resolve to try, once again, to make the players protect them from themselves. George Steinbrenner gave Dave Winfield, San Diego Padre free agent outfielder, an unprecedented ten year contract worth approximately $23 million. Atlanta Braves' owner, Ted Turner, the ambitious cable television mogul, signed journeyman outfielder Claudell Washington to a five-year no-trade contract escalating to $600,000 a year.

Increasing salary arbitration awards also caused more hand-wringing and moaning by the owners. After the 1979 season, the Cubs' relief ace, Bruce Sutter, had won a $350,000 salary raise at the arbitration table that enabled his agents to negotiate a long-term deal in 1980. "We didn't think we'd win arbitration," Jim Bronner, one of Sutter's agents, admitted openly, "and by all rights, we shouldn't have. It was our finest hour."

Early in 1981, management moaned again when a salary arbitrator awarded Detroit Tigers outfielder Steve Kemp $600,000 instead of the $360,000 submitted by the club. Ownership watched helplessly as the gap grew alarmingly wide between player and owner bids. In the first years of salary arbitration, the system had worked reasonably well because both sides had to be realistic because the arbitrator could not split the difference; he chose one bid or the other. After the Messersmith decision, free agency caused a rocketing of salaries and there was nothing in the Basic Agreement that prevented arbitrators from using free agent salaries for comparative purposes in making their judgments. In fact, in the 1980 settlement that averted a strike, the union had been able to reduce the eligibility requirement for salary arbitration from three years to two years.

Adding to the malaise of management was a sense that membership in their exclusive club of ownership was changing rapidly. In the past two years, nine franchises had been put on the market. Two of the more maverick departed owners might not be missed by the old guard, Oakland's Charlie Finley and the White Sox' Bill Veeck, but early in 1981 came the news that the Phillies' Ruly Carpenter, a member of the DuPont family that had owned the franchise since the 1940s, intended to sell. Carpenter had tired of bickering with players and agents and missed the good old days when he felt closer to the players. Sportswriter Tracy Ringolsby quipped, "That once-stable, rarely-changing family of club owners has become about as stable as a Latin American government."

On February 17, 1981, Ray Grebey called a press conference at his New York office to announce the formal enactment of Attachment 9 into the Basic Agreement. As far as he was concerned, the owners had at last won major league compensation, but Grebey stressed that only three players in the most recent 1980 re-entry free agent draft — outfielder Dave Winfield, pitcher Don Sutton, and catcher Darrell Porter — would have required major league compensation based on the performance criteria. He claimed it was nothing for the union to get agitated about.

He had to be kidding. "Do you mean to tell me they're ready to shut down the industry just because they want compensation for three or four players?" Marvin Miller rhetorically asked Ralph Ray of *The Sporting News* as the war of words began to escalate. "Come on! How can anyone believe that? What they want to do is stymie free agency for the overwhelming majority of players." Miller also took umbrage at the PRC's placing Attachment 9 into the contract with a xeroxed copy of a fourteen month old proposal. "It is a classic example of not bargaining," he declared. Increasingly, Miller took up the complaint that the owners' main motive was to break the union.

With the dreaded attachment now officially in the Basic Agreement, the Players Association acted quickly. On February 24, its executive board authorized a strike for May 29, but unlike 1980, the players decided to complete the exhibition schedule. Orioles third baseman Doug DeCinces, American League player representative, best captured the mood of the players when he observed, "We want to go to the last possible second and give them every opportunity to resolve it."

Increasingly, it became a time of rhetoric and not negotiation. "I have never seen the owners more unified and prepared for a strike," George Steinbrenner warned. "Unless he handles this right, it could be the Waterloo for Marvin Miller." Miller responded, "If his heart bleeds for the Padres [Dave Winfield's former team], let him do something unilaterally. We won't object. Let him sell one of his players to San Diego for $1."

While Steinbrenner was extremely volatile and wont to change his mind quickly, the owners were more united than ever because they had both a strike fund and strike insurance. Since the start of the 1979 season, they had put 2% of their gross revenues into a strike fund that had reportedly grown to $15 million. After the 1980 settlement, the owners allocated $5 million to purchase over $50 million of strike insurance from Lloyd's of London. The players, too, had a contingency fund drawn from its bubble gum card licensing revenue, but it was much smaller.

The 1981 season started on time, and on April 7, federal mediator Kenneth Moffett returned to the talks. But there was only minimal progress towards a compromise on compensation. The players had yielded by now to accept some kind of major league compensation, and the owners had moved a little by saying that signing clubs could protect more than 15 players on their 25-man major league roster and perhaps even more than 20. But the owners still wanted direct compensation for a free agent transaction, something like a trade, and that remained unacceptable to the union.

The players once again raised the idea of a pool, from which a team could indirectly pick a major league replacement for a lost free agent, but the hard-line owners were not buying that. "The pool is something the association withdrew over a year ago," Grebey said, "and can't be taken seriously."

Kansas City Royals' owner Ewing Kauffman, a pharmaceutical industry kingpin, offered a revealing insight into the snubbed paternalistic mind that had driven ownership to the brink. Defending the need for compensation to Ralph Ray of *The Sporting News,* Kauffman asked, "How would Mr. Miller feel if he put 100 students through law school, then received none of their services after they graduated?"

Moderate Harry Dalton tried to preach compromise. "I hope that we are not about to witness another macho test of wills," Dalton said to a pool of reporters in what he thought was an off-the-record comment shortly after the start of the 1981 season. "From what I hear, the players association is genuinely looking for a compromise if we'll just give them something that they can accept without losing too much face."

The Washington Post picked up this remark and Grebey fined Harry Dalton $50,000 for breaking the owners' gag rule on the negotiations. When asked for a comment, Marvin Miller observed, "I think I always realized that truth had a price, but I never realized it was that expensive." Miller added, "I just find it hard to picture grown men imposing such a gag on themselves. These are the same people who will tell you how to conduct a strike vote."

Most observers of the baseball scene thought a strike more likely now than a year earlier, yet they were surprised at how little the strike was being discussed among the players unlike 1980. But to those who still questioned the players' solidarity, pitcher Rudy May, the Yankees player representative, warned, "Man, don't the owners know that there's going to be a whole generation of ballplayers' sons who grow up with the middle name Marvin? After all that this man has done for us, who's going to be ungrateful enough not to lose some paychecks if we have to?"

Then, 24 hours before the May 29th strike deadline, it seemed that Marvin Miller had pulled another rabbit out of his hat when William Lubbers, chief counsel for the National Labor Relations Board, asked for a temporary restraining order preparatory to an injunction preventing the owners from implementing their compensation proposal. In the summer of 1980, the union had requested the NLRB to bring an unfair labor practice charge against baseball because it had refused to open its economic books while at the same time constantly wailing in public about a pending economic disaster. Lubbers' call for an injunction indicated that he agreed that compensation in the form of Attachment 9 should not be implemented into the Basic Agreement without an examination of baseball's financial condition.

The strike deadline was put on hold as an entourage of lawyers from both sides and the national press corps journeyed to the upstate federal courtroom of Judge Henry Werker where the NLRB case had been randomly dispatched. On June 10, 1981, Judge Werker denied the injunction, ruling, "There has been no convincing evidence submitted that the issue of compensation is an economic one warranting the disclosure of financial information." Attachment 9 would stand. As had happened too many times earlier in judicial rulings on the baseball business, Werker concluded his decision by crying, "PLAY BALL!!! SO ORDERED" (capitals and exclamation points in original).

In effect, Werker's ruling triggered the start of baseball's first industry-wide midseason strike. A desultory last-ditch meeting between players and owners in New York City proved as fruitless as all the others. Early on the morning of June 11st, Commissioner Bowie Kuhn walked down the street and sadly gave a thumbs down sign to an inquiring fan. Moments before, Marvin Miller had gone before the television cameras to say, "We have accomplished nothing. The strike is on."

Players on the road faced varying complications in getting back to their home cities or their permanent homes. Some embittered clubs let players fend for themselves in making travel arrangements. This posed a considerable problem for some athletes who had been so used to having basic life skills taken care of that they lacked the elementary knowledge of finding a travel agent in a telephone book. More benevolent clubs like the Orioles helped the players make arrangements. "My reasoning was simple," Orioles' traveling secretary Phil Itzoe said. "Someday we're going to have this unfortunate situation behind us and we are going to be operating as a baseball team."

The Orioles had been one of the clubs most desirous of avoiding a strike. Since 1979, they had been owned by Edward Bennett Williams, the famous Washington trial attorney who was not as wealthy as most of the other owners. He had heavy interest to pay on a loan and stood to lose a lot of money in a strike. Williams prided himself on a good working relationship with Doug DeCinces and shortstop Mark Belanger, two Orioles who were leaders in the Players Association. Williams liked to say that the three of them could have settled the labor issues in a few hours. Ignoring the threat of Ray Grebey's $500,000 gag rule, Williams was often openly critical of the administration of the Player Relations Committee. "They could foul up a two-car funeral," he once snapped. But Williams was basically a lone voice in the wilderness, dismissed by Grebey as "a loose cannon."

Both sides dug in for what they expected to be a long strike, a test of wills and a war of attrition. Only three desultory meetings were held in the first eight days of the strike. When mediator Moffett was asked why he hadn't called more meetings, he replied, "Things are getting nasty in there. You don't call meetings when nothing good will come out of them."

Accused of having a Svengali-like influence over the players, Marvin Miller withdrew himself from the bargaining table. Until the end of June, the players were represented instead by Belanger, De Cinces, Bob Boone, and Steve Rogers, ace pitcher of the Montreal Expos. Also on the bargaining team was Donald M. Fehr (pronounced "fear"), the lawyer who had successfully argued the Messersmith-McNally case in federal court in 1976 and had replaced Richard M. Moss as Association counsel in 1978. All members of the union bargaining team were used to ownership hardball tactics and by now they comprised a veritable hard line of their own.

Ten days into the strike, with 153 games already canceled, the owners' strike insurance started to kick in. The policy would pay $100,000 for every canceled game up to 500 games and would not expire until August 8. The healthy franchises were used to receiving $100,000 every home date, and the fabulously successful Los Angeles Dodgers regularly took in between $300,000-$500,000 per gate. On the other hand, the labor costs of all the teams would be reduced during a strike. Some poorer franchises like Calvin Griffith's Minnesota Twins actually stood to make money during the strike.

Unlike the 1972 strike, public and press opinion tilted towards the players with both national sports weeklies expressing anger at management. Under a banner headline, "*STRIKE!* The Walkout the Owners Provoked," *Sports Illustrated* editorialized, "This is a struggle in which the workers fought to preserve the status quo and avoid a strike, while the bosses sought radical change and courted a walkout." Less vociferously, *The Sporting News* lamented editorially that the owners had not reacted favorably to the players' compromises on compensation. It was also very critical of the gagging of Harry Dalton, observing, "We need discussion, not a $50,000 fine."

Roger Angell lamented in the *New Yorker* the loss of the "river" of baseball during the strike, the daily "box scores, and the averages and the slowly fluctuous standings." But he offered a penetrating profile of the management mindset that had provoked the strike.

"The players are getting too much money for their own damned good. These salaries are insane — they're ruining the game. Sure, we know who bid the contracts up to where they are now, but now it's got to stop," Angell presented this composite argument (reprinted in his book, *Late Innings*). "And these are just kids — don't forget that. Look at the way they all vote one way as soon as Marvin Miller gives them his spiel. They're country boys and he's a fast-talking city slicker who can outsmart them all. Hell, he's outsmarted us, so far. Now it's time to teach them a lesson. Let's stick it to them just once and see what happens. Let the season go down the tubes, if that's what it takes. We'll hang tough and show them what life is all about. Look, I like these kids — don't get me wrong — but they shouldn't get paid so damned much money and have all those girls on the road and get on TV all the time, when all they're doing is playing ball. . . And they shouldn't be able to quit working for good when they're thirty-five — can you beat that!"

A guest *New York Times* columnist was less detached, urging both sides to give up "your squalid little squabbles. Reassume your

240

dignity and remember that you are the temporary custodians of an enduring public trust," the writer begged. "You are evidently so enthralled by your mucky pelf and your self-serving stratagems that you have forgotten what your trusteeship means," concluded Angelo Bartlett Giamatti, president of Yale University, who five years later would enter baseball as President of the National League en route to his tragically short reign as commissioner of baseball.

A *Wall Street Journal* editorialist penned a poem on June 15th, "Casey on Strike".

> The sneer is gone from Casey's lips, his teeth
>   are clenched in hate,
> He pounds with a cruel vengeance his contract
>   on the plate.
> "It's not a game; it's just a job; that's what it
>   come to be,"
> This is what the slugger said " . . . and we'd
>   be agents free."

The poem ended,

> Oh, somewhere in this favored land the sun is
>   shining bright,
> The band is playing somewhere, and some-
>   where hearts are light,
> And somewhere men are laughing and the kids
>   have what they like,
> But there is no joy for most of us—when
>   Casey's out on strike.

Significantly, the poetry notwithstanding, *The Wall Street Journal,* that bastion of capitalism, published many articles that made a common point: the owners do not know how to run a business efficiently and they should not expect their employees, the players, to bail them out. Columnist Lindley Clark, Jr. borrowed from Shakespeare and dismissed ownership talk about competitive balance as "a tale told by an idiot, full of sound and fury and signifying nothing." He noted that if baseball had competitive balance, why did it take the Phillies 97 years to win the World Series? He lamented that the players seemed to be hung up on competitive balance, too, or else they could go to court to destroy the notion of compensation. "When the contracts expire let the players be free to sign with whom they please," Clark wrote. "That's the way it works in any business and business is what baseball is."

Since the late 1960s, many professors and researchers at the famed Wharton School of Business at the University of Pennsylvania had been fascinated by the workings of the perplexing baseball business. Wharton researcher Vincent Carroll informed *Journal* readers that baseball's problem was an internal one between owners in larger and smaller markets. He suggested that one possible solution to the dispute was to tax a team in a larger market that signs a player from a smaller market. (But when Wharton professors had come up with a similar revenue-sharing proposal in 1970, Bowie Kuhn recalled in his 1987 autobiography, *Hardball,* veteran Pittsburgh Pirates owner John W. Galbreath was furious. "If this gets adopted, it would eliminate control by the owner over his own franchise," Kuhn remembered the millionaire horse-breeder and home developer fuming. "I might as well sell the club.")

On July 1, Marvin Miller returned to the bargaining table, claiming that he did not want to make his absence an issue in the talks. If the All-Star Game scheduled for Cleveland on July 14 was to be saved, there had to be a quick settlement. But on the Fourth of July, talks broke off. New York Mets player representative Rusty Staub summed up the differences, "We are on different planets." A successful New York restaurateur in the offseason, Staub once wistfully observed, "We do no good tearing down our game every few years like this," but he added, "If I ran my business like baseball, I would not survive."

To complicate chances for a settlement, the NLRB hearings started early in July in downtown New York City. Although Judge Werker had denied an immediate injunction, the NLRB still intended to press its case on the owners' unwillingness to give necessary economic data to the union. In another measure of the continuing awe of outsiders at the baseball business, NLRB administrative law judge Marvin Welles stunned the courtroom during a

242

break in one of the sessions by asking Bob Boone and Mark Belanger for their autographs.

One fan vented his rising frustration in a letter published in the July 6 issue of *Sports Illustrated* that blasted the "overpriced, egotistical, and self-indulgent" players. Two weeks later, utility infielder Greg Pryor, the Chicago White Sox player representative, tried to answer the charges of William Ocel.

"I have worked at the same job for 11 years: pro baseball player," Pryor wrote. "My average salary for my first seven seasons in the minor leagues was $6,600 per year. Overpriced?" Pryor explained that in 1977 he had been allowed to choose a new employer because the 1976 Basic Agreement gave free agency rights to six-year minor leaguers as well as six-year major league veterans. Pryor left the Yankees and signed with the White Sox. Yet, after 10 years as a pro, "My average salary from 1971 to 1981 is way up to $25,000 per year. Overpriced?"

"This strike is not designed to benefit players who have signed multi-million-dollar, multi-year contracts," Pryor went on. "They have already received the benefits of their free agency, and if a secret ballot were taken, I believe many of them might vote not to strike," he added frankly. "Instead, the strike is for the benefit of all those present and future players who may become free agents."

Unlike many players, Greg Pryor had some union experience in his background, having an uncle who led a plumbers and pipefitters local in Ohio. Recollecting in 1990, Pryor said, "The players were not trying to get anything else in 1981. We were just trying to retain the benefits that we had achieved through the bargaining process in previous negotiations."

On July 15th, the day after the postponed All-Star Game, Secretary of Labor Raymond C. Donovan came to New York to enter the talks. It was a move that surprised many observers because Ronald Reagan's first Presidential administration had pledged itself to a policy of not "interjecting" itself into disputes in the private sector. In a 1990 interview, mediator Kenneth Moffett explained that Donovan's presence had been requested by John McMullen, the Houston Astros' owner, who knew the Secretary of Labor from mutual associations in New Jersey. Representatives of Vice-President George Bush's office were cool to the idea, Moffett recalled, because Donovan's prior business operations were under intense public scrutiny at the time. It is a measure of the kind of behind-the-scenes clout a baseball owner has that McMullen prevailed and Donovan joined the talks.

The Secretary told both sides in a brief opening statement that he wished that the talks would continue under his aegis. But they continued to get nowhere in New York. A few days later, both sides accepted Donovan's invitation to continue discussions in Washington. Moffett, who was also busy mediating the airline controllers' strike at the time, thought the move away from the media hotbed of New York was a good idea. "Any time you have a total disclosure to the media," Moffett explained to Jane Leavy of the *Washington Post,* "there's going to be posturing." Moffett noted that many of the New York sessions had begun with arguments over what principal had said what to which reporter. When the sides arrived in Washington, Donovan got both sides to agree to a news blackout.

The Washington talks seemed to be making progress along the lines of pooled compensation when the conflict of personalities reared its ugly head once again. Asked about the idea of a pool that mediator Moffett had mentioned in a press briefing, Grebey exploded, "It is not Moffett's idea, he got it lock, stock, and barrel from Marvin." To which Miller replied, "He has told a lot of lies in these negotiations, but this is the worst one."

The talks broke off and both players and owners dispersed for regional meetings. For the first time there was a smattering of news about player dissatisfaction. Dodgers second baseman Davey Lopes told the *Los Angeles Times* that the negotiations were a "circus," adding, "The last thing I want to do is pick up a paper and read Doug DeCinces' synopsis about the players' feelings because he is not qualified and he doesn't what he's talking about." The media had been filled with talk that the season was soon going to be canceled, and Lopes was very concerned. "This forget-the-season attitude really eats at me," he railed. "Before we do that, brother, we better stop and take a vote."

Lopes had been frustrated partly because the media blackout in Washington had kept the players unaware of developments. A regional meeting of the players in Los Angeles calmed Lopes down, and afterwards, he issued a statement totally supporting the Players Association. Except for some resentment that certain players like the Dodgers' Steve Garvey and the Yankees' Tommy John had contractual clauses that paid them during the strike, the players held fast. (Don Baylor waited until the publication of his autobiography in 1989 to utter his belief that players should have stuck together totally, with none being paid during the strike.)

By the end of July, both sides were getting edgy and hoping to end the strike. "George Steinbrenner is telling a reporter that Ray Grebey is fired," Peter Gammons reported in the *Boston Globe,* "and agents concerned with finding lines of credit for their clients are calling Marvin Miller's office." Agent Steve Greenberg, the son of Hall of Fame player and former owner Hank Greenberg, was serving as an intermediary during the strike, and he now estimated that only 15 of the 26 owners still maintained confidence in Ray Grebey's ability to make a settlement. Lee MacPhail was given the go-ahead by commissioner Bowie Kuhn to meet with Marvin Miller to get a feeler as to what the players would accept as a strike settlement.

On July 28, a clear signal of an impending settlement came when some players, who had been at a regional meeting at the Players Association offices, drifted over to the Doral Inn, the New York headquarters of the stalled talks, to meet informally with owners and their representatives. In the early morning hours of July 29, a strike settlement was announced along the lines of pooled compensation. The owners won the "warm body" of a major league player in that each team could only protect 24 men on its 25-man major league roster. But the players association had won the point that the compensation could not be direct but indirect in the form of the pool. The players agreed to drop the NLRB case in exchange for full service credit for days lost during the strike towards their pension and free agency eligibility. Unlike the 1980 settlement, where the leaders of both sides had exchanged perfunctory handshakes, Marvin Miller and Ray Grebey did not shake hands on the morning of July 29, 1981.

The All-Star Game was re-scheduled for August 9th (a day after the strike insurance was slated to run out) and two days later, the season would resume. In keeping with the tradition of the modern history of the Players Association, the union allowed the owners to devise the schedule for the resumption of play. Because teams had played an unequal number of games at the time of the strike, the concept of a "second season" was introduced with all 26 clubs starting the post-strike period at 0-0. Teams who were in first place in their divisions on June 12 were proclaimed winners of the "first season." An additional round of playoffs was added at the end of the season, a contest between the winners of the "second season" and "first season" to decide who would meet in the divisional play-offs for the right to enter the World Series.

Total economic losses in the strike were estimated at $28 million in player salaries, and $72 million in owners' revenue even when the strike insurance monies were subtracted. Both sides now waited with some concern to see if the grumbling fans would come back to the ballparks. *Wall Street Journal* sports columnist Frederick L. Klein noted that a Kalamazoo, Michigan, radio station asked its listeners if they wanted baseball scores reported on news broadcasts and a resounding 95% phoned in no. Before the strike, total major league baseball attendance had been up over 1 million fans, and another gate record was forecast. After the strike, for the first time since the mid-1970s, attendance dropped 11%, and the Saturday afternoon national TV Game of the Week ratings fell one significant point.

The financial problems were soon joined by structural flaws in the split-season format. Many observers, including White Sox manager Tony LaRussa, an attorney, noted that it could be in the interest of a team that won the first half to lose selected games in the second half to an inferior opponent so that a better rival not make the playoffs. "If it turns out you have to lose a game to get in there," LaRussa said, "I could not tolerate nor would I ask my players to lose a ball game; so the best way to do it is to refuse to take the field." Commissioner Kuhn admitted the problems, and there was even talk that the system might be altered.

Baseball stumbled through "the second season" without change, and then faced the additional embarrassment that the team with the best overall record in baseball, the Cincinnati Reds, did not even make the playoffs. The Yankees, the Montreal Expos, the Billy Martin-led Oakland A's, and Los Angeles Dodgers won their way into the regular playoffs, and then at least television executives were happy when the cities in the largest markets, New York and Los Angeles, fought their way into the World Series. After dropping the first two games, the Dodgers swept the next four, thereby avenging their two losses to the Yankees in 1977 and 1978.

When baseball resumed in 1982, attendance picked up as if nothing had happened. Nearly 45 million paying customers went through major league baseball turnstiles, breaking the 1979 record by more than a million. Two Midwestern cities from small markets, St. Louis and Milwaukee, were represented in the World Series.

An imminent changing of the guard on both sides of the labor fence offered the hope that the bitter personality conflicts of the past might be avoided. Marvin Miller followed through on his retirement and in January 1983, Kenneth Moffett, the federal mediator, took on the unenviable job of trying to replace a legend. In April 1983, ending the speculation since the end of the strike that his days were numbered, Ray Grebey departed from the Player Relations Committee. Effective January 1984, his replacement would be the retiring American League President Lee MacPhail, a moderating force on the management side who only took the job when given the unanimous support of all 26 owners.

Baseball was also soon to have a new commissioner. In August 1983, realizing that he lacked the votes for re-election to a fourth term, Bowie Kuhn resigned. Waiting in the wings was the self-made millionaire Peter Ueberroth, a travel entrepreneur who was currently preoccupied with the job of director of the 1984 Los Angeles Olympic Games. Ueberroth's mission would be to make baseball even more profitable than the Olympic extravaganza.

In the fall of 1983, arbitrator Peter Seitz died. In a posthumous essay in *The American Scholar,* the general circulation magazine of

Phi Beta Kappa, Seitz recalled the angry reaction to his Messersmith-McNally decision that "sounded like the last five minutes of Götterdämmerung, the Twilight of Baseball." Eight years later, he happily noted, "The number of hot dogs, bottles of beer, soft drinks, and tickets sold in baseball stadiums has escalated to unprecedented heights, and the competition among baseball teams has never been keener." With new management and better marketing on baseball's mind, it seemed possible that the bitter ideological battles of the past years might be fading. The hope proved illusory.

16

OLD WINE IN NEW BOTTLES:
FROM STRIKE TO COLLUSION TO LOCKOUT

*"The players' definition of give-and-take bargain-
ing is we give and they take."*
—*Barry Rona, management's labor counsel,
shortly before the 1985 baseball strike.*

*"Acting in concert with regard to free agency
rights is prohibited whatever may be the economic
situation of the individual clubs."*
—*Arbitrator Thomas Roberts, September 21,
1987, finding the owners guilty in the Collusion
I case.*

*"He is what he is, a .500 pitcher with a 4.00
ERA."*
—*Agent Alan Meersand, after negotiating a three-
year $3.6 million contract for pitcher Walt Terrell
in the restored free agent market of 1989-90.*

It was early in 1983, and Marvin Miller was clearing files out
of the Players Association office. Kenneth Moffett had recently
taken over as the executive director of the Association, but Miller
was agitated over a new rule that the baseball owners had passed
requiring every club to establish at least a 60-40 ratio of equity to
debt. "Think about that for a moment," Miller exclaimed to *New*

York Times sportswriter Joseph Durso. "They're saying that when you get to that point, you have no more money to pay salaries. They're again flirting with the antitrust law. In any other business, they'd go to jail for that." Durso concluded, "Don't think Marvin Miller has lost any hop on his rhetoric."

Kenneth Moffett must have felt like George Selkirk and Babe Dahlgren, the men fated to follow Babe Ruth and Lou Gehrig. "I've stood in awe of Marvin for 20 years," Moffett told Murray Chass of the *New York Times* shortly before taking on his new job. "We go back to the early 60s when he was working with the United Steelworkers and I was a mediator in Cleveland."

Moffett himself came from a union background, his father and grandfather having worked in the hard coal mines outside of Harrisburg in eastern Pennsylvania. After graduating from the University of Maryland, Ken Moffett's first job had been as a staff representative with the United Mine Workers District 50 office in Baltimore and Richmond, Virginia, but Moffett soon chose a career in mediation. By the time of the 1981 baseball strike, Moffett had risen to the rank of acting director of the Federal Mediation and Conciliation Service.

Initially, Moffett had not been interested in the Players Association job. After the strike ended, both he and Miller provided the players with a list of qualified candidates from the union world. When it became clear to Moffett, a registered Democrat, that the Reagan Administration wanted him out within six months from his current mediation post, he asked the players to be included in the interview process. After he won the job, some baseball management officials raised their eyebrows, questioning the propriety of a neutral in a strike going to work for one of the partisans. "It happens all the time," Moffett told Chass. "We have a history of directors who do that. But they all have gone to management. I'm the first to go to labor."

Moffett's temperament was not as confrontational as his predecessor. During his first weeks on the job, he explored the delicate subject of certifying agents for players. The right to an agent had been included in the 1970 Basic Agreement, and since the coming of free agency in 1976, the agent had joined the player and the owner as an influential third party in the baseball business. But many agents were ill-equipped for the technical tasks of contract-writing and tax planning, and some had even proven unscrupulous. Moffett hoped to work discreetly with management on saving from players from poor representation, but nothing came of agent certification in 1983 because "too many players wanted to stay on the good side of their agents," Moffett reflected in 1990. (The Players Association did establish the right to certify agents in the 1985 Basic Agreement.)

Establishing a joint union-management anti-drug program was another area that Moffett started to explore. Stories of athletes' cocaine addiction had become almost daily items on the sports pages. The National Basketball Players Association was in the process of agreeing to a 1983 program that would expel any players found guilty of three offenses. Drug problems were especially severe in the fierce and painful world of professional football, but one of the many casualties of the lengthy but unsuccessful football players' strike of 1982 was that there were still few restrictions on the power of football commissioner Pete Rozelle to unilaterally suspend players for alleged drug abuses. "I agreed with Marvin Miller about the basic principle that a union should not be forced to discipline and prosecute its members," Moffett recalled in 1990, but the former mediator was concerned about the tragic aspects of drug abuse. He hoped he could make some sensible inroads into a painful and sensitive area.

Shortly before Moffett headed for his first official visit to the players in spring training, Marvin Miller called to ask him if he could use Association offices to write a letter to the player representatives clarifying his role as a consultant. Moffett replied that he did not think it was a good idea. Before he headed south, Moffett asserted his independence dramatically by changing the locks on the Association offices.

While Moffett was touring the spring training camps, the news broke of the new television contract for major league baseball. It was a billion dollar network television deal for broadcasts over the next five years shared as in the past by the National Broadcasting Company and the American Broadcasting Company. When phoned for a comment by Murray Chass, Moffett called the figures "incredible," adding, "That is more money than was thrown around in talks I sat in with Ford and Westinghouse and General Electric." If the prior formula of one-third of the TV money into the players pension was maintained, the fund was due for a whopping increase from $15.5 million to $66 million.

Word started to circulate around the Players Association grapevine that Moffett was not going to be a tough enough negotiator with the owners. In late April 1983, Jerome Holtzman, a rare sportswriter who had been always sympathetic to the Players Association, reported in the *Chicago Tribune* that Mike Marshall had sent a letter to all 26 player representatives warning them about Moffett's inexperience. The feisty reliever was now out of baseball, having been cut by the Twins after the strike, but he had won all his salary from 1981 and 1982 when the National Labor Relations Board ruled in behalf of his complaint that he had been released for union activities. Marshall told Holtzman that he did not necessarily think Moffett should be replaced, but, "It is up to the players to educate Mr. Moffett."

In September 1983, Moffett moved to New York to be closer to his job, but he never got to represent the Players Association at the bargaining table. Shortly before Thanksgiving, the executive board of the Players Association announced the firing of Kenneth Moffett and the two lawyers he had brought to the Association from the mediation service, David Vaughn and Nancy Broff. Named as Moffett's interim replacement was Marvin Miller. "The process of educating the members hadn't been followed as diligently as should have been," board member Steve Rogers explained to *Sports Illustrated* which called Moffett's ouster "a stunning move . . . [and a] palace coup." Don Baylor told Murray Chass, "We were going sideways." Another unidentified player asked, "What is a union leader, an advocate or a mediator?" Association counsel Donald Fehr, mentioned as the most likely to succeed Moffett on a permanent basis, criticized the ousted leader's work habits, citing his walking out on a grievance hearing and his delay in moving to New York. (The hearing in question was on the owners' 60-40 equity:debt ratio that had so disturbed Miller. The union ultimately lost the grievance and fired arbitrator Richard Bloch who ruled against them, but the 60-40 provision is still an ownership rule as of 1990.)

Marvin Miller denied that he had any role in the coup. Since Moffett had locked him out of the Association office, "I had written nothing to players or anybody on player association matters," Miller told Chass. "I had undertaken no phone calls. I had held no meetings." Miller insisted that his return was only for two weeks until the players chose a successor at their annual meeting, but when asked by the Associated Press what would happen if the players could not decide on a replacement, Miller replied, "We'll face that when we get to it."

Moffett was shocked by his ouster after less than eleven months on the job. He told Chass that his willingness to work on the drug problem with management concerned his rivals in the union, Fehr and Mark Belanger, the retired shortstop whom Moffett had brought in as a special assistant but had now joined the dissidents. "I think Don and Mark were afraid if this thing flew," Moffett said, "I might establish a power base and it would be difficult to get rid of me."

In comments in *Sports Illustrated*, Moffett further defended his role in seeking a mutual program in a troublesome area. "Drugs aren't a win-lose type of situation," he declared. "These are kids who are messed up and need help, and there are ways to do this short of confrontation. You can't go to the mat on every issue." Yet going to the mat on every issue had been the style in baseball labor relations for the last two decades. It was now clear that with the interim return of the advocate Miller—who had taught the "kids" and "boys" to be men at the bargaining table—that at least one of the sides in the negotiations for the next Basic Agreement was going to be a hardliner. At the players' meeting in Maui in early December 1985, Donald Fehr was voted acting executive director with Marvin Miller returning to his role as consultant.

When acting director Fehr returned to the mainland, baseball's drug controversy erupted once again. On December 15, 1983, baseball commissioner Bowie Kuhn (still in office prior to the arrival of Peter Ueberroth) announced the suspension for one year of the

Dodgers' ace relief pitcher Steve Howe. Howe had tested positive on three urinalyses during the past season and had been suspended three times. Kuhn said that he had added the additional suspension because "we are going to do what is reasonably necessary to protect our game."

Kuhn's action came as Willie Wilson and Jerry Martin, Kansas City Royals outfielders, began serving three month prison sentences in Fort Worth, Texas, for having purchased cocaine. A third Royal, first baseman Willie Mays Aikens, was to start a sentence in January after finishing a drug rehabilitation program in Baltimore, and onetime All-Star pitcher Vida Blue, released by Kansas City during the 1983 season, was due for sentencing momentarily.

The conviction of the Royals players had shocked the Middle American bastion of Kansas City. The sentencing federal magistrate, J. Milton Sullivant, mentioned the players' "special place in society" as a factor in his deciding on a prison term for the purchase of a relatively small amount of the illegal drug. The fairness of the prison sentences was hotly debated in and out of baseball. "Willie Wilson apologized to me personally," said Kansas City catcher John Wathan (who became the club's field manager in 1988). But veteran pitcher Steve Renko, the American League player representative, told Mike Littwin of the *Los Angeles Times*, "The publicity, the damage to their careers, the fact that no one will ever let them forget what they have done, that seems plenty of punishment." Renko added that many prominent lawyers and doctors who had drug problems were not punished.

Many in the players union were justifiably paranoid about the plans of some owners to use drug violations as an excuse to invalidate long-term contracts. In September 1980, commissioner Kuhn had indefinitely suspended Ferguson Jenkins, the star Texas Rangers pitcher, because he refused to talk to baseball's security officials about his arrest in a Toronto, Canada, airport for possession of cocaine. Jenkins argued that his statements might prejudge his judicial case that was not scheduled to be heard until December. The union grieved the suspension before baseball's impartial arbitrator, Raymond Goetz, who promptly reinstated the pitcher. Citing "the relatively light nature of the charge against Jenkins," Goetz ruled that it was unfair to take away a man's employment before he was brought to trial.

In informal and confidential chats with players, Roger Angell noted in *The New Yorker* that perhaps at least half of the major leaguers were willing to be tested to remove any suspicion. "I have nothing to hide," was a common refrain. Yet there was great doubt as to the sincerity of most owners in their words against drug abuse. In his memoirs, Lee MacPhail frankly recalled the problem of clubs who "wanted to be tough on drugs but they did not want to be involved in any way in confronting their own players."

The Players Association filed a grievance on behalf of Steve Howe while realizing that the player was in dire need of assistance. Meetings continued on a mutual drug assistance program that was finally put into writing later in 1984. It allowed for drug testing of players who reasonable cause suggested might be abusing illegal substances. It was the start of aiding employees in a very sensitive and difficult area.

The arrival of the Miller protege, Donald Fehr, did not affect the changing of the guard at the Player Relations Committee. In January 1984, Lee MacPhail took over as the third director of the owners' beleaguered labor arm. "I'm not really elated about it," MacPhail admitted in an interview shortly before he took on his new assignment, "but somebody has to do it. I think it is important that the owners, players, and Players Association have a good long-term relationship, and that we can work out an agreement that's fair to both sides and without any disruption of play."

Meanwhile, on October 1, 1984, fresh from his success as the organizer of the Los Angeles Olympic Games, Peter Ueberroth, a onetime water polo player at San Jose State University, splashed onto the scene as baseball's sixth baseball commissioner. Soon to be named Time magazine's 1984 Man of the Year for being "the embodiment of the entrepreneurial spirit that is flourishing in the United States," Ueberroth faced a crisis on his very first week on the job. The major league umpires union, headed by the combative Richie Phillips, was demanding more pay for post-season appearances and threatened a strike if not satisfied. Ueberroth stunned management by granting the umpires raises and also increasing the regular season pay for veteran umpires to over six figures. Ueberroth thus momentarily quieted Phillips, who had prepped for the job of representing umpires (and pro basketball referees) as a homicide detective in Philadelphia.

Needless to say, Ueberroth was not going to find matters as simple in trying to use suasion with the players union. Talks for a renewal of the Basic Agreement that had expired at the end of 1984 were going slowly as usual. The voices were lower, which was perhaps an encouraging sign. Lee MacPhail said that the division of television money was going to be difficult and that the owners wanted arbitration reforms, but he did not see any problems with individual owner payolls. "It is up to the separate clubs," he said.

Then, late in February 1985, management changed course. Crisis negotiations returned to baseball when MacPhail called a press conference at the Player Relations Committee offices to announce that baseball's finances were in perilous condition and the owners had decided to open the books to show the problems to the players. Whereas just a few weeks earlier MacPhail downplayed any structural problem in the game, now the siren call of inability to pay was being raised for the first time by the owners. The union prepared itself, skeptically, to examine the data that MacPhail said would be forthcoming immediately. "There may be some information we feel isn't appropriate," MacPhail said, "[but] we'll give them everything within reason they asked for." Acting union leader Fehr warned that it might take until June before the union had made some judgment on the figures. Both sides agreed to continue negotiating while the season started on time.

On June 4, 1985, after visiting the players on all the teams for a second time (the first time had been in spring training), Fehr announced that the union executive board had voted to call a strike after the games of Tuesday night August 6 if a new Basic Agreement had not been signed. The date was chosen because the players would have received most of their salary by then, but the owners would not receive 80% of the television money until post-season competition.

In mid-June, Roger Noll, a Stanford University economics professor and an established academic authority on the baseball business, completed a 47-page report for the union based on the owners' financial figures. After studying the available data for most of the clubs, Noll concluded that the baseball business "seems simultaneously to be experiencing robust growth and declining increases in player salaries."

Management reacted with disbelief, charging that Noll had long been an ally of the Players Association and a witness for the union at Congressional hearings that were investigating whether baseball should be allowed to keep its antitrust exemption. The owners brought forward a report by their own expert, New York University economics professor George Sorter, who said that baseball lost $27 million in 1984. Other management experts claimed that baseball as an industry was heading towards a total loss of almost $240 million by 1988.

Rookie commissioner Ueberroth had not taken an active role in the negotiations, except to urge both sides to keep talking. In late July, as the strike deadline neared, Ueberroth journeyed to Cooperstown to preside over the annual Hall of Fame induction ceremonies that were enshrining outfielders Lou Brock and Enos Slaughter, shortstop Arky Vaughan, and knuckleball pitcher Hoyt Wilhelm. "I am waiting to hear the words 'common ground' and 'compromise,'" Ueberroth said of the stalemated talks. As the spokesman for the fans, Ueberroth declared that there must not be a strike. When these words were relayed to union consultant Marvin Miller, he replied, "Exactly which fans elected him?"

Back at work at the commissioner's office on August 1, Ueberroth announced that he was proposing two points to the negotiators to avert a strike. First, he called for the establishment of a $44 million escrow fund, a midpoint between what the owners were offering and the players wanted for the pension fund. Urging the union to drop its strike deadline, Ueberroth suggested that for every day after August 10 that the dispute was not settled, the sides should agree to give $1 million to amateur baseball. Ueberroth's second point essentially agreed with the owners' call for a ceiling of salary arbitration awards, with the exception of "a superstar clause" exempting an extraordinary player from such a limitation.

Previously, Ueberroth had opposed salary caps of any kind as against free enterprise. The owners, however, had lusted for some kind of control on salary increases ever since the dual pressures of free agency and salary arbitration had pushed their salary bills ever higher. The National Basketball Association had recently gotten its players union to agree to a salary cap, so hope sprung eternal on baseball ownership's side that the union might relent.

Consultant Marvin Miller dismissed Ueberroth's ideas as "grandstanding" and the work of an "amateur" who went public with his proposal before telling each side privately, but the sides continued to talk. Ueberroth explained, "All I am doing is putting the bread on the table with the hope they can break the bread." With the main issues economic, salary arbitration eligibility and pension contributions, public opinion was not on the side of the players in 1985. *The Sporting News* released a poll showing that a large majority of the fans thought that the players were being greedy. Many fans and owners asked why players with an average salary of about $360,000 a year were so concerned about a pension.

On Sunday August 4, two days before the strike date, two milestones in baseball history were established when Tom Seaver won his 300th game and Rod Carew belted his 3000th hit. It was as if the gods of baseball were saying that the sport and its legends would survive the momentary disruptions off the field.

After the games of Tuesday night August 6, 1985, the players did strike again for the fourth time in 14 years. Yet this was to be the quickest baseball strike ever. Within 48 hours, commissioner Peter Ueberroth announced to a packed New York press conference with millions ostensibly watching on TV that all games lost to the strike would be made up by either doubleheaders or games on off-days, and the post-season would proceed on time.

On the surface, it looked like both sides had won some things and lost some others — in short, that real bargaining had at last come to baseball. The players won a hefty increase of almost $21 million into the pension fund, but that was far short of the $66 million or one-third of the television money they had been seeking. The players won a sizable increase in the minimum salary to $60,000, and saw their World Series shares increase noticeably when commissioner Ueberroth had his office give up the 15% cut off the top that former commissioner Kuhn's office had always taken.

A major gain for the owners came after they dropped the idea of the salary cap on an arbitrator's award, when the players gave back a year on salary arbitration. Beginning in 1987, only players with three or more years major league experience would be eligible for that important process. (Economist Gerald Scully reports in his 1990 book, *The Business Of Major League Baseball*, that two-year players' average salary went up from over $213,000 in 1985 to almost $310,000 in 1986, but in 1987, the average dropped 38% to under $192,000.)

There were also two significant changes relating to free agency in the 1985 settlement. Management willingly gave up its right to major league compensation for a lost free agent, settling instead for amateur draft choices. So disappeared the pool that had been the compromise at the end of the bitter 1981 strike. Only seven players had been claimed from the pool in its four years of existence, but one of them had been Tom Seaver, whom the Mets had left unprotected after the 1983 season. When Dennis Lamp, a journeyman White Sox free agent pitcher, was signed by the Toronto Blue Jays, the Chicagoans immediately grabbed Seaver out of the compensation pool. (The incident became a cause celebre in New York, and only the Mets' front office knows to this day whether it was an innocent or a deliberate mistake.)

The other change in the free agent system was the abolition of the re-entry draft and the grant to free agents of the right to sign with any of the 26 major league clubs. The union pushed for this liberalization of the rules, but it did not foresee that the absence of a public draft could aid the owners' desire to cut down on free agent spending; without an open selection of players, the owners could refuse privately to negotiate with any free agents.

The sporting press generally decided that the owners had lost again. "Players win on called third strike" was how Jerome Holtzman's *Chicago Tribune* story was headlined on Thursday August 8. Murray Chass saw the defeat of the salary cap a big victory for the players in his analysis in The New York Times. Many owners were indeed grousing that they had the players on the run for the first time, but let them get away. Eddie Chiles, the Texas Rangers owner who had expressed some sympathy for the players in the 1981 showdown, now grumbled, "We should have dealt with unions like General Motors or the government with the air controllers." Another mogul told Holtzman, "We could have gotten the whole thing, but Ueberroth forced the settlement for his own personal benefit."

Peter Ueberroth refused to take credit for the settlement, praising instead the teams headed by Donald Fehr and Lee MacPhail and his counsel, Barry Rona. But the popular view was that Ueberroth, dubbed "The Lone Ranger" by some owners, had saved the day. *The Sporting News'* cover headline of August 18, 1985 summed up popular perception best: "It's Over, For Pete's Sake."

In spite of the settlement and the rewarding of Donald Fehr with the permanent job as executive director of the Players Association, it was clear that the players' solidarity had not been what it used to be. On the eve of the strike, players were openly saying that they did not think arbitration was a strike issue. "If I don't go to arbitration next year, so what?" said Don Mattingly, whose Yankees were in a close pennant race with Toronto. "I'll probably go the next year." Jim Gott, relief pitcher of the San Francisco Giants, added, "We all know that salary arbitration is unfair, anyway." Another contrast in player solidarity in 1985 and 1981 can be seen in Greg Pryor's 1990 recollection of the two strikes. The writer of the incisive letter to *Sports Illustrated* in 1981, Pryor had since joined the Kansas City Royals, and recalled that he was on a golf course in Kansas City with teammates George Brett and Bud Black when news of the end of the brief strike reached them on the 9th hole. "We said let's tee up for the last nine holes before they call us back to work," Pryor remembered. He added, "We think that we won our division that year because we missed having to face the Tigers' Jack Morris on the day the strike started."

The players had hardly been back to work a day when fierce disagreements erupted between the labor committees as to what had actually been decided in the hectic last hours of the strike. Part of the problem may have been due to the absence of Donald

Fehr from some of the last crucial meetings because of a mysterious illness that ultimately was diagnosed as resulting from a previously undiagnosed case of diabetes. The fundamental flaw was that trust, never in great supply in baseball's labor relations, was rapidly evaporating. The union felt that it had been gulled into giving up the extra year of salary arbitration on the basis of false financial figures brought forth by the owners. As a result of these disagreements, the 1985 Basic Agreement was never put into writing. "It is absurd to think that we functioned for ten years without a written agreement," baseball's current commissioner Fay Vincent said during an August 1990 interview, "but we did."

The retirement of Lee MacPhail as director of the Player Relations Committee shortly after the 1985 settlement did not help the situation. While MacPhail had always accepted management's biases throughout his long career in baseball club and league offices, he was universally respected throughout baseball. Barry Rona, his replacement, had been a longtime counsel to the PRC, and his experience in the game had been virtually limited to the contentious labor relations field. Insiders noted a rising animosity on the part of Rona's counterpart, Donald Fehr, who believed that he had been tricked by Rona into giving up the extra year of salary arbitration. Soon the Rona-Fehr relationship was almost as bad as the Miller-Grebey one.

To add to this unfortunate state of affairs came the anti-drug crusade of commissioner Peter Ueberroth who urged all players to support his call for mandatory drug testing. Ueberroth said that he had a "personal obligation to families everywhere whose children idolize baseball players, to the game of baseball and to the players directly." He claimed that within a few years, all of society would be looking to baseball as a model program for fighting drug abuse. "In the short term and the long term, we will be successful. Flat successful," Ueberroth told *New York* magazine writer Nancy Collins. "Successful *period*. The only important thing is that we become the first sport to put this problem behind us" (italics in original). Ueberroth even talked about using AWAC's fighter planes to keep cocaine and other illegal drugs from crossing our borders.

There had been a delicate balance created on the management-union drug committee, but it was destroyed in September 1985 when Ueberroth, deliberately skirting the union, sent a letter to each individual player asking him to support his program of drug testing. George Steinbrenner personally delivered Ueberroth's letters to the New York Yankees clubhouse, but player representative Dave Winfield intervened, telling his boss that the letter was an unfair labor practice. "The union must be consulted first," Winfield said. Steinbrenner stalked out, and Winfield proceeded to toss the letters into the waste basket.

The players were deeply divided and troubled about the drug problem, but Ueberroth's actions were almost universally seen as grandstanding. Don Baylor told Murray Chass that many players thought Ueberroth had played an important role in settling the strike, but he lost that support with his heavyhanded actions about drugs. "I don't think the commissioner realizes how far he got set back," Baylor concluded.

Undoubtedly, one of the reasons for Ueberroth's action was his concern about the black eye baseball would absorb when several major league players were due to testify in a Pittsburgh federal courtroom at the trial of Curtis Strong, a Philadelphia caterer who was accused of being a major supplier of cocaine to players. Ueberroth's fears were realized in September 1985 when nightly television news programs highlighted major league baseball players, under a grant of immunity from prosecution, baring the lurid story of their involvement with cocaine.

Ueberroth was under heavy pressure to hit the drug abusers with severe penalties. He deliberated on a decision during the off-season, and at the start of 1986 spring training, Ueberroth announced suspensions for all 19 players implicated in the Pittsburgh scandal. He said that the penalty would be waived if the players agreed to donate a portion of their salary to anti-drug programs. Only the Mets' first baseman Keith Hernandez initially indicated that he would challenge Ueberroth's terms, but then he succumbed to the intense club and media pressure and agreed to the fines. When asked to comment by Ross Newhan of the *Los Angeles Times*, union consultant Marvin Miller said, "Apparently we don't have players with guts enough to defend themselves."

Even more detrimental than the drug controversy to baseball's labor relations scene was the disappearance of the free agent market after the 1985 season. There were no bids whatsover for the services of Kirk Gibson, the Detroit Tigers outfielder, a game-breaking player and hard-nosed competitor who was a key member of the 1984 world champions. Nor did a good relief pitcher, Donnie Moore of the California Angels, receive one offer. Gibson and Moore returned to their original teams, receiving pay increases but not the kind of gigantic hikes free agents had come to expect. White Sox catcher Carlton Fisk, a potential Hall of Famer, received only one legitimate bid from another team, the Yankees, before deciding to remain in Chicago.

The Players Association did not see the elimination of the 1985 free agent market as a simple matter of management's fiscal prudence. In February 1986, it filed a grievance with baseball's arbitrator Thomas Roberts, protesting management's most recent action. Soon the word "collusion" was entering the sports pages almost as frequently as "compensation" had six years earlier. In both cases, the word symbolized the growing distrust between the parties to the labor agreement.

Article XVIII, Section H of the historic 1976 Basic Agreement that created the first bargained changes in the reserve system stated, "The utilization or non-utilization of rights under this article XVIII is an individual matter to be determined solely by each Player and each Club for his or its own benefit. Players shall not act in concert with other Players and Clubs shall not act in concert with other Clubs." Ironically, it was the owners in 1976 who insisted on this language because they were worried that a players' agent might get his clients to act in concert. A high-powered agent with many players in his stable might insist, for example, that a team sign one of his less talented players before he offered the services of his more desirable client.

As history unfolded, it turned out to be the owners who were violating the spirit of the provision. The Players Association hoped for a swift judgment of collusion and damages to the players whose

263

market value had been reduced by the curtailing of the free agent market. Arbitration decisions take time, of course, and in June 1986, while the collusion case was still being studied, the owners fired Thomas Roberts as arbitrator. Allegedly, they were protesting his decision that drug testing clauses in individual player contracts were unconstitutional, but Barry Rona had admitted that the drug clauses were voluntary, leading the Players Association to believe Roberts' firing was only a stalling tactic to prevent his ruling on collusion. So, confident that Roberts had been unfairly fired, the union agreed that Richard Bloch, the arbitrator it had fired over the 60-40 equity-debt grievance, should rule on the legality of Roberts' firing. In September 1986, Bloch reinstated Roberts, declaring that there was no precedent for firing an arbitrator in the middle of the case.

The owners had bought time, however, for Roberts would not rule on the case that became known as Collusion I until September 1987. Meanwhile, in the off-season of 1986, the case that became known as Collusion II was playing in baseball's once-vibrant free agent theater. Most baseball observers considered this crop as more appealing than the previous year's. At least nine players were considered prime candidates for new employers, pitchers Ron Guidry and Doyle Alexander, catchers Lance Parrish, Bob Boone, and Rich Gedman, slugger Bob Horner, second baseman Willie Randolph, and two outstanding outfielders from the Montreal Expos, Andre Dawson and Tim Raines. Yet once again, no bids were forthcoming.

The owners demonstrated their new found solidarity even further when no club put in bids for Raines and Gedman after December 8, 1986. In the 1985 Basic Agreement, the union had agreed to a provision that said a free agent not signed by his team or offered salary arbitration by December 8 could not be re-signed by his old team until May 1. It did not foresee that the owners might use the provision to bring unwanted unemployment to the free agent. To paraphrase what Cubs general manager James Gallagher had said before the amnesty for Mexican League "jumpers" had been declared in 1949, "The sight of Tim Raines and Rich Gedman languishing at their homes will keep players from trying the free agent market again."

Early in 1987, Andre Dawson had also not found a new employer. He had not re-signed with Montreal because he desperately wanted out of Olympic Stadium where the astroturf had taken a terrible toll on his knees. In Richard M. Moss, Dawson had a creative and knowledgeable agent, an experienced hand at tilting with baseball moguls. The first counsel to the modern Players Association, Moss had been with Marvin Miller every step of the way from 1966 to 1977. He had argued and won the arbitration cases of Catfish Hunter, Andy Messersmith and Dave McNally, he had negotiated Nolan Ryan's first multimillion dollar contract in 1979, and he had won for Dodgers' southpaw Fernando Valenzuela the first million dollar arbitration victory in 1983.

Knowing that Andre Dawson wanted to finish his career on a grass home field and that the prospect of day baseball in Wrigley Field in Chicago was very appealing to his client, Moss headed for the Cubs' home base in Mesa, Arizona with spring training already underway in 1987. Moss informed Cubs president Dallas Green, a former journeyman pitcher and a stalwart member of the baseball's old guard, that Dawson wanted to play for the Cubs so badly that he would sign a blank contract. The Cubs could fill in the salary. Shamed into making a bid at such a bargain basement opportunity for a valuable player, Green offered Dawson a contract for $500,000, almost half of what he had earned in his last year in Montreal. (Dawson went on to be voted the Most Valuable Player in the National League in 1987 and ultimately received a long term contract.)

Richard Moss also tried to break the free agent log jam for another client, the Tigers' ace righthander Jack Morris. He offered Morris' services on a one-year basis to four clubs of the pitcher's choice, including the Twins, who played in his home area of St. Paul, Minnesota, and the Yankees. George Steinbrenner salivated at the prospect of getting a proven workhorse for his beleaguered pitching staff, but he would not break ranks with his partners. Morris returned to the Tigers but won a whopping $1 million raise in salary arbitration when the Tigers refused to give him a long-term contract. Ultimately, as with Dawson negotiations, Moss won a longterm contract for his star.

In a May 1, 1987 article in the *Wall Street Journal,* Moss told reporter Hal Lancaster that the owners had been "teaching free agents a lesson: If you become a free agent, nobody will make you an offer and it might end your career." The veteran players' advocate went on to suggest that there were darker conspiracies being planned by the owners. Sharing his dark vision from his "stark aerie" on a Southern California mountaintop that Lancaster noted was so steep "that it was not unlike scaling the Himalayas in search of a guru," Moss warned that with the free agent market killed, the owners planned next to scuttle salary arbitration. They will simply not offer a contract to those three to six year players still eligible for salary arbitration, and then they could be frozen out like the free agents had been, he forecast.

The owners are flirting with anti-trust violations, the agent concluded, and he expressed the hope that the pending Collusion I grievance could result in the arbitrator giving the players the right to sue for treble damages as granted by antitrust law. Moss hinted that the players had also been seeking out "substantial people" in major cities to become backers of a competing major league. So came to light the notion of an "agents' league," as management people would come to deride it. Such a new league was reported as a possibility for 1990, but in 1989, plans for the new circuit were postponed indefinitely.

Moss' forebodings were not paranoid. Since the early 1980s, many teams had tried to cut down arbitration losses by hiring the independent consulting firm of Talbot "Tal" Smith, a former general manager for the Houston Astros. While Smith's services aided many teams in winning arbitration cases, the problem of losing even by winning in salary arbitration remained acute for the owners. It was not inconceivable that a unilateral attack on salary arbitration might be in the works.

In March 1987, the owners won a rare recent legal victory when the United States Supreme Court refused to overturn a federal appellate ruling in Chicago that granted the owners' exclusive ownership of television rights. "Any traditional right of players to control their own publicity or use of their likenesses is preempted," the local court had ruled.

Whatever cause there might have been for celebration in ownership circles on the television issue faded on September 21, 1987. On the same day that, coincidentally, pro football players went out on strike in another unsuccessful effort to gain free agency, reinstated arbitrator Thomas Roberts handed down the verdict of guilty against the owners for collusion against the 1985 free agent market. Roberts did not find the proverbial smoking gun, but he based his judgment on the compelling circumstantial evidence that after three management meetings in 1985, the free agent market all but disappeared.

Roberts cited first a meeting on September 27, 1985 in Itsaca, Illinois that commissioner Peter Ueberroth had chaired. The cost of player development was the subject on the baseball agenda, but Roberts inferred that a plan to restrain the market for free agents was also hatched. Roberts then mentioned a memorandum that retiring Player Relations Director Lee MacPhail had circulated to the owners in St. Louis on October 22, 1985 at their annual World Series meeting. In his farewell address, MacPhail had written, "We must stop day dreaming that one free agent signing will bring a pennant," but he noted wearily, "This requires resistance to fan and media pressure and is not easy." At the same meeting, Peter Ueberroth encouraged an informal poll of the owners who pledged not to offer longterm contracts to players.

In his ruling, Roberts noted that before the owners' World Series meeting, the Kansas City Royals had wooed free agent outfielder Kirk Gibson, and some of their officials had even taken him on a hunting trip. After the St. Louis gathering, the interest in Gibson "suddenly cooled."

Roberts cited as the final evidence of the conspiracy against free agents an action taken by the owners at their winter meeting in San Diego in December 1985. After Lee MacPhail handed out a list of available free agents, Roberts wrote, "Every major league club abstain[ed] from the free agent market until an available free agent was 'released' by his former club upon the announcement that the former club was no longer interested in his services." The arbitrator concluded his 16-page decision by saying, "Acting in concert with regard to free agency rights is prohibited whatever may be the economic situation of the individual clubs."

Responding to the defeat, Barry Rona said, "One of the great difficulties I have with the decision, to be blunt, is figuring out what we have to do different to be in compliance." Other management spokesmen expressed similar sentiments, saying that no one could force them to spend unwisely when they had learned a lesson. One of Lee MacPhail's most earnest points in his memorandum had been that some owners had been pledging deferred compensation to players until well in the 21st century. Given the rapid turnover in ownership, MacPhail thought that an especially foolhardy managerial judgment.

When to no one's surprise the union and management could not decide on appropriate damages, arbitrator Roberts on December 21, 1987 offered a so-called "second look" free agency to the free agent class of 1985. Kirk Gibson, still the most valuable member of that group, took advantage of his new opportunity by signing a long-term contract with the Los Angeles Dodgers. He was instrumental in their pennant and 1988 World Series victory, his pinch-hit home run in the bottom of the ninth inning of the Series' first game against the Oakland Athletics one of the most dramatic moments in baseball history. But Roberts granted only seven of the 62 eligible free agents a "second look" because the others had been eligible to become free agents again since the collusion had occurred.

The same scenario was acted out in Collusion II when arbitrator George Nicolau ruled on August 31, 1988, that the class of 1986 free agents had been conspired against. In a lengthy 81-page decision, Nicolau was far more harsh on the owners' conspiracy. "Everyone 'understood' what was to be done," the arbitrator wrote. "There was no vestige of a free market, as that term is commonly understood." Nicolau cited the example of Tigers' free agent catcher, Lance Parrish, whom the Phillies wanted to sign but Detroit wanted to keep. Nicolau noted that American League President Dr. Bobby Brown and two powerful owners on the Player Relations Committee, Milwaukee's Bud Selig and the White Sox'

268

Jerry Reinsdorf, had called up Phillies' president William Giles whose interest cooled, although Parrish ultimately signed with the Phillies.

Nicolau named other management names, too, old owners and new ones, in a ringing denunciation of "a pattern of uniform behavior . . . in deliberate contravention of club obligations" under the Basic Agreement. In hailing the decision, Donald Fehr called the collusion a "story of deceit, dissembling and conspiracy." Like arbitrator Roberts before him, Nicolau offered a "second look" to fourteen free agents, but Bob Boone was the only ballplayer who took advantage, moving from the California Angels to the Kansas City Royals for the 1989 season.

A Collusion III case was filed for the 1987 free agent group because while there had been some movement from league to league, most noteworthily, slugger Jack Clark of the Cardinals moving to the Yankees, there was still a pattern of restricted movement and declining salary increases. The Collusion III case was also won by the union early in 1990. The ultimate monetary damages that collusion will cost management will run well over $200 million.

Meanwhile, the Player Relations Committee was preparing for the next crisis by advising clubs to put lockout clauses in any long-term contracts negotiated beginning in 1988. Management wanted players to agree to non-payment in case of a lockout or a strike. Some player agents were able to get neutral clauses inserted, i.e. pay during a strike or lockout would be determined by an impartial arbitrator. Many agents also negotiated longterm contracts with a very low salary for 1990 so that in case of a major work stoppage, the player did not lose much money. With 1990 two years away, the signs for another major confrontation were unmistakable. When the genial William Giles was asked by the *Philadelphia Inquirer* to describe the state of baseball's labor relations in the late 1980s, he replied, "The worst ever."

Yet amidst all the rancor and turmoil, the popularity and prosperity of baseball was reaching new heights. Peter Ueberroth's marketing prowess was paying off. The new Major League Baseball Promotion Corporation was bringing in unprecedented amounts of revenue. In 1989, total major league attendance would soar over

55 million people with another 23 million people flocking to see minor league baseball. College baseball in the same year would count over 12 million spectators. Bubble gum cards, always big sellers in the youth market, doubled in sales during the 1980s, and purchasing such cards was now considered by some analysts a better investment than the stock market.

"Baseball's doing better than I told it to," Ueberroth told *Esquire* writer Mike Lupica in 1988, adding, "These words aren't going to look too good on paper." But Ueberroth, the Lone Ranger, really did not care what many people thought. He was a doer, a man whose favorite word was pro-active, as opposed to re-active.

Early in 1988, Ueberroth called a press conference to announce another staggering television contract for baseball. The Columbia Broadcasting System, hoping that baseball would boost its sagging ratings, had purchased the exclusive rights to network baseball from 1990 to 1994. For the first time, a full season of baseball games would also be broadcast on cable television, the Entertainment and Sports Network (ESPN) paying $400 million for the right to broadcast over 160 games a year.

Ueberroth was hailed for his achievement, but he was giving clear signals that he was only going to be a single- term commissioner. Rumors of high political aspirations always followed him around, either a Republican candicacy for Senator of California or even the Presidency of the United States. Ueberroth grew irritated at the constant rumors; intimates said that he did not have the patience to glad hand votes for any elective office including election as baseball commissioner. Although he said that he enjoyed reading baseball's box scores as much as stock market quotations, Ueberroth had never really warmed up to the game's traditions and its collection of characters. Needless to say, the steady stream of collusion judgments did not make his decision to leave any harder.

For a change, however, the transition to a new commissioner in baseball was easy and relatively painless. A. Bartlett Giamatti, National League President and an eloquent elegist of the game, was voted unanimously as Ueberroth's successor effective at the end of 1989. With the television contract in place and some major controversy on the way with the investigation of Pete Rose's gambling activities, Ueberroth left office early in the spring of 1989, returning to the private sector as head of Contrarian Industries in Newport Beach, California.

While president of Yale University, Bartlett Giamatti had led the institution through an intense 5-week employee strike. Union leaders on the Yale campus had not been enthralled by Giamatti's performance, and it is quite possible that he would have had his confrontations with the ballplayers' union. Yet few players or anyone in the baseball business could have disagreed with what Giamatti told *Business Week* in a cover story in early April 1989. "The greatest problem in baseball today can be expressed in one word: mistrust," he said. "Mistrust among owners, among players, mistrust of owners by players and owners by agents. It is corrosive."

In a position that had not been filled with men of vision, Giamatti gave promise of posing clearly the challenges of the future. He was a traditionalist who liked the game on grass and detested the designated hitter, but he also realized that baseball had a new audience of younger people who liked the fastness of astroturf baseball and watched the game on new television technology. "That screen is going to have an enormous impact on the forms of leisure it transmits," Giamatti told *U.S. News and World Report* in October 1986. "All this is going to have to be understood and anticipated to keep an aging public and a public accustomed to another form of vision interested in baseball."

One of Giamatti's first acts as commissioner was to create a new post, deputy commissioner, and he filled it with Francis T. "Fay" Vincent, a former member of the Securities and Exchange Commission who most recently had been the president of Columbia Pictures. Vincent had come into the movie business in the wake of the embezzlement scandal of Columbia's prior president, David Begelman. Vincent's total inexperience in the movie business was considered a plus by the company's managers. Vincent was soon dubbed the Judge Landis of the movies, a connection not lost on his new and close friend, Bart Giamatti.

On August 24, 1989, with deputy commissioner Vincent sitting at his side, commissioner Giamatti announced the permanent suspen-

271

sion of Pete Rose because his gambling activities had not been "in the best interests of baseball." Eight days later while on vacation on Cape Cod, A. Bartlett Giamatti, 50, died of a massive heart attack.

Fay Vincent was named his successor immediately, baseball's eighth commissioner, and remarkably, third within four months of 1989. Vincent's early days in office were also tumultuous. Shortly before the start of Game 3 of the World Series between the Oakland Athletics and the San Francisco Giants, the Bay area was rocked by a severe earthquake, the most devastating since the 1906 San Francisco disaster. At least 59 people died and over 3,000 were injured, besides extensive property damage. Vincent postponed the Series for eleven days before deciding, with the consent of local officials, that it would be good for the spirit of the area for the games to resume.

In Vincent's first months on the job, he gave clear indications to the players that he wanted improved relations and better lines of communication with the Players Association. He chose as his deputy commissioner Steve Greenberg, the agent who had been an intermediary during the 1981 strike and who had deep baseball roots as Hall of Famer Hank Greenberg's son.

On October 31, 1989, literally on the eve of the beginning of talks for the new Basic Agreement, Vincent announced that Barry Rona had resigned as head of the Player Relations Committee. Named as Rona's replacement was Charles T. O'Connor, Jr., who had been counsel to the PRC for only about a year. O'Connor was a partner in the law firm of Morgan, Lewis, Bockius, and not associated with the corporate law firms of Willkie, Gallagher, and Farr or Baker and Hostetler that had represented the American and National Leagues for years and had advised the PRC during the major legal cases of the 1970s. It was another sign that the commissioner wanted to put the antagonisms and failures of the past behind him.

Although O'Connor did not know he was going to be the PRC point man for the 1990 negotiations until the last minute, he was familiar with the general thrust of management's position. "Revenue sharing" was one of the new catchwords. The idea was a variation of the "percentage of the gross" scheme that the football

272

players had put forward in 1982 to no avail and that the basketball players had agreed to in 1984 when shown real losses by the basketball owners at the bargaining table. At an early session, O'Connor asked Donald Fehr to give him a reasonable estimate of what percentage of baseball revenue the players would like to have. In basketball, it was close to 50%, but Fehr saw no reason to answer. As before, the players saw no reason for a change in a system that, with the end of collusion, was once again reaping sensational rewards.

George Steinbrenner had kicked off the 1989 free agent market by offering volatile pitcher Pascual Perez a three-year contract worth over $5 million. (Perez pitched only 14 innings in 1990 before giving out to a season-ending arm injury). Gene Autry brought down some more of his saddlebags stuffed with money to corral southpaw pitcher Mark Langston at $16 million for five years. (Langston, too, would prove a major disappointment in 1990 with a sub-.500 record.)

As in the late 1970s, the bidding for free agents brought higher salaries for those players who were not quite yet eligible to test the market. Twins' outfielder Kirby Puckett broke the $3 million a year barrier in a long-term contract as did Giants' first baseman Will Clark. Before long, six players were earning over $3 million. In early April, Don Mattingly broke the $4 million a year barrier, followed only two months later, by a $5 million a year five-year contract for the Oakland Athletics' outfielder Jose Canseco.

Salary arbitration awards in early 1990 also produced an aggregate gain of 98% for the eligible players, up from 71% in 1988. Although the owners had saved an average of $100,000 a player since the eligibility requirement for arbitration had been raised to three years in 1987, the hated process was still a bone in many hardliners' craw. But, now in 1990, the players were poised to get back that year for the younger members of the union.

It was hard for the owners to convince players that revenue sharing was needed when the all the owners seemed to be joining the spending spree. For instance, Milwaukee owner Bud Selig, the chairman of the Player Relations Committee, was one of the leading advocates of revenue sharing. He constantly urged the players to help the owners in smaller markets to compete. Yet while talking about restraint, in the winter of 1989-90, Selig anted up over $3 million a year to sign each of his longtime stars, outfielder Robin Yount and infielder Paul Molitor, to multi-year contracts.

Early in January 1990, Charles O'Connor informed Donald Fehr that the players would be locked out of spring training if an agreement was not reached by February 16. As always, progress was at a snail's pace in the early negotiations. The owners had not offered any pension increases, were asking again for salary caps on arbitration awards, and still had revenue-sharing on the table.

The impolite word "lockout" was not used by management until the eve of the deadline when Charles O'Connor said, "I concede at this stage it's a lockout." Management privately must have known that the lockout had only a long shot at being successful. The players did not get paid until the season started, and the union had prepared for the likelihood of a lockout by withholding licensing money as a potential strike fund. But remembering the experience of the in-season strikes of 1981 and 1985, when players had been paid but owners had not received most of their television money, management decided the lockout was its only chance to get an agreement from the union.

On February 16, 1990, the owners imposed the lockout. A few players on the New York Mets tried to work out in the club's new facility in Port St. Lucie on the east coast of Florida. When turned away, they went to play golf—"The First Annual Lockout Invitational," quipped Mets' pitcher Bob Ojeda. With no movement towards an agreement, Donald Fehr told the players not to hurry to the spring training areas to make the owners think that they were so eager to play. "Go fishing or play golf," he advised. When there was no movement in the first days of the lockout, lawyer Fehr warned that the first spring exhibition games were close to being "implicated."

Talks continued in New York through late February, many of them held in commissioner Vincent's office as a courtesy to Vincent who because of an injury in college walked with difficulty. The talks were reasonably civil and informal. "It's not shirts and skins," *New York Times* columnist Ira Berkow quoted Richard Levin, a public relations spokesman for the commissioner's office. "No one has trouble telling one side from the other." There was little movement, however, and Fehr warned that he planned to visit the players near the Florida and Arizona training sites before the end of February. Paul Molitor, a longtime Players Association activist, summed up the players' essential confidence. "They haven't come in our direction," he said. "We'll just have to wait and listen."

Press commentary was extremely critical of the lockout at a time of prosperity in baseball. Citing the massive influx of television cash, sportswriter Tom Callahan wrote in the *Washington Post*, "Baseball is almost embarrasingly flush." Callahan went on to enjoy the irony of former baseball commissioner Bowie Kuhn's recent flight to an obscure hideout in Florida to escape creditors. "Almost as exquisite as the name Marsh Landing is the thought of the word bankruptcy being returned literally to the doorstep of Kuhn," Callahan wrote of baseball's ex-commissioner who had never ceased to moan about baseball's fiscal problems.

Another Wharton School management professor twitted ownership's position in a *Wall Street Journal* opinion piece, "For Better Ball Nothing Beats Greed." Joseph W. Harder's study of eight 1988 arbitration award winners indicated that the so-called "overpaid" players had performed better than in previous years. Harder also noted that because of collusion, free agents since 1987 had actually earned 23% less than players with similar statistics who had not been free agents.

When commissioner Vincent convinced the owners to withdraw the revenue sharing concept from the table, there was hope that the lockout might be a short one. But on February 21, the owners' negotiators brought to the table a proposal that asked the players not only to accept salary arbitration caps but to waive the application of free agent salaries to arbitration awards. The owners had been trying without success for this concession for years. Murray Chass reported in the *New York Times* that the proposal was the work of Frank Cashen and Harry Dalton, moderate general managers who, after years of trying to stop the tide of salary increases, had promoted a measure worthy of King Canute.

275

The very next day, commissioner Vincent told the union to consider that yesterday had never happened. But there was still no agreement on pension contributions and the union was determined to win back that year of arbitration it had yielded in 1985. "I still hear about it from the younger players," said Fehr, as he left for the south and his visit to the players without an agreement.

The game of high stakes poker continued until March 18 when 24 hours before ESPN was scheduled to televise its first spring training exhibition game, the lockout ended with both sides announcing the acceptance in principle of a new Basic Agreement. It was essentially an extension of the previous contract except that the union did win back salary arbitration eligibility for certain two year players via a "manipulation window" that was put into the contract to enable approximately 17%, or about 12 players, to qualify for arbitration. The minimum salary was raised to $100,000 with a cost-of-living increase added for later years. To discourage future collusion, a treble damages penalty was spelled out in the contract.

Assessing the settlement in the *Chicago Tribune*, Jerome Holtzman marveled at another major victory for the union. By gaining back some arbitration rights for younger players, something most observers had thought impossible, Holtzman estimated that the union had gained $70 million over the next five years. "Fehr was shooting for the moon and he hit Mars," he quoted one wag. The result really was not too surprising, Holtzman argued. A professional union was matched against a Players Relations Committee consisting of "a banker [the Twins' Carl Pohlad], a car salesman [Selig], two real estate developers [Jerry Reinsdorf of the White Sox and Fred Wilpon of the Mets], and an ex-Navy commander whose expertise is marine architecture [the Astros' John McMullen whose tirades against union leaders had only traditionally served to unite the players]. A motley assemblage, all with different agendas." Holtzman concluded, "They can barely crack an egg. Even if they tried to break the union, they wouldn't know how." He chortled, "Next time around, [the union] will want more."

What will the next time around offer and what will be the shape of baseball in the 21st century? In spite of the frustrations of the lockout that cost the small spring training businesses of Florida and

Arizona millions of dollars, baseball did not seem to lose many fans as a result. Total major league attendance continued to surge. The creation of two expansion teams in the National League for the 1993 season promised to bring more money to the owners ($95 million was established as an entry fee), 50 more jobs for the players, and more opportunity for Americans to see the national game.

Baseball had another successful year in 1990 with interesting pennant races and the emergence of a possible dynasty in the Oakland Athletics. On the other hand, television ratings for the first year of the new contract were disappointing. Some people wondered whether television money, the fuel that had sparked the latest free agent spending, had peaked, while others still thought of pay TV as an untapped cash cow.

While new blood in high places has never meant much change in baseball's labor relations, it is hard not to feel optimistic about the new leadership on management's highest level. Commissioner Fay Vincent, who left Columbia Pictures a very rich man, seems to have both intelligent independence and a genuine love of the game. "I think being the commissioner of baseball is the finest job in the private sector," he has said on many occasions.

Vincent is cautiously optimistic that the economic study committee which was created in the 1990 Basic Agreement will be fruitful. Although aware of the past failure of such efforts in baseball, Vincent noted in an August 1990 interview, "Anything is progress. We don't have agreement on what the industry made." Donald Fehr and Bud Selig, the revenue sharing enthusiast, will serve on the committee, the commissioner said, as well as "four men of size and substance and standing."

Coming out of the entertainment business, Vincent can live with the reality of players making huge salaries, and he does not think that the fans really mind. "They don't think of Will Clark as an economic being," he says about the $4 million a year San Francisco Giant first baseman. Vincent often expresses the wish that people see business problems as economic not moral.

Charles T. O'Connor, the new Player Relations Committee director, shares that commonsensical approach. "Some employers cannot accept that his employees have chosen an intermediary,"

O'Connor observes. "But they get over it. It took baseball a long time to make a hospitable acceptance that their players wanted to be represented by a union."

This is not to say that new agreements in baseball will be smooth sailing. There is too much money involved and such a long history of conflict and greed on both sides that crisis will never likely be far away. It will be interesting to see if calm management can convince skeptical players that fundamental changes like revenue sharing are needed in the future. As San Francisco Giant outfielder Brett Butler, a member of the Players Association executive subcommittee, observed towards the end of the 1990 season, "If the owners could build a relationship where there was some trustworthiness, both sides could prosper tremendously."

Another hope for the future, however fanciful, is that the daily conditions of baseball can be addressed in an open fashion by both sides. Many people in baseball feel that the season is too long, and that a return to the longtime tradition of 154 games makes considerable sense. Yet the subject has never been seriously discussed probably because of the adjustments in lowered revenue and wages that both sides would likely have to make.

Another issue concerns the steady increase in the length of individual games. The three-hour contest is now commonplace. Can both sides address this problem in a true spirit of "the best interests of the game"?

Outside the contentious atmosphere of the bargaining room, many players have expressed concern about trends in the game. During the 1990 season, after he had been one of the leaders in the successful negotiations for the Players Association, Paul Molitor reflected, "I see a tremendous difference in players' approach to the game, whether it is veteran players with long-term contracts or younger players concerned about arbitration eligibility." While glad that players are prospering, Molitor feels that many players no longer know "what it is for teams to get together and win championships." He reflects, "It has taken away from some of the pleasures that ballplayers should have as players."

If players can express these concerns in an environment where the owners don't take the remarks as weakness, there is hope that the game will continue to flourish artistically as well as financially. "If I had the power," Greg Pryor reflects, "I'd put every player back on one-year contracts." Pryor recalls that he made the point when asked what he would do by Avrom Fogelman, who was briefly the Kansas City Royals' owner in the 1980s before bankruptcy forced his selling the team back to Ewing Kauffman.

It is interesting that a hero of this story in less prosperous days, John Montgomery Ward, felt the same way about the incentive spurred by one-year contracts. Whether the view is true or not, John Montgomery Ward still talks pertinently to the baseball situation. One hundred years after the failure of the players to run their own league, Ward is worthy of remembering in so many ways. Yet the clash of wills between resistant owners and newly enriched players would not abate.

Epilogue
The Cataclysmic Strike of 1994 and the Recovery

There was some good economic news about baseball in the first years of the 1990s. Major League attendance reached a new plateau in 1993 with over seventy million fans passing through the turnstiles, an increase of over fifteen million spectators from 1992. Admittedly, half of the gain came from the seven and a half million fans who attended games of the new franchises, the Florida Marlins in Miami and the Colorado Rockies in Denver, but the additional gain of millions of new paying fans in other cities showed that baseball still had a solid audience even if all the opinion polls said that pro football had eclipsed pro baseball as the country's most popular sport by a two-to-one margin. Licensing revenues were also growing in baseball, up to $3 billion in 1993, double the amount of 1990.

Yet the good news was dwarfed by the clearly visible war shadows for another coming labor confrontation. Both CBS and ESPN had lost money on the billion-dollar national television contract that had been former baseball commissioner Peter Ueberroth's parting gift, and the owners were bracing for a much less lucrative next TV contract. In April 1992 the last payment of the $280 million in collusion damages against free agents was due, but in fact there was considerable haggling going on over the amounts due to players who had suffered in the frozen market of the mid-1980s. With unfettered free agency restored, Major League salaries were, not surprisingly, on the upswing again.

By 1992, 174 players were earning over $2 million a year, compared to only 29 in 1990. A rapidly accelerating game of leapfrog was in progress for the title of the game's highest-paid player. Boston Red Sox pitcher Roger Clemens signed a four-year contract for $21.5 million, making him baseball's first $5 million-a-year salaried player. Oakland Athletics slugger Jose Canseco soon surpassed him in the highest salary stratosphere in baseball. Both Clemens and Canseco stayed with the teams that originally

281

signed them but had used the *threat* of free agency to match or surpass the salaries actual free agents were earning on the open market. "Where would it stop?" the beleaguered owners asked themselves.

Equally as important to the owners' sense of crisis was the escalating revenue disparity between the richest and the poorest of their brethren. In 1980 the gap was only $10 million between the legendary New York Yankees and the fledgling Seattle Mariners, who had only been a member of the exclusive baseball ownership fraternity since 1977. By 1991 the gulf between top and bottom revenue producers was $60 million and growing. As the inequity grew between the teams and the payroll costs seemed unstoppable, the owners looked again to try to stem the tide by the only method they seemingly knew: forcing the players to protect themselves from each other.

In November 1991 the Players Relations Committee switched negotiators again by hiring Richard Ravitch, a prominent New York real estate tax lawyer who had previously worked as a bargainer for the New York City Transportation Authority against many municipal unions. By offering Ravitch $750,000 a year, at least $100,000 more than Fay Vincent's salary, the owners were sending a clear signal that they considered the PRC chairmanship a more important position than commissioner. Vincent was miffed when he learned of the discrepancy in the pay scale and disputed the interpretation of hard-line owners that his office had no role in labor disputes. Like every prior commissioner since the autocratic Kenesaw Mountain Landis, Vincent believed in his authority to control matters "for the good of the game." He was not impressed when Ravitch often quoted Napoleon's dictum, "Better to have one bad general than two good ones." Vincent intended to assert the full authority of what he viewed as the Office of the Commissioner of Major League Baseball.

Vincent had placed high hopes in the results of a joint economic study committee that had been created as part of the 1990 Basic Agreement. However, when issued early in 1992, the committee's report reached no consensus on a better direction for the industry. The two members selected by the owners—Paul Volcker, former director of the Council of Economic Advisers for presidents Jimmy Carter and Ronald Reagan, and Rockefeller Foundation economist Peter Goldmark—expressed serious concern about the growing revenue gap between teams. However, the players' representatives—University of California labor law professor David Feller and Brookings Institution economist Henry Aaron—did not believe that the situation required sacrifices in players' income or that the athletes should necessarily have to contribute to any revenue-sharing program. In a sharply worded independent opinion, Henry Aaron (no relation to the all-time home run king) doubted that baseball was "on the brink of some vague sort of economic trouble," but he did write prophetically, "A governance structure of the clubs that is incapable of enforcing greater revenue-sharing is *the* problem. Unless that problem is addressed and solved, labor/management peace will never come to baseball."

With the gulf growing between big and small market owners and remaining traditionally vast between owners and players, Fay Vincent would have had to possess extraordinary political skills to save his job. However, the owlish, bookish man who had once considered becoming a priest lacked the charisma to become a leader of baronial owners who were determined yet again to assert their authority and finally put the aggressive players in their place.

It wasn't only the coming labor showdown that would thwart Vincent's hopes for a successful reign. He would be faced with virtually a perfect storm of thorny issues that even the most resolute and accomplished of executives would have found difficult if not impossible to solve. For the first time since the age of baseball expansion began in 1961, the American League wanted a share of the membership fees of $95 million apiece that the Florida Marlins and Colorado Rockies were due to pay the National League prior to their first seasons in 1993. After a thorough study, Vincent ruled that teams in the AL should receive 22 percent of the money in exchange for exposing 54 percent of their teams' players to the expansion draft pool.

The small market American League teams howled in protest. Minnesota Twins general manager Andy MacPhail questioned whether the commissioner understood how important player development was to a franchise in a smaller market such as Minneapolis–St. Paul. MacPhail told Vincent that he would rather give back the Twins' $3 million share of the expansion fee and hold on to his players. The young executive, a third-generation MacPhail in baseball after his grandfather Larry and father Lee MacPhail, was working for Minnesota owner Carl Pohlad, a billionaire banker ranked as one of the richest men in America and who was yet a leader of the owner-hawks who were constantly trying to cut the growth of player salaries.

The National League owners were pleased when Vincent's monetary award to the American League teams was not as extreme as had been feared, but NL president Bill White was in no mood to be conciliatory. White, a former St. Louis Cardinals All-Star first baseman and the highest-ranking African American executive in baseball, was still miffed that Vincent had intervened in the 1991 labor negotiation with the National League umpires, giving the arbiters larger raises and more vacation time than White thought reasonable. Dr. Bobby Brown, American League president and former Yankee third baseman, had also been disappointed by Vincent's action.

The trend was unmistakable. Fay Vincent was constantly finding himself in no-win situations. Early in the 1991 season, he suspended Yankees owner George Steinbrenner for two years for consorting with gambler Howard Spira in the bizarre effort to find damaging information about his own outfielder Dave Winfield. Though many Yankee fans were glad to see Steinbrenner temporarily out of commission because the team had not been to a World Series since 1981, Vincent's excessive use of the commissioner's power in his suspension of Steinbrenner raised the eyebrows of some owners.

Vincent lost more support when he heavy-handedly tried to impose a lifetime suspension on Yankee southpaw relief pitcher Steve Howe. There was no doubt that the six-times-suspended Howe was a very troubled young man with severe addiction problems. The pitcher appealed the suspension through the Players Association, and when it was learned that the commissioner's office had been negligent in supervising Howe's daily testing program during the off-season, baseball arbitrator George Nicolau rescinded the suspension. Vincent was incensed that Yankee manager Buck Showalter and general manager Gene Michael had testified in Howe's behalf at the arbitration hearing and summoned them to the Office of the Commissioner, even though Showalter was shortly to manage a day game at Yankee Stadium. Vincent threatened them with expulsion from the game for not taking management's side in the hearing and instead supporting the position of Howe's lawyer Dick Moss, the prominent agent and influential first counsel for the Players Association. According to John Helyar's thoroughly well-sourced *Lords of the Realm*, Michael retorted, "I didn't testify for Dick Moss. I testified for Steve Howe."

With Howe's suspension rescinded, the pitcher remained with the Yankees until early in the 1996 season; shortly afterward he retired from the game. In his 2002 book *The Last Commissioner: A Baseball Valentine*,

Vincent wrote, "The tragedy in all this is that nobody was worried about Steve Howe in any way; it was all about his arm, not about his head. I fear we will read about him again." Steve Howe would die on April 28, 2006, after his pickup truck turned over in Coachella, California. An autopsy discovered that he had toxic amounts of methamphetamine in his system.

The problems of drug-abusing players and the fierce protectiveness of the Players Association toward them would come to plague baseball in the years ahead. But in 1992 it was the less dramatic but economically important issue of sharing the cable television revenues from the two super-stations that ultimately led to Fay Vincent's undoing. According to one estimate, broadcasts of Ted Turner's Atlanta Braves games on WTBS and Cubs games by the Chicago Tribune Company's WGN (the same corporation that owned the Chicago team) were costing their National League rivals up to $250 million a year. There were rumblings that several of the teams not blessed with super-station revenue would soon not allow WTBS and WGN to broadcast their home games.

Meanwhile, the Cubs remained in the National League East division and the Braves in the National League West, a structure that dated back to 1969 when the two Major Leagues split into two divisions. Though Ted Turner was amenable to a shift to the NL East, the Tribune Company steadfastly opposed a Cubs' shift into the NL West because it feared that the later start of West Coast home games in the Chicago market would cut into the high ratings of its late evening news programs.

Most of the NL teams agreed with Vincent that the shift in divisions of Chicago and Atlanta made sense, and NL president Bill White was amenable to changing his league's unanimous voting rules on major issues to a more flexible three-quarters majority. Yet in a peremptory action in early July 1992 that Vincent later admitted was a mistake, he ordered the Cubs to move to the NL West. No chief executive in any business would look kindly upon such a dictate, and thus it was no shock when Cubs president Stanton Cook secured an injunction from a local Chicago court to block the directive. Vincent counter-sued, and soon the dispute headed for federal court.

A tipping point had been reached in the movement for a no-confidence vote in Vincent. Chicago White Sox owner Jerry Reinsdorf had long wanted a showdown with the Players Association without the meddling of a commissioner who he felt was too friendly with the union and who did not understand the imperatives of marketing. Reinsdorf, who also owned the Chicago Bulls in the National Basketball Association, a league that operated with a salary cap, was a Brooklyn native who grew up a fan of the great post–World War II Dodger teams. He had risen to prominence in the world of real estate investment and by managing what was called OPM, Other People's Money. Though his new Comiskey Park, opened in 1991, did not possess the architectural beauty and urban uniqueness of Baltimore's Camden Yards that opened the following year to wide-spread acclaim, revenues from his new ballpark enabled the White Sox to leap to second place on the list of baseball's most profitable franchises. Reinsdorf's partner was Eddie Einhorn, a highly successful cable TV entrepreneur who knew intimately the workings of a business that had become an ever-expanding cash cow for baseball.

After Vincent's autocratic action against the Cubs, Milwaukee Brewers owner Allan Huber Selig, who almost from birth everybody had called Bud, joined Reinsdorf's faction against the commissioner. A baseball-loving onetime automobile dealer, Selig had been instrumental in 1970 in obtaining another Major League Baseball franchise for Milwaukee to replace the transplanted Boston Braves, who had stayed in Wisconsin for only thirteen years before moving to Atlanta and the more advantageous southeastern U.S. television market. He had become the leader of the small market teams, who desperately wanted a good revenue-sharing package in the next Basic Agreement. The problem was particularly acute for the Brewers, who were located in a small-sized city with a limited television market surrounded by rural Wisconsin and hockey-loving Canada to the north, Lake Michigan to the east, the Twin Cities market to the west, and the two Chicago Major League behemoths to the south. Selig never missed an opportunity to warn of dire consequences to the less financially endowed franchises if revenue wasn't shared more equitably. Selig "had been on the phone for twenty-three years," the late Jerome Holtzman observed in his book *The Commissioners*, "canvassing every square foot of baseball's problems, particularly at the executive level."

Yet he was a conciliator by nature, always seeking a way to find common ground, and had been reluctant to join any anti-Vincent coalition. However, the autocratic manner in which the Cubs had been ordered out of the NL East convinced the Milwaukee owner to join forces with the rebels. Selig had never felt personally close to the New England–bred,

Yale-educated Vincent, who in turn was known to dismiss the Milwaukee native as just "a small town schlepper."

Selig and Reinsdorf would become a formidable tandem, Selig the leader of the small market–low revenue teams and Reinsdorf the big guy from the big city always willing to take on the union and a collective bargaining agreement that he felt was biased toward the players. His particular bete noire was salary arbitration, a process he derided as "making me pay what my stupidest competitor pays." He was particularly dismissive of Vincent's efforts at being accommodating toward the union, and he warmly welcomed Selig into his faction.

Vincent seemed to have saved his job in June 1992 when after a 7–2 vote in the Players Relations Committee, he agreed not to talk to union chief Donald Fehr separately without PRC approval and also not to sit in on any of the bargaining sessions unless specifically asked. However, when soon thereafter stories began appearing in the *New York Times* and *USA Today* in which Vincent was quoted as saying he had survived an attempted putsch, the moguls who wanted the commissioner's head moved in for the kill. Selig was among those owners particularly incensed when Vincent leaked embarrassing information about credit lines of at least $35 million that his office had established to provide needed injections of capital for several owners.

In late August 1992, almost three years to the day after Fay Vincent's good friend and predecessor Bart Giamatti had died of a heart attack, the owners announced an 18–9 vote of no-confidence in Vincent's leadership (the Cincinnati Reds auto dealer–owner Marge Schott abstained for no stated reason). His chief defenders were the New York Mets co-owner Fred Wilpon and Orioles owner Eli Jacobs and his right-hand man Larry Lucchino, representing big market teams that could function easily under the current system. However, Pittsburgh Pirates owner Douglas Danforth, former chairman of the board of the Westinghouse corporation, spoke for the majority when he declared that he had no confidence in the current leader's ability to help the financial fortunes of sagging clubs, to cut the tide of rising player salaries, and to prevent damaging leaks to the news media.

Vincent's initial impulse was to fight to uphold the powers of his office. He even contemplated a lawsuit, hiring the high-powered Washington lawyer Brendan Sullivan, a partner in the influential firm of Edward Bennett Williams, the late Orioles (and Washington Redskins football) owner. He soon decided against a long protracted legal struggle that he was sure he could win but would be damaging to the institution of Major League Baseball.

Vincent resigned on Labor Day 1992, and Bud Selig was named the acting commissioner. He pledged to unite the owners like the players had been for the past twenty-six years, but he had a huge task to accomplish. With collusion not too distant a memory and huge free agent contracts being handed out again, the union was more than ever disinclined to listen to poor-mouth cries from the owners. During his 1992 annual spring training trip to visit all the players, Fehr told his troops that if the owners paid every player $1 million the moguls would still have $750 million to divide among themselves.

As the player-owner relationship deteriorated in its familiar way, the rift between large market and small market owners was becoming increasingly and publicly obvious. Two incidents at the annual December 1992 winter meetings in Louisville, Kentucky, dramatized the point. Carl Barger, formerly president of the small market Pittsburgh Pirates and who had just assumed the same post with the expansion Florida Marlins, issued a fervent plea for revenue sharing and better treatment for the new franchises. After seeing the very slim pickings of talent offered by his new partners for his $95 million membership dues, Barger said caustically in so many words that the name of the game in baseball was to stick the expansion clubs with lemons as players. Not long afterward he collapsed and died of a heart attack.

Later in the Louisville meetings (which would be baseball's last for several seasons because the owners were dismayed at how player agents were utilizing the presence of the media to build up cases for their clients), Richard Ravitch won a vote from the owners to reopen the Basic Agreement a year early. Ravitch insisted that economic necessity required concessions from the players.

Veteran pundits on the baseball scene predicted that the decision to reopen would trigger a strike by the players sometime in 1993. The pessimists were premature because Ravitch had been able to garner only a 15–13 vote, a sign that the moguls were still divided on how to make their industry prosperous by achieving their oft-stated favorite goal of "cost containment." The division in their ranks was dramatically revealed at the end of the Louisville meetings when new Giants owner Peter Magowan, the supermarket mogul who had recently bought the team from Robert

Lurie to assure its permanence in San Francisco, shocked the gathering by signing Pittsburgh Pirates outfielder Barry Bonds, the biggest free agent on the market, to a record-setting $43 million six-year contract.

The same pattern was being followed since the birth of free agency in 1976. Collectively the baseball owners longed for the salary caps that had been agreed to in the other major sports—since 1983 in the National Basketball Association and 1993 in the National Football League—but individually baseball owners couldn't resist the lure of signing that one veteran free agent who assured rapturous off-season headlines that ostensibly would lead to success on the field in the coming season. No wonder the owners loved the idea of a salary cap to curb their enthusiasm and why it remained anathema to the players, who had only a few years to make big money and who didn't want to approve any agreement to curb their chances on an open market.

One of the ironies of the dominant Major League Baseball Players Association, founded by such a fierce trade unionist as Marvin Miller, was that it now consisted of some of the richest individuals in sports. In a 2005 interview on the bizofbaseball.com website, ex-commissioner Fay Vincent noted, "It's not unusual for the top three or four players on a team to make more than the owner by a substantial margin." Eugene Orza, the chief counsel for the Players Association, quipped, "If it was Samuel Gompers's idea to make Republicans, we sure have made a lot of Republicans." Yet union solidarity remained the abiding principle of the association, and if any individual members strayed from the viewpoint, a floor-to-ceiling portrait of Marvin Miller that hung in the union offices in midtown Manhattan provided a vivid reminder.

Though Bud Selig was trying his hardest to achieve owner solidarity to match the longtime unity of the Players Association, the only way he could build an owners' consensus on revenue sharing was to insist that the players must agree to a salary cap. Players Relations Committee chairman Richard Ravitch would soon produce a traveling slide show that he claimed would prove declining revenues for most Major League teams. Ravitch called for a new system in baseball that would discontinue salary arbitration but allow for free agency after four years. The plan, however, provided for "the right of first refusal" for a team potentially losing a free agent, a condition that existed in pro basketball and pro football but one that the baseball union had always staunchly opposed because it would limit the market for a free agent if his original team wanted to keep him.

A big feature of Ravitch's plan was something he called "pay for performance," or PFP, in which game statistics would be used to determine salaries for the younger players instead of arbitration. He stressed that under his proposed new system there would be less need for players' agents to take a percentage of the players' income. When pushed for more details, however, Ravitch admitted that Giants first baseman Will Clark, who had just signed a multiyear multimillion-dollar contract extension, would receive only half of his new riches if management's proposed system went into effect. Gene Orza quickly dismissed PFP as "rotisserie baseball for lawyers."

In early August 1993, nearing the first anniversary of his accession to the interim commissioner's chair, Selig gathered the moguls at a weekend retreat in Kohler, Wisconsin, eighty miles north of Milwaukee. Selig hoped that in this secluded setting the owners would at last agree to a revenue-sharing proposal. It was not lost on the newspapermen covering the conclave that Kohler was the home of the toilet manufacturing company that had endured a record-breaking eight-year strike by the United Auto Workers in the 1950s. One sportswriter asked irreverently, "Could baseball save itself from going down that well-known bathroom fixture?"

It became clear that a consensus was not being reached when over the course of the weekend the gathering broke into big and small market caucuses in different buildings at the Kohler resort. Milwaukee baseball writer Tom Haudricourt drew a mouth-watering metaphor, likening the moguls' attempt at revenue sharing to the rich owners having lobster thermidor for lunch and offering a piece of lobster to the poorer owners, who would in turn exchange half of their ham sandwich. When no consensus was reached over the weekend, the normally affable George W. Bush, the Texas Rangers managing partner who had tried to mediate the dispute, growled to the press, "I ain't saying nothin' about nothin'."

The 1993 season was played without interruption, and on the field it was an exciting year, with the Toronto Blue Jays repeating as World Series champions in dramatic fashion. Outfielder Joe Carter became the first player in baseball history to win a World Series with a come-from-behind bottom-of-the-ninth-inning home run that he belted off Philadelphia Phillies reliever Mitch Williams. Little did the players realize that it would be the last Fall Classic for two years.

The Basic Agreement expired on the last day of 1993, and though the owners did not lock the players out of spring training, there were no negotiations in progress for a new contract. In fact, since Richard Ravitch had announced the owners' desire to reopen the Basic Agreement in December 1992, there had been no formal bargaining sessions at all. The players did not see the need for major changes in the contract, and though the owners desperately wanted a better deal for themselves, they were still too divided to be able to bargain effectively for it.

In January 1994 Ravitch was able to announce that the owners had voted for a revenue-sharing agreement in which over $58 million would be placed in a pool for the aid of the weaker franchises. But as always the program was dependent on the union agreeing to a salary cap. When finally in June 1994 the two sides actually sat down at the same table for a bargaining session, Ravitch presented the linked proposal and predictably Donald Fehr rejected it.

Close followers of baseball's labor scene noted that the relationship between Fehr and Ravitch had become as poisonous as that between Ray Grebey and Marvin Miller thirteen years earlier. "Fehr and Loathing" became a nickname among some writers for the two current negotiators. Meanwhile, in lieu of any bargaining sessions, the Players Association zeroed in on Congress, where Fehr went to testify in behalf of overturning baseball's antitrust exemption. He found a particularly sympathetic listener in Ohio Democratic senator Howard Metzenbaum, who as a key member of the Senate Judiciary Committee tried to make antitrust law enforcement a big part of the agenda.

On June 28, 1994, Fehr announced that the union had voted a strike date for all games after August 12, 1994, if a new agreement had not been reached. The Players Association picked a strike date late in the season when its members would have received most of their salaries, and the owners would be most vulnerable because they had not received any of their lucrative postseason television money. Houston Astros player rep Ken Caminiti summed up the general feeling of resigned solidarity among union members when he said, "When Don says we go, we must go."

The game of high-stakes poker intensified in early August when management responded to the imminent strike date by withholding their regular contribution to the players' pension fund. It was as if the hard-line owners were showing the players yet again who was the boss and who really controlled the money. The union immediately filed a grievance with the National Labor Relations Board (NLRB) that it ultimately won. The owners then added on another provocation when they tied their call for revenue sharing and a salary cap to the players' willingness to share some of their lucrative licensing revenue. An anonymous owner who had witnessed brinksmanship for several years sighed that each side wanted to "feel like it's screwing each other." A few days before the looming strike date President Bill Clinton lamented to William Gould IV, who he had appointed chairman of the NLRB, "I think I'd be president for life if I could solve this dispute."

When the players walked out after the games of August 12, 1994, an exciting season was cut short. It had seen the small market Montreal Expos leading all of baseball with a 74-40 record and the New York Yankees in first place (after the longest period without a championship in their history). Roger Maris's home run record of sixty-one was in sight of Giants slugging third baseman Matt Williams, who already had belted forty-three, and the Padres future Hall of Fame right fielder Tony Gwynn at .394 was in range of the magic .400 batting mark not reached since Ted Williams's .406 in 1941. Never had a baseball strike been called so late in the season, when the pennant races were heating up and fans especially enjoyed baseball as a delightful and often dramatic end-of-summer experience.

As often happens in the initial stages of a strike, both sides hardened in their positions. One month later, Selig informed Fehr that the television networks needed to know immediately about playoff and World Series scheduling. When the union chief said that the gulf between the sides was too great on all issues, the interim commissioner announced on September 14, 1994, that the owners had voted overwhelmingly to call off the rest of the season, including the playoffs and World Series. Only the Cincinnati Reds' Marge Schott and the Baltimore Orioles' Peter Angelos abstained. The feisty Angelos, a lawyer who had made much of his fortune in winning suits for workers who suffered from asbestos poisoning, had strong general sympathies for unions in general. On the other side of the labor fence, Schott wanted to play the World Series with replacement players from the Minor League and semipro ranks. "We have lost twenty of these labor conflicts in a row," she said. "It's about time we won one."

Labor relations in baseball had reached its nadir. The warring sides had inflicted upon the game a body blow that neither World War I nor World War II had been able to accomplish—the cancellation of the World Series.

Baseball was now in uncharted waters. A seemingly endless strike continued, and none of the desperately needed money for the owners was coming in from postseason television revenue. The union's old war horses Marvin Miller and Dick Moss amped up their rhetoric. Moss announced that he, two U.S. congressmen, sports economics authority and Smith College professor Andrew Zimbalist, and other investors were creating a third league, the United States League, that would seek to begin play in 1995 with unsigned players from the striking Major Leagues. Miller urged that the NLRB issue a ruling making all the players free agents because of the unfair labor practices of the owners.

With the strike in full force, President Clinton enlisted Secretary of Labor Robert Reich and later called upon the retired renowned federal mediator William J. Usery in efforts to bring the sides together. However, after the midterm November 1994 elections, the Republicans won control of both houses in Congress. Although most of the players were sympathetic to the Republican principle of high earning power–low taxes, and many Republican as well as Democratic legislators agreed with the Players Association credo of a free market for free agents, the changing of the guard in the halls of legislative Washington was not encouraging. Neither was the retirement, after the 1994 election, of one of the bigger supporters of antitrust enforcement, Ohio's Senator Metzenbaum.

Shortly before Christmas 1994, Richard Ravitch announced that the owners considered an impasse had been reached in negotiations and that they planned to put into the contract the terms of their revenue-sharing proposal coupled with a salary cap. The union quickly countered by filing unfair labor practice charges with the NLRB.

President Clinton again tried to interject himself into the situation by proposing a meeting at the White House with both sides and an impartial arbitrator in attendance. He pleaded for an agreement to be reached no later than February 7, 1995, a date he selected because it was the one hundredth anniversary of Babe Ruth's birth. The sentimental gesture was rejected by both sides.

Early in 1995 the situation turned potentially very ugly when the owners announced their plans to hire replacement players for spring training and the regular season. They offered contracts, some for over $100,000 a year, to semipro players and hundreds of Minor League players who were not on the forty-man team rosters and thus not likely future members of the Players Association. The National Football League had used replacement workers in regular season games to bring the NFL Players Association to its knees during the 1987 pro football strike. Although baseball management realized that a 162-game baseball season was far different from football's 16-game schedule, there was no end in sight to the strike and contingency plans for a 1995 season had to be made.

Not all of management was united behind a strategy that was quickly branded by union loyalists as the hiring of scab labor. Peter Angelos announced that he would not use replacement workers, partly because of his sympathies as a union lawyer and also because he didn't want Orioles shortstop Cal Ripken's consecutive-games streak to be sullied by competing in games against ersatz Major Leaguers. (Ripken was due to pass Lou Gehrig's seemingly unbreakable record of playing in 2,130 games in a row sometime in 1995.) Paul Beeston, an influential management official with the Toronto Blue Jays, warned that there were laws in the Canadian province of Ontario that prohibited using nonunion workers.

Another split in the ranks occurred when Detroit Tigers field manager Sparky Anderson refused to participate after seeing the ragtag group of replacement players work out at the Tigers' spring training camp in Lakeland, Florida. Anderson and other less outspoken baseball officials believed that the sport would diminish itself if it passed off as a Major League product hitters who couldn't really center and drive the ball and pitchers who couldn't really pop a catcher's mitt or pinpoint the outer reaches of the strike zone.

Nonetheless, spring training with the replacement workers proceeded, and the Players Association continued to seek outside relief for their problems. A bipartisan group of three U.S. senators—Bob Graham (D, FL), Daniel Moynihan (D, NY), and Orrin Hatch (R, UT)—introduced a bill that would remove the antitrust exemption in matters of mandatory collective bargaining. But the new Republican majority in the Senate never seriously debated the bill. Newly installed speaker of the house Georgia congressman Newt Gingrich summed up the mood of the new majority in Washington when he said, "I'm not sure Congress is the right place to try to organize the national pastime."

On March 26, 1995, the Players Association finally saw an end to a nuclear winter that was morphing into a barren spring and worse. The NLRB voted 3–2 to issue an unfair labor practices injunction against the owners for unilaterally implementing new terms of workplace regulation without bargaining over them as mandated by law. The labor board urged a swift judicial verdict on the merits of the case. Through the random method of selecting a federal judge for any case, the name of Sonia Sotomayor came up. At forty years old, she was the youngest judge on the federal bench and coincidentally was serving on the same federal district court in New York City as Irving Ben Cooper, who had delivered the first negative judgment in Curt Flood's suit in 1970.

Sotomayor acted swiftly. In a strongly worded opinion issued a day before April Fool's Day 1995, Judge Sotomayor sided with the NLRB majority and gave a stinging rebuke to the baseball owners for declaring an impasse and implementing a salary cap and eliminating salary arbitration without input from the players' union. In a rare recent example of a judge in baseball's tortured labor history who used the poetry of the game to side with the players on labor issues, Sotomayor wrote, "Opening Day is one of the most beautiful days on the baseball calendar and it should not be disturbed because one side has failed to fulfill its duties under the collective bargaining mandates of this country." (In August 2009 Sotomayor was elevated to the highest court of the land as an associate justice of the Supreme Court of the United States.)

Once Sotomayor's decision was rendered, Donald Fehr immediately announced that the strike was over and that the players were willing to go back to work under the terms of the prior contract. There was still no new agreement, but the owners accepted the players' decision and immediately terminated all the replacement players. Nineteen would ultimately make the Major Leagues, most notably right-handed pitcher Rick Reed, who would help the New York Mets to playoff and World Series appearances in 1999 and 2000, and first baseman–designated hitter Kevin Millar, who would be a sparkplug on the 2004 World Series–winning Boston Red Sox. Neither Reed nor Millar would be allowed to join the Players Association and would not share in its licensing revenue.

One particularly sobering aftereffect of the strike was the dismantling of the Montreal Expos, who likely would have made the playoffs if the 1994 season had not been interrupted. Aware that the return of the previous terms and conditions of the labor contract would prevent them from keeping their star players, the Expos had a fire sale. Top reliever John Wetteland went to the New York Yankees, and top-notch outfielders Larry Walker and Marquis Grissom wound up with the Colorado Rockies and the Atlanta Braves, respectively. The Expos never recovered from these key losses, attendance plummeted, and in 2005 they were relocated and became the Washington Nationals.

In all, 232 days were lost to the strike, and owners' losses ran close to $1 billion in lost television and gate revenue. The players' cumulative losses ran as high as $300 million, and the median salary that was down to approximately $400,000 at the start of 1994 fell to $325,000 in 1995. Unlike after earlier strikes, angry fans did not immediately return. Most had considered the walkout a battle between millionaire players and billionaire owners and were angry at both. Attendance would be down approximately 20 percent in a 1995 season shortened to 144 games.

Yet the game on the field remained irresistible and as always provided many memorable moments. On September 6, 1995, Cal Ripken broke Lou Gehrig's consecutive-game streak when he played in his 2,131st straight game. When the game became official after the fifth inning, Ripken spontaneously jogged a victory lap around the edges of the stadium as the capacity crowd at Baltimore's Camden Yards roared its ecstatic approval.

Another great highlight of the season was the appearance of the Seattle Mariners in the playoffs for the first time. A doormat ever since their birth in 1977, the Mariners made up over ten games on the California Angels in the last two months of the season, beat them in a playoff game, and then swept the Yankees at home after losing the first two games of the five-game divisional series. Behind rising young stars such as outfielder Ken Griffey Jr., designated hitter Edgar Martinez, and the storklike pitcher Randy Johnson, they turned Seattle baseball-mad for the first time in its history. Once considered a city ripe for abandonment (though Bud Selig never favored that drastic action after losing his beloved Milwaukee Braves to Atlanta in 1966), baseball in Seattle caught on so convincingly in the last months of the 1995 season that city and state officials approved funding for a new outdoor stadium with a retractable dome, Safeco Field, that in 1999 replaced the dreary indoor Kingdome. Another sign of baseball's amazing ability to heal from its self-inflicted wounds was visible in the 1995 World Series when two longtime doormats, the Atlanta Braves and the Cleveland Indians, battled for baseball's top prize, with the Braves winning in six games.

Attendance throughout baseball picked up in 1996, though still not to prestrike levels. The game on the field was continuing to provide thrills, heartbreak, and solace for its many fans. The Oakland Athletics' Mark McGwire smashed fifty-two home runs, and the Orioles' Brady Anderson, who had never hit more than twenty-one in a season and never again would hit more than twenty-four, slugged fifty. It was the first time that two sluggers in one league had hit fifty home runs since Roger Maris and Mickey Mantle in 1961. In 1996 the Yankees finally broke through to win their first World Series since 1978, denying a repeat victory to the favored Braves.

There was still no new signed Basic Agreement. The old guard remained in command at the Players Association, with Don Fehr and Gene Orza in the highest positions, but there was a new negotiator for the owners in Randy Levine. Like Richard Ravitch, who had departed during the 1994–95 strike, Levine was a New York lawyer who had experience bargaining with the municipal unions as a close associate of New York's Republican mayor Rudolph Guiliani.

Also assisting management's side was Rob Manfred, a lawyer who had first started working in baseball in 1987 on the collusion cases as a law partner of Chuck O'Connor in the Washington DC firm of Morgan, Lewis, and Bockius. When O'Connor became Players Relations Committee chairman in 1989, Manfred worked alongside him; Manfred believes that from then until the present day he has attended virtually every significant meeting concerning the business of baseball.

"I did not expect a new agreement in November 1996," Manfred recalled in a September 2009 phone interview. "I came to New York with only a briefcase and expected to return that night. I wound up staying for two weeks." With the bitterness of the long strike fading into the rearview mirror, both sides were coming to the realization that a new agreement was necessary even if neither one could get everything they wanted.

There were revolutionary aspects being discussed that came to fruition beginning with the 1997 season. A luxury tax was agreed upon; starting in 1997 and lasting through 1999, owners whose payroll exceeded $51 to $59 million would be forced to pay a 35 percent levy into a central fund that would be distributed to low-revenue teams. The Players Association was concerned that the lower-paying clubs would pocket their share of pooled revenue and not devote it to player salaries, but the union refused to accept a salary floor suggested by management because it might become a prelude to a salary cap that still remained anathema to the Association's side. Nonetheless, the acceptance by the union that some drag on salaries was necessary to allow the poorer revenue teams to compete was a major concession.

Another innovative part of the agreement was the decision to begin interleague play starting in 1997. Along with this intriguing if controversial change that would disrupt nearly a century of intraleague scheduling was a restructuring of each league into three divisions. The six division winners and a wild-card entry in each league—the team with the best record in each league that was not a division winner—would be eligible for an eight-team postseason. In the rearrangement, the Cubs would leave the NL East. However, they would not move to the NL West but into a new NL Central division with longtime rival the St. Louis Cardinals. The Braves would move into the NL East, creating new rivalries with the Mets, the Phillies, and the new Florida Marlins.

Written into the new Basic Agreement would also be an understanding that both sides would work together "to grow the game," a phrase that came out of the 1992 joint economic study report. It meant that an effort should be made to expand Major League Baseball's role on the international stage, a fitting gesture for a sport in which the number of Latin American players, primarily natives of the Dominican Republic and Venezuela, was fast approaching majority status. Beginning in 2006 and continuing in 2009 and every four years thereafter, a World Baseball Classic was scheduled early in spring training. Both the clubs and the union agreed that a player should perform for the team representing the country of his birth or for a country where the player could claim some kind of blood affiliation.

What was also noteworthy about "the growing of the game" phase of the new agreement was that the players agreed to contribute about 2.5 percent of their licensing revenue to the concept. Two and a half years after the owners' demand for a share of players' licensing revenue had been seemingly the last straw before the August 1994 walkout, the players were now willing to share some of their largess for the greater good of the game.

There was some drama before the agreement was finalized. One of the sticking points that remained was the players' insistence on receiving credit for time lost during the 1994–95 strike. Management militant Jerry Reinsdorf remained adamantly opposed to the concession and to any settlement that did not include a salary cap. He led an 18–12 vote that rejected a new agreement in early November 1996. Yet almost immediately after the vote, Reinsdorf dipped into the free agent market and plucked slugger Albert Belle away from divisional rival Cleveland, making Belle baseball's first $10 million-a-year player by signing him to a five-year $55 million contract.

Reinsdorf's coup was a striking example of how an individual owner's perceived self-interest could trump longstanding ideology. Not surprisingly, most of Reinsdorf's baseball partners were not pleased with his profligate action, and before the end of November 1996 the vast majority of owners decided that a new Basic Agreement was better than none at all. They voted 24–4 for a contract that included the union winning back its service time.

The Basic Agreement formally went into place during spring training 1997. Two months earlier in January 1997, Curt Flood had died two days after his fifty-ninth birthday. The former Cardinals center fielder who had sued baseball had found some peace in his last years, but he still died regretting that none of the players had come to his trial or given any genuine moral support. In October 1998 he achieved a kind of immortality when Congress passed the Curt Flood Act, which stripped away the baseball owners' antitrust exemption in the areas of mandatory collective bargaining. Both the owners and players lobbied in Washington for this bill, another sign that both sides wanted to put at least the antitrust aspect of their bitter past labor battles behind them.

Another sign of normality came on ownership's side in 1998 when the interim tag was removed from Bud Selig's title and he was elected permanent commissioner at a salary of nearly $3 million a year. As baseball's profitability soared in the next years so did Selig's salary. By 2007 his annual take was nearly $17.5 million a year, more than any player except for three New York Yankees—Alex Rodriguez, Derek Jeter, and Jason Giambi, who were all playing for a team whose payroll and access to cable television riches far exceeded any other Major League club. Yet Selig was no longer publicly wringing his hands at the teams' rising salary ledgers, going so far as to observe that no one extravagant contract was likely to disturb him again.

The takeoff year for baseball's resurgence was undoubtedly 1998, a year during which baseball attracted new fans and won back many old ones with the dramatic home run chase of Mark McGwire and Sammy Sosa. Reunited on the St. Louis Cardinals with his former Oakland Athletics manager Tony LaRussa, McGwire broke Roger Maris's home run record in early September on his way to a previously unimaginable seventy-home-run season. It seemed like a feel-good story when McGwire befriended the family of the late Maris and invited them to his home run coronation. Sosa also broke Maris's record later in September and finished with sixty-six home runs.

There was a disturbing moment in the middle of the summer of 1998 when Steve Wilstein, a veteran reporter for the Associated Press, found a bottle of androstenedione (hereafter shortened to "andro") in McGwire's locker. A chemical originally invented by the disgraced East German scientists to aid the performance of both their male and female athletes in the Olympic Games, andro was definitely an illegal anabolic steroid. It had been recently banned by the National Football League and in 1988 had cost Canadian sprinter Ben Johnson his Olympic medals after he tested positive for it. Though Congress had passed the Anabolic Steroids Act in 1990, and Fay Vincent in 1991 and Bud Selig in 1997 had both issued warnings about the danger and illegality of the drug, there was as yet no provision against it in the Basic Agreement.

It seemed an inescapable fact that in the late 1990s preventing steroid abuse and taking a stand in behalf of an even playing field were simply not priorities for either side on the baseball labor fence. Crowds were coming back in droves to the ballparks to witness the home run heroics. In fact, there was more criticism of Steve Wilstein's reporting that andro was in McGwire's locker than of the slugger's taking unfair advantage. Many of Wilstein's sportswriting colleagues criticized him for snooping at McGwire's locker, manager Tony LaRussa wanted to revoke Wilstein's clubhouse credential, and union honcho Gene Orza said andro would not be discussed "at a time when Mark McGwire's chase of the home run record might be compromised." *ESPN: The Magazine*, founded in 1998, featured either McGwire or Sosa on four of its early covers, and in December McGwire and Sosa were named *Sports Illustrated*'s co-1998 Sportsmen of the Year.

Home runs were glamorous and attracted the general fan as opposed to the baseball purist, who preferred watching the so-called small ball highlighting pitching and defense with just enough offense to win games. A 1999 national Nike sneaker commercial neatly summed up the growing attitude inside baseball and certainly the culture at large. Atlanta Braves finesse pitchers Greg Maddux and Tom Glavine were seen chatting with Heather Locklear, the sultry star of the television series *Melrose Place*, but when massive he-man Mark McGwire strolled by, Locklear abandoned the scrawny pitchers for the slugger. "Hot chicks dig the long ball" was the commercial's tag line.

The youth-oriented Fox television network was becoming so enamored of baseball's programming potential as a lead-in to their lucrative other shows that before the start of the 2001 season they anted up over $2 billion for the next five years of baseball's postseason after offering only $565 million for five years in 1995. In addition to rising network television revenue, there was an explosion in the so-called new media centered on the internet, cell phones, and other technology of the new millennium. Commissioner Selig revealed his increasing ability to create effective owner consensus by getting all thirty owners to agree to share equally the lucre from this burgeoning new media market. (In 1998 the exclusive club of baseball ownership reached thirty when the Tampa Bay Devil Rays joined the American League and the Arizona Diamondbacks joined the National League.) In 2009 Major League Baseball launched its own cable television network, promising baseball all day all the time. It was another example of the sport once considered a stepchild to impatient television executives becoming a leader on the cutting edge of new broadcast technology.

There was so much money available in the game for both sides that another work stoppage seemed increasingly unlikely. More continuity from management had helped to regularize the relationships between the sides. In 1998, the same year Bud Selig accepted the title of permanent commissioner, the Players Relations Committee was dissolved into a new structure headed by lawyer Rob Manfred, who was named the executive vice-president for labor relations. In 1999 the offices of the two Major Leagues were incorporated into the one umbrella corporate entity of Major League Baseball.

During the 1999 season Major League Baseball caught an unexpected break when most of the members of the umpires' union, counseled by the always-confrontational lawyer Richie Phillips, handed in their resignations en masse in the quixotic hope of obtaining a better contract. Not surprisingly, baseball officials instead accepted the resignations gladly, being rid of several umpires they had wanted to dismiss and shortly also of their contentious adversary Phillips, who had badly miscalculated. A new union was formed with a friendlier attitude toward management. Several of the umpires did sue to win back their old jobs, and four of them were ultimately successful.

Of course, matters were more constant at the Players Association. Executive director Donald Fehr and Gene Orza, who now held the title of chief operating officer, stayed on the job, but they increasingly found a more congenial and genuine bargaining environment. In 2002 and again in 2006, the Basic Agreement was extended without a work stoppage. There are bound to be conflicts in any labor-management situation, especially in the fishbowl atmosphere of Major League Baseball with so much fame, fortune, and celebrity surrounding the participants. Increasingly, though, both the union's and the owners' spokesmen were minimizing their public disagreements and putting on the best face together in the unceasing glare of the limelight. Fehr did announce during the 2009 season that he would be retiring before the start of the 2010 season. Union counsel Michael Weiner, who had arrived on the scene during the collusion controversy of the mid-1980s but who didn't carry around the baggage of the Association's first two decades of battle, was Fehr's overwhelmingly approved replacement.

The groundswell about steroid abuse built nearly into a tidal wave throughout the first decade of the twenty-first century; how both sides handled the issue may be a good point at which to end this latest excursion into baseball's imperfect diamond. The differing views of management and labor reflect how both sides had come to disagree while being agreeable and interested in a healthier environment for the sport. Rob Manfred told Howard Bryant in the sportswriter's indispensable 2006 book *Juicing the Game*, "The goal isn't to catch people. The goal is to keep them doing it [using banned substances]." For Donald Fehr, a precise and logical man who did not suffer fools gladly, the issue was more complicated. He loathed the term "performance-enhancing drugs," although he admitted he was concerned about anabolic steroids that posed both a health risk to the athlete and likely an unfair advantage to a player on the field of competition. Unlike the always-outspoken Marvin Miller, who doubted that steroids could have a positive effect on performance, Donald Fehr had expertise in this area; he was on the board of the United States Olympic Committee, which enforced strict drug testing provisions on its athletes. But according to Bryant, Fehr abstained from votes on drug testing issues because he felt strongly about the right to privacy guaranteed in the U.S. Constitution. And as Gene Orza and Marvin Miller always reminded him, a union should not be responsible for policing its members. Nonetheless,

Fehr did agree to reopen the labor contract three times after the 2002 Basic Agreement to increase the penalties against players who failed drug tests.

Pressure from Congress and the public was intensifying in the wake of sensational disclosures of steroid abuse in baseball. Slugging third baseman Ken Caminiti, the 1996 National League MVP with the San Diego Padres, told *Sports Illustrated* in a June 3, 2002, cover story that he had used steroids during his career and that they had helped him recover from many injuries. "I've made a ton of mistakes," Caminiti told writer Tom Verducci. "I don't think steroids is one of them. . . . At least half the guys are using steroids." Caminiti, who would die of a drug-induced heart attack in October 2004, emphasized that journeyman players must take PEDs to compete with others who might take their jobs. Just a few days earlier the retired slugger Jose Canseco told a national Fox television audience that 85 percent of the players had taken some kind of performance-enhancement drugs.

The numbers were undoubtedly exaggerated for shock value, but enough players were growing upset that all Major Leaguers were being tainted with the substance abuse brush that the Players Association agreed to random testing during the 2003 season. If more than 5 percent of the players tested positive, there would be more stringent testing and punitive measures for failed tests put into the labor contract. In November 2003, not long after a surprising World Series in which the upstart Florida Marlins upset the Yankees and won their second championship in their short eleven-year existence, word came to Commissioner Selig that somewhere between 5 and 7 percent of Major League Baseball players had tested positive for illegal performance-enhancing drugs.

The test results were supposed to be anonymous and destroyed by the union once the results were recorded. Somehow they remained in the possession of baseball's testing laboratory for several days, and they were subpoenaed by federal authorities investigating the San Francisco Bay Area Laboratory Cooperative (BALCO)—believed to be a den for the manufacture and distribution of illegal performance-enhancing substances. Baseball stars Barry Bonds, Jason Giambi, Benito Santiago, and Gary Sheffield were among the athletes who testified before a BALCO case grand jury in San Francisco. In January 2004 U.S. attorney general John Ashcroft issued a forty-two-count indictment against the owners of the BALCO laboratory. Victor Conte, the founder of the laboratory and previously a bass player in the rock group Tower and Power, was convicted and would serve several months in prison.

Barry Bonds had become the biggest name in baseball after belting seventy-three home runs in 2001, shattering Mark McGwire's new record of seventy within three years. Idolized by most San Francisco fans, Bonds was unpopular in the rest of the country. He was protected by his manager Dusty Baker and his owner Peter Magowan, who needed his drawing power as the team moved into its expensive new beautiful downtown stadium in 2000. Bonds's almost grotesque oversized head seemed to give convincing circumstantial evidence that his offensive prowess had been chemically enhanced.

Also in 2001 Mark McGwire retired from baseball. He had been victimized by a series of injuries, the most serious being patella tendonitis, a condition not usually suffered by baseball players and suggesting suspiciously that his body had broken down from the cumulative effect of the unnatural substances he likely had been taking. He admirably refused to accept the salary from the last years of his guaranteed contract that he would not be able to fulfill. Before he went into seclusion in a gated community in southern California, McGwire made a telling remark that too many contemporary players were allowing their agents to choose where they should play instead of making for themselves the choice of their new professional home.

McGwire would stay out of the limelight until subpoenaed to testify before Congress on St. Patrick's Day 2005. The story of steroid abuse in baseball would simply not die. The media would not let it die, and many older fans hung their heads sadly about what the game had come to with all its inflated offensive statistics. "I am not here to talk about the past" was McGwire's litany, one that he would repeat over and over again before Congress and a national television audience. What could he say in an era when the truth had been hidden and only spin masters offered advice? Another infamous moment at the hearing came when Rafael Palmeiro, considered a likely Hall of Fame candidate with over five hundred home runs and three thousand hits, pointed his finger at the committee and the television cameras and said, "I never took steroids." A few months later in August 2005 he tested positive for one of the stronger steroids, winstrol.

As the first decade of the twenty-first century moved on, the baseball public seemed both jaundiced and pained as the names of other Major League players who had tested positive in baseball's first random testing program of 2003 began being leaked to a press eager to spread the word of the disgrace of onetime baseball heroes. The Players Association sued in a northern California federal court against the government's unwarranted presentation of those anonymous tests before the California grand jury. The union won a major verdict in the late summer of 2009 when the court ruled that the seizure of that list by the federal investigator Jeff Novitzky was unconstitutional. As of the fall of 2009 the federal government had not decided whether to appeal the case to the Supreme Court. Both baseball management and the union condemned the leaking to the press of names from that list as felonious acts that should be subject to the full prosecution of the law.

The union and management were also in agreement that congressional grandstanding on the issue served no good purpose. If Congress had not passed the Dietary and Substance Health Education Act of 1994 (D-SHEA), the problem of abuse would have been far easier to control. The onus of removing the most dangerous substances from nutritional supplements had been taken from the manufacturing companies and placed instead on the overworked federal Food and Drug Administration (FDA); a Pandora's box had been opened. Such dangerous substances as creatine (which Brady Anderson openly admitted he had used in building himself up to his fifty-home-run season in 1996), andro, and ephedra would not be banned until early in the twenty-first century. During spring training in 2003, a Baltimore Orioles Minor League pitcher had died of an overdose of ephedra as he unwisely tried to speed up his preseason conditioning program.

Commissioner Selig was indignant that baseball was receiving the brunt of public criticism despite the sport having started a widespread Minor League testing program in 2001 and finally getting the Major League players to agree to some testing in 2003. Penalties of fifty games for the first violation, one hundred games for the second violation, and a lifetime suspension for a third infraction were the toughest in pro sports. Selig also commissioned Maine's George Mitchell, the former Democratic Senate majority leader and currently a member of the board of directors of the Boston Red Sox, to investigate thoroughly steroid abuse in baseball. Although the Players Association discouraged any of its members from cooperating with the investigation, Mitchell moved ahead. He received the vital cooperation of Brian McNamee, Roger Clemens's personal trainer who had been arrested for possessing illegal drugs, and Kirk

305

Radomski, a former New York Mets clubhouse worker who had similarly been apprehended by federal authorities.

Mitchell's report was released on December 13, 2007, and stated frankly at the outset, "Everybody in baseball—commissioners, club officials, the players association, players—shares responsibility." He called for more vigilance in clubhouses and for baseball to institute a department of investigation to track down abuses before they grew too widespread. He also called for amnesty for past violations, a condition that was a vital part of the agreement that Mitchell had brokered in Northern Ireland that on Good Friday 1998 put into writing (and so far into practice) the end of centuries of warfare between Ulster Catholics and Protestants. "I learned that letting go of the past and looking towards the future is a very hard but necessary step towards dealing with an ongoing problem," Mitchell told Richard Sandomir of the *New York Times* at the time of the release of his report.

Certainly most of the fans remained in a forgiving mood. Major League attendance soared over eighty million in 2008, and even the great economic recession of 2009 caused a drop of less than seven million paying customers. Something about the game of baseball remained indelible and optimistic. When his number 31 was retired by the Chicago Cubs in the middle of the 2009 season, future Hall of Fame pitcher Greg Maddux expressed sentiments about the current scandal in the game and baseball's enduring beauty. "I never thought if a guy got a hit off me it was because he was on steroids. It was because I made a bad pitch," Maddux told the Wrigley Field crowd. He concluded elegiacally: "I always considered it a privilege to wear the uniform. This game gives you so much when you're playing, and when you stop and it keeps giving, you feel a little guilty. I tried to do it right, or the way I thought it was right." As baseball heads into the second decade of the twenty-first century, maybe both sides on the labor-management front can now say the same thing.

Bibliographical Notes

Two lively and beautifully written histories by Robert Smith, *Baseball* (New York: Simon and Schuster, 1947) and *Baseball in America* (New York: Holt, 1962) are the best places for any interested student of baseball's past to begin. Harold Seymour's first two books in a projected four volume series, *Baseball: The Early Years* (New York: Oxford University Press, 1960) and *Baseball: The Golden Age* (New York: Oxford, 1971) are indispensable though often tedious source books. David Voigt's two volumes, *American Baseball: From Gentleman's Sport to the Commissioner System* (1966) and *American Baseball: From the Commissioners to Continental Expansion* (1970), both from Norman: The University of Oklahoma Press, are livelier reading but are marred by shoddy editing and overgeneralizations. Paul Gregory's *The Baseball Player: An Economic Study* (Washington D.C.: Public Affairs Press, 1956) has some good information on early baseball owners, as does Lee Allen's fine *The American League Story* (New York: Hill and Wang, 1962).

Helpful monographs include Eliot Asinof's gripping *Eight Men Out: The Black Sox and the 1919 World Series* (New York: Holt, Rinehart and Winston, 1963). Asinof's first book was a novel, *Men on Spikes* (New York: McGraw Hill, 1955) but it is based on true stories of minor leaguers denied opportunity because of the reserve clause. Bill Mead's *Even the Browns* (Chicago: Contemporary Books, 1978) is a lively and useful account of World War Two baseball. Fred Stein's *Under Coogan's Bluff: A Fan's Recollection of the Giants Under Terry and Ott* (Alexandria, Va., published by the author, 1978) also sheds light on baseball conditions during the 1930s and 1940s.

J. G. Taylor Spink's biography *Judge Landis and 25 Years of Baseball*

(St. Louis: Sporting News Publishing Company, 1947; reissued in 1974) is a standard source. Unfortunately, there is no archive of Landis materials. Bill Veeck's irreverent books are extremely readable and insightful about the baseball business which he observed and participated in for decades. They are both written with Ed Linn: *Veeck—As In Wreck* (New York: Putnam 1962) and *The Hustler's Handbook* (New York: Putnam, 1965), especially the chapter "Harry's Diary—1919," which probes the unbelievably Byzantine maneuverings which led to Landis' appointment as Commissioner and the demise of Ban Johnson.

Lawrence S. Ritter, *The Glory of Their Times: The Story of the Early Days of Baseball Told by the Men Who Played It* (New York: Macmillan, 1966) is the first and remains the best of the many oral histories of baseball. Jerome Holtzman's interviews with sportswriters, *No Cheering in the Press Box* (New York: Holt, Rinehart, and Winston, 1973) is a useful compendium, as is Donald Honig's *Baseball: When the Grass Was Real* (New York: Coward, McCann and Goeghegan, 1975) and *Baseball Between the Lines* (New York: Coward, McCann and Goeghegan, 1976), books which carry the oral history technique into the 1950s.

Two rollicking reminiscences by sportswriters are especially noteworthy: Harold Parrott's devastating *The Lords of Baseball* (New York: Praeger, 1974) and Harold Rosenthal's mellower memoir of the 1950s, *The Best Years of Baseball* (Chicago: Contemporary Books, 1979).

Lionel S. Sobel, *Professional Sports and the Law* (New York: Law-Arts Publishers, 1977) is an extremely important book by a University of Southern California law professor. It covers the legal issues of today's sports world in a fine historical perspective. Sheldon Gallner's earlier *Pro Sports: The Contract Game* (New York: Scribners, 1974) is a very helpful guide to the new world of sports agentry. The April 1978 issue of the University of Utah's Law School magazine, *The Journal of Contemporary Law*, has two important articles: Thomas M. Boswell and Richard B. McKeown provide a short history of the reserve system in "From Trial by Law to Trial by Auction" while Paul W. Shapiro trenchantly analyzes the arbitrary power of the National Association in "Monopsony Is Never Having to Say You're Sorry." Charles Maher's four-part series on labor in professional sports in the *Los Angeles Times,* February 12-15, 1973 is an excellent introduction.

Hard and accurate material on baseball ownership has always been deliberately difficult to obtain, but the first Celler Sub-Committee on the Study of Monopoly Power investigation in 1951 (82nd Congress, first session) is a good place to start. It is published in the House Judiciary Committee Hearings, volume 38, as *Organized Baseball* (Serial 1, Part 6 — Washington: Government Printing Office, 1952). The 1957 Celler inquiry is included in volume 59 of the House Judiciary Committee Hearings (85th Congress, first session). Other House and Senate Commerce and Judiciary Committees have published testimony from the many inquiries of the 1950s, 1960s, and 1970s.

Two archival collections deserve special note: the Emanuel Celler Papers at the Library of Congress (Washington, D.C.) and the Happy Chandler Papers at the University of Kentucky, Lexington. There are two very helpful senior theses at the Princeton University Library: Richard S. Armstrong, "The Unionization of Baseball" (1947) and Michael R. Blankshain, "The Labor Market in Major League Baseball" (1978). Peter Craig's massive Oberlin College thesis, "Organized Baseball" (1950) can be found at the Library of Congress.

Periodicals consulted include *The Sporting News* (1886-present), *Sporting Life*, the *New York Clipper*, and *Baseball* for the earlier periods. (The *Clipper* provided the most dispassionate coverage of the Players League war of 1890.) In later periods, *Business Week, Colliers, Forbes, Fortune, Life, Look, Newsweek, Saturday Evening Post, Sport* and *Sports Illustrated* have been probed. The reporting of Murray Chass, Leonard Koppett, and Red Smith in *The New York Times* has provided good background for recent years, as has Curt Flood's autobiography, *The Way It Is* (New York: Trident Press, 1971).

The capsule portraits in *Current Biography* (New York: H. W. Wilson Company, published monthly and annually since the mid-1940s) have afforded many valuable nuggets of information.

The end of the twentieth century may go down as a golden age for writing about baseball as well as baseball writing. There is a growing list of books that provide serious insight into baseball as a perplexing business while maintaining a warm feeling for the game on the field. Among those recent books that were especially helpful were James Edward Miller, *The Baseball Business: Pursuing Pennants And Profits In Baltimore* (Chapel Hill, University of North Carolina Press, 1990), Gerald Scully, *The Business Of Major League*

Baseball (Chicago, University of Chicago Press, 1989), Neil Sullivan, *The Minors* (New York, St. Martin's Press, 1990), and Steve Mann's essay, "The Business of Baseball," in John Thorn and Pete Palmer, *Total Baseball* (New York, Warner Books, 1989 edition). Kenneth M. Jennings, *Balls And Strikes: The Money Game In Professional Baseball* (New York: Praeger, 1990) was also helpful although it could have benefited from more careful editing.

Anything that Roger Angell has written about baseball is worth savoring. Of special use for the chapter on the 1981 baseball strike was his essay reprinted in *Late Innings: A Baseball Companion* (New York, Simon and Schuster, 1982). Veteran sportswriter Leonard Koppett makes a lot of sense in his book, *Sports Illusion, Sports Reality* (Boston: Houghton, Mifflin, 1981).

Autobiographies are always fascinating sources, although they must be treated as understandably biased accounts. Two works by major management participants in this story are essential: Bowie Kuhn, *Hardball: The Education Of A Baseball Commissioner* (New York, Times Books, 1987), and Lee MacPhail, *My Nine Innings* (Westport, Conn., Meckler Publishing Company, 1989). On the players' side, Don Baylor with Claire Smith, *Don Baylor: Nothing But The Truth* (New York, St. Martin's Press, 1989), the paperback version of Keith Hernandez with Mike Bryan, *If At First* (New York, Penguin Books, 1987), and Dave Winfield with Tom Parker, *Winfield: A Players' Life* (New York, Norton, 1988) are noteworthy.

Many a sportswriter has moaned that you need to know labor law to understand baseball these days. Some excellent texts are now available in addition to the Lionel Sobel book noted earlier (that was supplemented in 1981). Legal scholars Robert C. Berry, William B. Gould IV, and Paul D. Staudohar have made a major contribution with *Labor Relations In Professional Sports* (Dover, Mass., Auburn House, 1986). Paul Staudohar is the sole author of *The Sports Industry And Collective Bargaining* (New York, Industrial and Labor Relations Press of Cornell University, 1986, 1989). Berry and Glenn M. Wong have produced two volumes of *The Law and Business of the Sports Industries* (Dover, Auburn House, 1986).

University of Tulsa law professor Ray Yasser has a fine volume of case studies, *Sports Law: Cases and Materials* (Lanham, Md.,

310

University Presses of America, 1985) that includes the 1976 federal court ruling that upheld the Messersmith-McNally decision. Purdue University industrial relations professor James B. Dworkin has written the history, *Owners vs. Players: Baseball and Collective Bargaining* (Dover, Auburn House, 1981). See also Dworkin's articles in the March 1986 *Arbitration Journal,* and the August 1988 *Labor Law Journal.* Glenn Wong, a law professor and a baseball arbitrator, surveyed baseball grievance arbitration cases in the March 1986 *Arbitration Journal.* Marvin Miller and Ray Grebey went at it again in the December 1983 issue of *Arbitration Journal.*

David Kaplan contributed a perceptive portrait of Donald Fehr in the October 29, 1989 *New York Times* magazine. Roger Cohn offered a similarly fine portrait of Fay Vincent in the same magazine on June 10, 1990.

Last but not least, a tip of the cap goes to the *Baseball Encyclopedia* (New York, Macmillan, 1st edition, 1969, 9th ed., 1990). It is a volume that enables baseball research to be performed effortlessly and enjoyably.

GLOSSARY OF TERMS

American Baseball Guild — the ballplayers' union that labor activist Robert Murphy tried to form in 1946, but did not succeed; its program for improved minimum salaries and a pension plan were taken up successfully 20 years later.

Antitrust exemption — the Supreme Court ruling of 1922 that grants professional baseball exemption from the normal anticompetitive restrictions of other businesses engaged in trade and commerce under antitrust laws.

Arbitration, grievance — since 1970, the right of players to have disputes settled by an impartial outsider except those issues deemed "in the best interests of baseball" which are still heard by the commissioner of baseball.

Arbitration, salary — since 1973, the right of players to have a single-year's salary determined by an impartial outsider who chooses either the player's or the owner's last bid; no splitting the difference is allowed.

Baseball Players' Fraternity — an abortive attempt for an union of players from 1912 to 1918; led by David Fultz.

Basic Agreement — the governing rules of player-owner relations, established for the first time in 1968; its renewal every four or so years has been the occasion for bitter player-owner negotiations.

Brotherhood of Professional Baseball Players — the first attempt for a baseball players union in 1885; it expired with the failure of the Players League after 1890.

Collusion — "secret agreement for fraudulent purpose," according to the dictionary; what the owners were found guilty of by impartial arbitrators in the late 1980s in refusing to negotiate with veteran free agents.

Compensation — the major demand of management in the 1981 strike who clamored for a major league player to "compensate" a team for the loss of a major leaguer to free agency.

313

Compensation pool — the compromise solution that ended the 1981 strike in which each team placed certain major league (and/or minor league) players into a pool from which a team that lost a free agent could select a replacement; abandoned at the owners' request in the 1985 Basic Agreement.

"Competitive balance" — a shibboleth of baseball owners for a century, describing restrictions on players needed for equal competition in a league.

Draft, amateur free agent — established in 1965, the method by which most baseball players enter the industry; starting with the team with the worst record in the previous season, each club selects rights to amateur players who have a year to sign; if they don't sign, they return to the unsigned talent pool.

Draft, professional reentry free agent — established in the 1976 Basic Agreement, it provided for a similar order last-going-first selection of major league veterans with more than six years experience; abolished by mutual consent in the 1985 Basic Agreement.

Federal League — a competing third major league that lasted only during the 1914 and 1915 seasons.

Major League Baseball Players Association — chartered in 1954, given permanent leadership in 1966, it is a federally protected union that has brought unparalleled riches to its individual members, the major league players.

Major League Baseball Players Benefit Plan — the players' pension plan — considered perhaps the best employee benefit package in the nation.

Mexican League — a competing third major league that threatened the existing leagues in 1946 and 1947.

National Agreement — the pact that ended the trade war between the new American and the established National League in 1903.

National Commission — the tripartite body that ruled baseball under the National Agreement from 1903 to 1920; consisted of the two league presidents and a third person selected by the other two.

Office of the Commissioner of Baseball — created by the owners in 1920 to replace the National Commission in the wake of the World Series scandal of 1919; the power of the office is extraordinary, but when challenged in court, it has been upheld.

Option — a clause in the uniform baseball contract that was used until 1976 to keep the services of a player for an additional year (also known as the "renewal" clause); Option is also a method by which major league teams keep rights to players by optioning their services to minor league clubs for a period of years.

Players' League — a major league that competed with the existing National League for one season, 1890, disbanding because of inexperience.

Players' Protective Association — another short-lived players' group founded by Harry Leonard Taylor that lasted only from 1900 to 1902.

Reserve system — the method from 1880 to 1976 by which the owners bound the services of the players to one club indefinitely and without mutuality; the reserve clause or the reserve rule is that part of the reserve system that compelled a player to sign a contract binding him perpetually or else he was not allowed to play.

Waivers — the offering of a player's services to other clubs in reverse order of standing in the pennant races; goes into effect only when the original club decides it no longer wants the player's services.

Index

318

Index

Index

Index

321

Index

Index

Index

324

Index

Index

326

Index

Woodward and Armstrong, *The Brethren,* 213

Wrigley, Philip K. Jr., 147, 186

Yawkey, Thomas, 77, 119, 147, 185, 190

Yawkey, William, 77

Yastrzemski, Carl, 204

Young, Cy, 16, 61, 196

Young, Dick, 216

Young, Nick, 31, 67, 108

Yount, Robin, 273

Zeller, Jack, 122

Zimmer, Charles ("Chief"), 61, 64-66